Praise for
The Coming Biotech Age

"The pressure of competition frequently forces executives to focus almost exclusively on current economic developments in today's markets. In reality, successful economic performance requires an understanding of technology and its application in markets as they will change over the next several decades. Fortunately, a new book, *The Coming Biotech Age: The Business of Bio-Materials,* provides executives with an excellent framework for assessing the forces that will determine future markets in their industries."

KENNETH MCLENNAN
President
Manufacturer's Alliance/MAPI, Inc.

"A cutting edge look at the key technologies that will drive business in the next millennium. Oliver's book provides a clear way to stay ahead of the curve."

WILLIAM A. JENKINS
VP, Business and Finance
Cal Tech

"An insightful and stimulating look at how the technologies of biology translate into the economies of the 21st century."

DR. GEORGE RATHMAN
Chairman
ICOS

"A fascinating book, *The Coming Biotech Age: The Business of Bio-Materials* will be of interest to investors and financial advisors alike who are searching for a crystal ball's view into the next exploding economic wave. Bio-Materials will be to tomorrow's stock market what the Internet and e-business is to today's. Every investor who wants a glimpse into the next economic explosion should read this book."

DAN COHOLAN
VP & Managing Director, Head, Global Communications & Technology Group, Investment Banking, RBC Dominion Securities
Royal Bank of Canada

The Coming Biotech Age

Also by Richard W. Oliver

The Shape of Things to Come: Seven Imperatives for Winning in the New World of Business

The Coming Biotech Age
The Business of Bio-Materials

Richard W. Oliver

McGraw-Hill
New York   San Francisco   Washington, D.C.   Auckland   Bogotá
Caracas   Lisbon   London   Madrid   Mexico City   Milan
Montreal   New Delhi   San Juan   Singapore
Sydney   Tokyo   Toronto

Library of Congress Cataloging-in-Publication Data

Oliver, Richard W.
    The coming biotech age : the business of bio-materials / Richard W. Oliver.
       p.   cm.
    Includes index.
    ISBN 0-07-135020-9 (cloth)
    1. Biotechnology industries—Forecasting.   2. Biotechnology—Forecasting.
  3. Bioengineering—Forecasting.   4. Molecular biology—Forecasting.   I. Title.
  HD9999.B442 O44   1999
  338.4'76606—dc21

                                        99-053282

McGraw-Hill

A Division of The McGraw·Hill Companies

1 2 3 4 5 6 7 8 9 0   DOC/DOC   9 0 9 8 7 6 5 4 3 2 1 0 9

ISBN 0-07-135020-9

It was set in Garamond by North Market Street Graphics.

Printed and bound by R. R. Donnelley & Sons Company.

 This book is printed on recycled, acid-free paper containing a
minimum of 50% recycled, de-inked fiber.

For Kim and Carrie

Their children may live forever.

Contents

Acknowledgments

Trying to predict the future of a new economic and technological revolution is an arduous undertaking. I was fortunate to have a large number of people help me. They gave freely of their time, energy, and insights.

To the literally hundreds of people interviewed for the book and those whose ideas I harvested from their writing, thank you for guiding the way and keeping me on track. Unfortunately you are too numerous to name individually. I trust that I honestly portrayed your ideas throughout the book.

For the less glamorous task of research and editing, however, the list is shorter, and the individuals deserve special recognition for their many contributions: Kim, Beryl, and Sutton Brothers; Richard Daverman; Sharon Felton; Mary Glenn; Jeanne Kahan; Tim Leffel; Clark Lu; Norman Moore; Peter Miller; Herb Nachman; Susan Oliver; Jane Palmieri; Jeff Qian; Russell Brothers; Cindy Smith; Phil Sweetland; Kyoko Taguchi; Kenneth West; and Ron Weiss.

Special mention is due to Jeremy Leonard, an economist with the Manufacturer's Alliance for Productivity and Innovation (MAPI) in Washington, DC, who was on special assignment to help me think through the economic impact of the Bioterials Age. His excellent work is evident in Chapters 3–7.

As always, I feel particularly indebted to the Owen Graduate School of Management, Vanderbilt University, for the opportunity to work on such a time-consuming project. In particular, the late Dean Marty Geisel and acting Dean Joe Blackburn deserve special thanks.

Thanks finally to my mentor and teacher, the late Marshall McLuhan, who taught me how to think about technology and the future, but more importantly, inspired me to write about it.

Richard W. Oliver

The Coming
Biotech Age

Introduction

The Bioterials Century

Chemistry and physics were the sciences that drove the technologies and economics of the twentieth century. They created and enhanced both the industrial and information technologies that underlay the vast economic progress of the world, and much of its political, social, and cultural change as well. Now, the biological and advanced materials sciences are creating a new economic engine—"bioterials" technologies—that will dramatically drive the economics of the twenty-first century.

There are vast differences in scale and scope, though, between this and earlier economic eras. The bioterials economy will grow faster, be more global, more pervasive, and more powerful than any before it, even the Information Age.

The Bioterials Age will complete the triumph of economics over politics, which was begun in the Information Age. It will unleash forces stronger than nationalism and more powerful than the combined armies of the world.

For politicians and public policy makers, bioterials will create issues of immense complexities with global ramifications for the environment, trade, and public welfare.

The technologies of bioterials will challenge our very definition of life.

New products from bioterials technologies will be more important than the car or the computer.

Bioterials will demand a new public literacy—BioLiteracy—and a citizenry actively engaged in its development and direction. Every person in the world will be called on to make a personal decision about his or her own genes and perhaps those of others.

1

In less than a generation, virtually every company will be a bioterials company—either an integral part of the development and use of the technology or dependent on it for survival and success.

The centrality of bioterials to the economy and every company mandates that every manager, every worker, in the twenty-first century be intimately conversant with the technology's potential to restructure and transform individual companies and major industries.

Bioterials—"Sci Fi" or Sure Bet?

A writer intent on predicting such a future needs to be judicious in drawing the line between the "seeable," based on the extension of known information, and pushing that information too far into that realm of imagination we call science fiction. "Sci fi" though, is not without value. The National Aeronautics and Space Administration (NASA) used large doses of science fiction to conceptualize its nearly $100 million Deep Space 1 experimental probe launched in 1998. It used *Star Wars* metaphors for its propulsion systems and an artificial intelligence system reminiscent of Hal 9000, the computer that "starred" in *2001: A Space Odyssey*. This book has used no such stimulants. It does, however, attempt to "push the envelope" of current thinking and ask "what if."

Today, as in earlier eras, our view of the future, our asking the "what if" questions, is often constrained by our past. As a writer, futurist, or simply a dreamer, I worry that I lack the necessary imagination and vision in approaching this task. I think, however, that I am neither alone nor historically unique.

Who in 1899 could have predicted the computer and the Internet?

To begin not only a new century, but also a new millennium, calls for even greater vision. But, who in the year 999 could have foreseen the car, the skyscraper, the printing press, baseball, tin cans, or even grand opera and postmodern art?

Surely the next century, and the next millennium, will bring vast changes that no one can foresee. But, this book makes a start. As such, it makes many claims about the future. The most important of those claims is that we are at the end of the Information Age and about to embark on a new economic and technological period, the Age of Bioterials.

Cells Trump Electrons

Central to this idea is that the economy and societal issues of the twenty-first century will be dominated by biology and the new materials sciences, rather than the chemistry and physics that determined so much of what we did, or believed, in the twentieth. In other words, I argue that in the coming years biology will eclipse electronics, and that cells and "quarks" (among the dozen or so smallest known particles) or subatomic matter will trump digits as the "drivers" of our lives. Although others before me, in academia and the media, have proclaimed the next century to be one dominated by biology, I believe this book transcends those visions in three fundamental ways.

First, my claim is not solely to the biological technologies, products, and services focused on all things organic. I am concerned as well with the materials sciences, whose embryonic activities at the subatomic level are aimed at fundamentally changing the inorganic materials in our lives. Thus, the unit of analysis here is matter—organic and inorganic. Attention is turned, therefore, not only to those universities, companies, and government researchers working at the cellular level on organic material and tissues—plants, animals, and human—but to those exploring the subatomic universe of minerals, plastics, paints, and the like. Although information and awareness about new materials sciences activities is in comparatively short supply, I will endeavor throughout the book to remind readers that it is *matter* that concerns us here, not just biology.

A second point of differentiation from earlier works is that I will focus primarily on the *economics of bioterials* rather than on the technical, scientific, or ethical aspects. There are several existing volumes that do that job quite thoroughly. Although it is impossible to write a book about bioterials without lapsing occasionally into the "gee whiz" technical stuff, I'll endeavor to keep that confined to what's necessary to understand the commercial impact.

Thirdly, earlier works focusing particularly on the life sciences aspects of biotechnology have in the main been negative. They have been quick to point out the potential dangers of biotechnologies, and at least one has called for severe curtailment, if not total abolishment, of all biotechnology research. I take a more positive approach.

The history of technology is one of relentless advancement. At no period in history have sufficient forces been marshaled to stop new technologies, despite many attempts. No technologies, in and of themselves, are either good or bad. That comes from how we use them. Clearly, the issues associated with the manipulation of organic matter raise new, in some cases almost unthinkable, challenges. But, stopping the research won't solve them. The best approach is to understand their potential and work to shape and channel them into productive directions for society. This will require a better-informed citizenry—a BioLiterate society—and is one of the motivations in writing this book.

Bioterials: Conquering Matter

In an earlier book, *The Shape of Things to Come: Seven Imperatives for Winning in the New World of Business,* I argued that the end of the Information Age called for rethinking our approach to information technology, not only as organizational beings, but in our personal lives as well. I urged people to let go of their last hesitations, "seize the modem," and make information technologies an integral part of everyday life. Despite its futuristic title, the book in many ways chronicled the here and now, providing seven imperatives for success in a world dominated by mature, ubiquitous information technologies. The book's last chapter was a brief nod to the future era of bioterials. At its most conceptual, the book argued that in the *Industrial Age we conquered space,* in the *Information Age we conquered time,* and in the *Bioterials Age, we would conquer matter.*

This current volume expands on this last proposition. Although primarily oriented to the economics and business aspects of bioterials, the book will also be of interest to policy makers and others interested in the ethical and social issues that result with the fast and pervasive influence of bioterials. Although the inorganic materials technologies should be relatively noncontentious, innovations that alter organic matter, whether plant, animal, or human, will prove to be problematic. In fact they already are. Despite my decidedly pro business and pro technology perspective, I try, in fairness, to point out the legitimate positions held by those who oppose such innovations. Although I can make no promise of resolving those issues, I do hope to fairly stake out their respective claims.

The "Periodic Table" of Biology

I argue in this book that bioterials will bring about changes on a scale different than any technologies before them—quantum changes, not incremental ones. I further argue that while the initial impacts are only now becoming apparent, the "inflection point" of rapid change is very close. Within a very few years, perhaps as early as 2005, we will begin the massive upward swing of knowledge and proliferation of new products and services indicative of the growth phase of any new technological era. The growth phase of bioterials, however, will dwarf all previous technology shifts in scope, scale, and velocity.

As we draw near the complete mapping of the human genome (the entire spectrum of some 100,000 human genes) and the comparable strides in the materials sciences, we are at a point akin to the scientific and commercial impact that the periodic table of the elements had on chemistry or the splitting of the atom on physics. Those inflection points drove the rapid discovery of new science, transformed economics and industries, and ultimately our lives. The bioterials growth phase will be almost vertical in its slope and global in its economic impact. It will swiftly create economic opportunities and advantages of almost unimaginable proportions, but mature just as rapidly as we reach the quarter century mark.

To extend my own views of the future and better understand the next century, I have had the good fortune to meet and hear the dreams of many of the researchers, scientists, and business people intent on imagining the unimaginable about the bioterials century. I owe them a huge debt. Although they are creating the new world of the twenty-first century, I hope to merely explore it. I trust this book will repay them in some small measure for sharing their insights with me.

The collective wisdom of those scientists, researchers, engineers, and business people convinced me beyond any doubt that the Bioterials Age will take us farther, faster, and create more change than any technology before it.

I make such claims with only one hesitation. I worry that I am underestimating the scope, scale, and speed at which bioterials will change our lives.

1

The Twenty-First Century

The Age of Bioterials

The world is about to exit the Information Age and enter the new era of "bioterials." The marvels of the Bioterials Age will be more global in their impact than the Internet. Its products will be more important than fire, the wheel, or the car, and faster and more productive than today's biggest supercomputers. The bioterials era will generate more new knowledge in a shorter period than history's collective wisdom, and the power of its technologies will eclipse that of the combined armies of the world.

The new age of bioterials will transform the global economy. Early in the next millennium, bioterials technologies will replace information technologies as the new engine of world economic growth.

In fact, the transition has already begun.

The End of the Information Age: Biology Trumps Electronics

During the last three decades of the twentieth century, it was commonplace to refer to our economy as the Information Age, and to a whole set of companies in computer, telecommunications, digital electronics, software industries, and the like as "hi tech." As the value and availability of information grew, it became rather fashionable for commentators to extol the glorious future of these technologies and argue that we are "at the dawn of a new era of information."

They are wrong. As we begin the new millennium, it is becoming more evident daily that we are at the end, not the beginning, of the Information Age. Information is important, and always will be. However, in the coming era information will be like electricity, cheap and ubiquitous. In this new era, information will be a valuable tool, but only a tool, and one that has receded into the background. Again, like electricity, it will be conspicuous only by its rare absence.

There are three overarching "technologies" at the heart of today's rapidly maturing information economy. The first is digitalization or the converting of content, whether voice, data, video or image, into a common digital form that can be sent individually or collectively over a common set of transmission media. The second is software, to manipulate, control, and direct the flow of this information. The third is the microprocessor or computer chip, the core driver and storage device for the other two. Essentially these three technologies rapidly drove down the cost of information, while simultaneously driving up its functionality and ease of use at an equally accelerating pace. Each of these technologies is maturing rapidly. We have the Internet, for example, because these technologies are mature, not new.

It has been well documented that a technology or a product (and, as it turns out, even an economy) follows a life cycle. (See Figure 1-1.) Early in that cycle, one or two suppliers exclusively control the product or technology. Thus, the technology or product is rare, typically very expensive, found for sale in a few exclusive outlets, and is often intended for use in a very limited set of applications. Communications

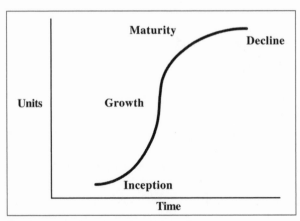

Figure 1-1. Typical product life cycle.

(advertising, promotions, and the like) about the technology or product is first about its discovery, followed shortly with "instructional" information about how to use it. It is generally at this discovery or inception stage that we label such products and technologies as "hi tech."

At the end of a technology and product life cycle, the reverse is true. The product is inexpensive, widely available from many suppliers, and advertising messages are about its many uses. Competition among suppliers is on the basis of brand image, typically extolling the virtues of (small) differences or new, varied uses and applications. And that, quite clearly, is the state of information technologies today.

Despite being only some 50 years old, it is obvious that the core "product" of the Information Age, the computer chip (or microprocessor), is aging rapidly. (See Figure 1-2.) Everywhere around us, the signs of a maturing information economy are starkly evident. In 1999, the number of chips made for devices other than computers (cell phones, appliances, cars, etc.) exceeded those going into computers. And yet, the production of computers themselves continues to grow. The result is that every part of life, economic and noneconomic, is alive with cheap and abundant computer power.

The cost of information has declined so rapidly, and is so widely available, that many have been heard to complain that they "are drowning in information." I, for example, had never even seen a computer, or even a calculator, when I graduated from college just 30 years ago. The computer, once a scarce and expensive device, is now found on every office desk, scattered widely throughout facto-

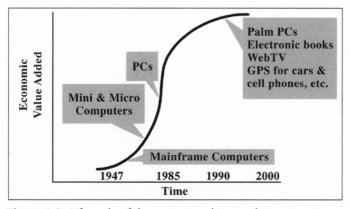

Figure 1-2. Life cycle of the computer chip: product categories.

ries controlling every function and process, and in half the homes in the United States. The next generation computer is expected to drop below $800, and the one after that below $500. And the software that runs a computer offers almost unbelievable functionality, essentially for pennies. As cheap, or cheaper and more functional than a TV, a computer is within the reach of virtually every person in the United States, indeed within the reach of many throughout the world.

Rather than being hard to find, the microprocessor, and indeed the computer, has become ubiquitous, and available for sale on virtually any street corner. And, many information services have become so cheap as to be almost free. Unlimited Internet connections are available for a mere $20 per month, and long-distance telephone charges are now routinely 10 cents a minute or less for anywhere in the country. It will not be long before a call anywhere in the world will be a "local" call. And, as a key driver of technology advances, new research and product developments in digitization, software, and microprocessors are aimed at further improving their functionality and costs but not at new science.

By virtually any definition, then, information technologies and the companies they spawned are rapidly maturing. Information technologies will continue to be important to the smooth functioning of our economies and society, just like cars, steel, oil, and electricity. But on the basis of their availability, cost, use, further development, or potential, these technologies and their product manifestations no longer deserve the epithet of "hi tech." Although still exciting in many of their applications, and important to virtually all aspect of our lives, information technologies and electronics are being trumped in every way. Bioterials is the new technological era. Bioterials is the new engine of the economy.

We are about to "flip" from the Information Age, which lasted only 50 to 60 years, to the Bioterials Age, projected to last only about half that time. Figure 1-3 graphically portrays the various economic eras. The horizontal axis outlines the major technologies, agrarian, industrial, information, and now bioterials, and approximately when they began and ended. The impact of these technological eras are plotted on the vertical axis as globalization and economic value added. While globalization is self-evident, *economic value added* refers to the amount an individual produces beyond that needed to support him- or herself. Each successive era has become more global, and as

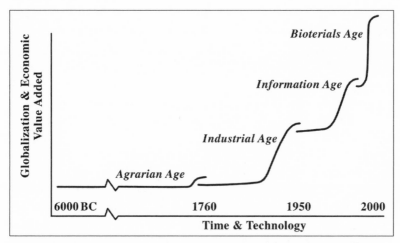

Figure 1-3. Technology creates economic eras. (*Adapted from Exhibit 2.1 in* The Shape of Things to Come *by Richard Oliver, McGraw-Hill, 1999.* SOURCE: *CSX Index. Reprinted with permission. All rights reserved.*)

will be demonstrated, has created more economic value added (expressed interns of GDP, or Gross Domestic Product, per capita and life expectancy). Importantly, the technologies have their greatest impact and are at their maximum power in the late stages of their growth phase and into their mature phase. Thus, in this analysis, the major technology "set" is taken to be the engine of the economy and a force for global economic integration.

While it is quite clear that information technologies increasingly became the major economic engine of the past five decades, a whole new set of technologies—biology and advanced materials—are poised to become the new engine driving the economy. Their scope, scale, and importance in our business and political lives supersede those of the electronic era with every passing day.

The new hi tech is bioterials.

Bioterials: The New "Hi Tech"

Two indicators in anyone's definition of "hi tech"—research and development (R&D) spending and patent approvals—underscore this new reality. Industrial Age firms (such as automobile makers, energy and steel producers) spend about 5 percent of their revenue dollars on R&D. Information companies typically spend between 10 and 15 percent. Bioterials companies, on the other hand, spend 15 percent at a minimum, just to be in the game, and those expenditure levels are increasing daily. Some companies, in the early stages of their development, spend every dollar of income, and then some, on R&D. (By contrast, many new Internet firms also spend all their money, but they devote it to acquiring customers, not new knowledge!) No other industry spends for research at a rate close to bioterials companies.

The other indicator of new knowledge generation is new patent approvals. Patents are only a rough (and most likely understated) proxy for the development of new knowledge, but a proxy nonetheless. New patent approvals in the area of information technology are slowly decreasing as a percentage of all approvals, whereas those for biotechnologies are increasing daily. In fact, they are increasing dramatically. As much of the R&D at this point is focused on the life sciences, patents in those areas dominate. Those in the materials sciences are only now beginning to gather critical mass. Although bioterials are clearly the new hi tech, a question remains.

Just what is meant by bioterials?

Bioterials?

Biotechnology

The term *biotechnology* and its abbreviation, *biotech,* crept into the language in the late 1960s and early 1970s. It was first applied to that set of technologies and companies that were concerned with understanding and "mapping" the human gene set. Their goals were somewhat diverse judging from the broad range of attitudes and ideas expressed by scientists, government officials, and a few enlightened businesses at the time. Stated goals related primarily to improvement of people's health by understanding the functions of genes and changing and directing them toward building healthier bodies.

Like many new terms, biotechnology has taken on different meanings over time. Some uses imply finer shades of meanings, although others broaden and enlarge the areas that are meant to be included in its use. Today, the term biotechnology is generally used to describe a wide range of technologies and businesses whose aim is to understand, alter, or direct the function of a wide set of organic cells, including plant, animal, and human. The diversity in the use of the term can be seen most clearly in the wide array of areas studied in university, private, and governmental labs. Or, in the equally wide array of organizations (some 2000 or more in the United States and about the same number around the world) that describe what they do as biotechnology. There is little agreement on a precise definition. During research for this book, one major obstacle was dealing with the varied and strongly held opinions on just what is included in the definition of biotechnology.

This book further confounds the problem with the new term, bioterials. A very close term, biomaterials, is in wide use in the health care field to describe those technologies related primarily to human tissues. My intent on coining a new term (a contraction of biotechnology and materials) is not an attempt to further confuse, but to try to capture the exciting work that is going on in several diverse fields of endeavor beyond medical subjects. This new term, bioterials, also highlights the "blurring" of the sharp distinction between organic and inorganic matter.

Advanced Materials

The biotechnology activities described here aim at "conquering" all things organic. Less known, but equally exciting, is research in the materials science area, aimed at "conquering" inorganic materials. Major research and commercial efforts in this field have been under way for some time to create what have variously been referred to as "advanced materials" or "smart materials." Thus, my use of the term, bioterials, includes the entire spectrum of matter.

At its most simplistic level, advanced materials research activity is essentially an extension of the work of the early material sciences but with a dramatic twist. The traditional science was largely concerned with creating applications for existing materials using their unique characteristics. The new science is radically different. It starts with the commercial application, then "designs" the atomic architecture of a new or improved material to meet that commercial need.

Some scientists and private labs are working on new materials for photonic and information storage applications that will greatly enhance the speed and efficiency of information management. Others are developing materials for a host of otherwise mundane industrial uses such as the world's smallest and strongest fiber or materials with fantastic new "surface" and "interface" properties that are many times stronger than conventional adhesives. Still others are developing new materials that are more porous or harder than any substance currently in commercial use.

Cornell University, among others, is leading in the development of "nanomaterials," that is, materials many times smaller and more useful than anything currently in use in today's "micro" world. Significant advances are also taking place in the area of smart materials, used for packaging, medical, or other applications, that change their properties for different applications or environmental conditions. Still other efforts are under way to redesign the atomic structure of paints, ceramics, and plastics so that they are better, cheaper, faster, and more useful than anything known to man. Exciting developments are also under way that make these materials environmentally "friendly" and use radically new manufacturing approaches such as "self-assembly."

Although this whole range of new inorganic materials developments will be discussed more fully in Chapter 7, it is worth noting here that, in a number of areas, the distinction between organic and inorganic materials is beginning to blur. At the intersection of biology and electronics, for instance, scientists are developing electronic noses, tongues, and ears whose components are primarily inorganic, but whose functions and applications are organic. In the Bioterials Age, the sharp demarcation between the organic and the inorganic disappears at the edge of each category, creating a whole new class of hybrid organic-inorganic matter.

For the purposes of this book, then, I use the term bioterials to include the combination of the two fields—biology and new materials sciences. Taken together, the almost breathtaking advances of each of these disciplines in the past few years *hold the promise of nothing less than "conquering" matter.*

GeneBanks: Dreams and Dollars

Almost as fascinating as the new technologies themselves are the "architects" of the new Bioterials Age, the scientists and engineers who are redesigning everything, animal, vegetable, mineral, and human, and the financiers who are making it possible for the dreamers to dream big dreams. I call the first group the "BioVisionaries" and have devoted several special sections to them throughout the book. They come from countries around the world and work most often in multidisciplinary teams in expensive, sophisticated government, university, and private labs linked to other researchers around the globe. The scope and scale of their efforts stand in sharp contrast to the heroes of the Information Age, who often worked alone or in small, highly motivated groups in the isolated "garage" incubators of Silicon Valley.

Interestingly, scientists who are at the cutting edge of biology use the term "GeneBank" to refer to the huge cache of information about genes. A bank is certainly an appropriate metaphor for this storehouse of knowledge, because the sums of money associated with this industry will be the largest in history. Thus, Chapter 11 turns attention to the "BioCapitalists" who are supplying the lifeblood—money—for these bioterials discoveries. Almost as much as the visionaries in the lab, the new breed of investors—individuals and companies willing to take long odds for a huge payoff—are shaping this new era. The deals and the capital structure of many of these biotech endeavors follow a fundamentally different path than those of the industrial or information eras. Universities and governments play larger and more pivotal roles, although deals between the largest pharmaceutical companies and the smallest biotech labs are essential for the development of the industry. In addition, large commodity chemical companies such as DuPont and Monsanto are re-inventing themselves as biotech "life sciences" companies and will play a major role in the shape and evolution of the industry.

We won't need to wait very long to enjoy the fruits of these new efforts. The scientific discoveries of the new technologies of bioterials are rapidly being commercialized. Notwithstanding the long governmental approval times in the drug discovery and in some agricultural areas, commercialization of bioterials will happen faster than virtually any other technological area, largely driven by the costs of research—in many cases three to five times or more faster than any technology before it. Early in the new century, we will witness the fastest rate of technology commercialization in history.

However, there are a small but growing number of people who question not just the speed of these developments, but whether we should be undertaking them at all!

The Bioterials "Genie"

Even industry detractors agree that biotechnologies have the potential to eradicate world hunger and disease and to overcome the most difficult medical dilemmas. They argue, however, that even those lofty outcomes are not sufficient to let the "biological genie out of the bottle." This book will argue the opposite. The genie is already out of the bottle and our efforts are best directed to mastering the genie, not the futile attempt to rebottle it. In one sense, however, those opposed to biotechnology are right. Its impact and issues will be beyond any other issues humans have ever had to deal with.

One ignores the political and social ramifications of new technologies at one's peril. Clearly, the unwanted by-products of industrial technologies created a political debate of huge proportions about the safety of the environment. In fact, it created some of the most impressive global political arrangements (several hundred global environmental protection agreements), and spawned the first global political movement—the "greens," today found in virtually every developed nation.

Information technologies have created no less a controversy. The debate today centers around the power of information technology to know and inform on every aspect of our lives, reducing personal privacy to a few computer keystrokes. Although technology and economics lead, politics doesn't always follow willingly. Historically, in the tension between economics and politics, politics had the last word—at least until now. Information technology began the push for economics over politics; bioterials will finish the job. Everywhere in the world, markets are freer than ever before and individual sovereign governments' control over monetary and fiscal policy slips away daily under the assault of the global financial system.

A major theme of this book is that the bioterials revolution now upon us is faster moving and its impacts are more profound that anything that has come before it. Despite being driven primarily by economic goals (I ask forgiveness here from the many scientists who are motivated by the pure search for knowledge), bioterials will raise issues that will challenge our very definitions of life.

In earlier economic eras the political, social, cultural, and ethical issues that attended development in technology, and the commercial pursuits that followed, seemed almost manageable if we (the public and our elected policy makers) worked hard at them. In the Industrial Age, the major issue was the impact its new technologies had on the environment. In the Information Age, with its pervasive and invasive technologies, individual privacy arose as the central issue of the times.

In both cases—environmental pollution and personal privacy—it seemed possible, with the right set of policies (however difficult in deriving), that we could skillfully strike a balance between the respective rights of society and those of the individual. Even today, some 40 years after Rachel Carson first alerted us to the dangers of environmental pollution in her book *Silent Spring,* we continue to craft legislation that encourages citizens and producers to clean up the environment and keep it that way. And at the end of the Information Age, we are now debating laws that protect that right to individual privacy without impeding commercial pursuits. Overriding these activities is a sense that, done carefully, we can have some measure of control over a technology genie's more unsavory aspects.

Bioterials will prove to be an entirely different kind of genie.

Systemic Issues: Growing from the Inside Out

Bioterials issues will differ not just in form and substance but in their ability to fundamentally alter nature. Like everything else about this new era, the ethical issues of the Bioterials Age will be *systemic—* growing from the inside out, affecting all aspects of the organism, whether that organism is the individual or society. The issues already identified seem almost overwhelming in their capacity to make us think the unthinkable and discuss the ineffable. Even more disturbing, though, is that the most difficult issues are yet to surface. Some, like human cloning and ownership of genetic information, will take on dimensions not yet obvious.

Thus, although this book is primarily about the economic importance of the new Bioterials Age, it will also venture, however briefly, into the social transformations that always attend the economic. Unfortunately, these technologies are even more perplexing in their ethical aspects. The Bioterials Age portends change of global proportions in every part of our lives. It will create new ethical and moral issues that touch the very definition of life, such as the ability to predetermine not only the sex, but the health and personality characteristics of our children as well.

As difficult as it is to predict the new economic realities, "bioethics" will create a huge "Chinese Wall" that threatens to divert, stall, or regress the evolution of bioterials research and commercialization.

However, as argued in Chapter 12, even though some impacts on human belief systems will border on the ineffable, their evolution is irreversible. Research may be stalled or diverted, but not stopped. In the whole of human history, no person, no group of Luddites, no political force has successfully impeded the inexorable march of technological progress. Like all technologies before them, bioterials technologies will out; they are unstoppable.

And, in the debates over the use of biotechnologies such as gene manipulation and cloning, astute observers are already noting that banning a particular practice or line of research in one area will simply result in its transfer to more accepting locations, perhaps eventually even off the surface of the planet.

BioLiteracy

Our best approach is to learn to understand, harness, and direct technologies, rather than throwing up our arms in a vain attempt to vanquish them. We will have no more luck trying to stop them than we could a rogue tsunami wave. But we need to act fast. The full force of the Bioterials Age is not 100, or 50, or even 15 years away. It will, potentially, be upon us in only 5 years.

Many social commentators argue that we need to ensure that our students become "computer literate." However, as computer technologies are improved daily, much of the difficulty of being "literate" from a computer standpoint disappears. Soon, most computers will be voice activated, keyboards will disappear, and the software will be so sophisticated that computers will bend to our will without much effort or knowledge of their workings on our part. On the other hand, we will be confronted daily with new innovations from the biological and new materials sciences. Our knowledge of such technologies, their impact and scope, will be at a premium. We will require an informed citizenry to carefully guide and direct these developments so we can harvest their riches and avoid, to the extent possible, their negative side affects.

Students and those currently in the workforce must become increasingly knowledgeable about these new technologies lest they become obsolete in this fast moving economy. At the transition from the Industrial Age to the Information Age, many workers found themselves stranded in jobs being rapidly given over to computers and robots. We found, at the time, that steel and auto workers did not make good computer programmers. We need to look ahead and ask: Will computer programmers make good biologists? The answer, I suspect, is no.

Those issues thus described grow from the relatively simple at the inorganic end of the spectrum to the exponentially more complex as we progress to the manipulation and control of organic materials—from plants, to animals, to humans. Chapter 12, "BioEthics," will attempt to lay out the questions, if not answers, related to the ethical challenges confronting the bioterials industry. If not solved, or at least managed, these ethical dilemmas, the "Chinese Wall" of bioterials, will impede the full realization of the era. No discussion of the Bioterials Age would be complete without an examination, however brief, about the likely ethical issues of the era. However, it is to the economics of the era that most attention is directed.

GeneFactories: BioEconomics

This book is intended primarily as a "first report" on the economic impact of the emerging biological technologies and their cousins in the new material sciences. While much of the industry is shrouded in the mysteries of the biotech lab, it is racing at top speed to the systematized production capabilities of today's most sophisticated factories. Despite the growing interest in biotechnologies on the part of the popular media, no other book has yet addressed the economic impact of bioterials, although several address scientific or ethical issues.

The biotech industry is generally defined as having four segments: human health care products, agricultural biotechnologies or "agbio," instruments and suppliers lab products, and chemical and environmental. This book uses a larger definition, and includes the entire area of new materials, and the use of biotech processes for industrial production. Such a definition puts emphasis on the importance of biology to basic manufacturing, and on the rapidly developing potential for "mass production" of health care and agbio approaches—or what might be called *GeneFactories.*

The Economic Laws of Bioterials

The biotech revolution began in earnest in 1973, when scientists Herbert Boyer and Stanley Cohen successfully recombined DNA from one organism with that of another. The "magic" of both the technology and the economics of biotech is the fact that virtually every cell has the power to replicate itself millions of times. The economic power of that magic is just now coming into focus.

The new laws of the Bioterials Age suggest that the underlying economics of this era will be even more profound than those of either industrial or information technology. The Bioterials Age will transform everything from the cellular and atomic within to the far reaches of every extremity and at a speed never before imaginable. Despite it being very early in this technology cycle, three fundamental economic laws (described more fully in Chapters 3 to 6) are coming into sharper focus:

The First Law of BioEconomics: The Daily Doubling of Knowledge. In the mid-1970s, early in the development of biotechnologies, knowledge in the industry (as expressed by patent approvals, a proxy measure for commercially useful scientific discoveries) took about 8 years to double. By 1997 that rate had been reduced to less than 4 years. Early in the new century that will become less than a year, and by 2005, biotechnology knowledge will likely double on a daily basis. This will occur as a result of the mapping of the human genome, expected in 2000–2001. This is the "inflection point" of the bioterials era, akin to the completion of the periodic table in chemistry, the splitting of the atom in physics, or the invention of the transistor in electronics. With the explosion of knowledge that follows, we will conquer matter.

The Second Law of BioEconomics: The Global Scope of Bioterials Is Inversely Proportional to Its Subatomic Scale. R&D activity often produces benefits beyond the entity performing the research, because the innovation has applicability across industries, or the entity performing the R&D is unable to capture all economic benefits. Most often, however, the additional benefits are reasonably predictable, as the other potential applications are widely known. Biotechnology R&D differs markedly from other kinds of R&D because the end results are much more difficult to identify and predict in advance. Unlike traditional fields of research, few characteristics and regularities are yet known about the new materials under study. However, the areas of real commercial impact of biotechnologies already account for more than a third of the world's GDP. Thus, while bioterial scientists work in the "nano world" of cells, molecules, atoms, and subatomic particles, their impact is global in scope.

The Third Law of BioEconomics: Accelerating Vertical Growth Rates. The first economic era, that of "hunting and gathering," lasted from the human's first appearance on earth until about 7000 years B.C. That time period marks the transition to the Agrarian Age which lasted until 1750, when mechanical technologies created the Industrial Age. The Industrial Age lasted some 360 years, until the advent of the Information Age. Information technologies drove the economy for only some 50 or 60 years, to be displaced now with bioterials. The Bioterials Age will last only about 15 to 30 years, but its economic returns will dwarf everything that has come before it. The economic returns from the adoption of energy and production technologies in the Industrial Age increased arithmetically, although those from the Information Age increased geometrically. As resources committed to biotechnology R&D increase, the commercial fruits of this research will increase exponentially.

Industry Asymmetries

In addition to the evolving laws of bioterials, there are now some structural attributes of the industry, such as the asymmetric size of firms and small markets with huge potential, that are already quite evident. Although they will be discussed more thoroughly later in the book, a brief overview of the industry is valuable at this point.

Small, but Numerous, Firms Focused on R&D. Since the development of recombinant DNA in 1972, over 2000 organizations (profit and non-profit) have been founded in the United States, and about the same number worldwide, to explore and take advantage of biotechnologies aimed primarily at the life sciences (agriculture and health care). About two-thirds of the companies are considered "mainline" biotech-nology firms with the primary goal of commercializing biotechnology R&D. The rest are companies engaged in biotechnology research but whose primary line of business is different (for example, certain phar-maceutical, agricultural, and pollution abatement companies). Of the strictly biotech firms, some 30 percent are publicly traded, 54 percent are privately held, and the remaining 16 percent are joint ventures.

Most of these firms are small, with 30 to 100 employees. They are often focused solely on R&D, and rely on bigger players, such as pharmaceutical firms, to handle marketing and distribution of their products and services. However, a few larger biotech firms, such as Amgen, Genentech, and Genzyme, currently account for significant sales volume in end-user markets.

Reinvention of Major Players from Related Industries. A number of major firms, such as DuPont, Monsanto, and Novartis, are rapidly reinventing themselves from commodity chemical companies to biotech, or life sciences, concerns. Dow Chemical, on the other hand, appears to be focusing more on the industrial applications of bioterials. For some this will be their entire focus, although for others, such as DuPont, life sciences are one part of a larger portfolio of activities. Likewise in the pharmaceutical industry, major players are either entering the field with their own R&D, or more often, developing strategic relations with the smaller, research-oriented biotechs.

Astronomical Research Intensity. Biotechnology firms are by far the most research intensive of all major nondefense industries. Estimates of current annual biotech R&D spending range from $7.7 to $10 billion. On average, biotechnology firms spent $69,000 per employee on R&D in 1995, compared to $7651 for all corporations. The top five biotechs spend an average of nearly $100,000 per employee per year, whereas the top pharmaceuticals spend $40,000 per employee per year. Expressed in terms of total operating cost (on average) for biotech firms, R&D accounts for an astronomical 36 percent. To pay for this research, the biotechs have an insatiable appetite for cash. They raised some $5.5 billion in 1997 and nearly as much in 1998, although the mix of venture, public, debt, and partnership funding is changing.

Small, but Rapidly Growing, Markets with Huge Potentials. The largest markets currently for biotechnology products and processes are pharmaceutical products, agriculture, and environmental remediation, with sales of $15 billion. Market activity is highly concentrated in medical applications, which account for over 90 percent of current sales. Ten-year projections suggest that the market for biotech products will more than triple in real terms and that medical markets will continue to account for nearly 90 percent of sales. The size of markets likely to be profoundly affected by biotech innovations is much larger than the biotech market itself. The major sectors most impacted are health care, chemicals, agriculture, mining, and environmental remediation. Together, they account for nearly 15 percent of the U.S. GDP. However, the potential impact of the larger category of bioterials is even more profound. Bioterials will eventually have a significant impact on the entire spectrum of manufacturing, an additional 15 percent of the economy, although research efforts in these areas are in the embryonic stage.

The economics of bioterials will transform not a limited number of domestic economies over a long period of time, but will revolutionize the entire global economy in a very brief, but intense explosion. It will work *genetically* to transform the world from the inside out. Its transforming powers are already evident. Business futurists are already describing the new corporate organization form as organic, using biological terminology such as "mutations" to drive home the need for radical changes. Senior managers of many large organizations are also turning to biological metaphors to adequately describe the nature and speed of change in their businesses. Some have been heard to argue that change within their organizations must be *organic* and that their response to the marketplace changes *genetic*.

The biological metaphor is also creeping into all walks of life and language, just as new words and expressions ("tune in and turn on" or "that doesn't compute") challenged conventional thinking and speaking in the Information Age. As we near our conquest of matter, however, more than our language will change.

Transforming Technologies

Major technologies create and transform economies, and they also transform much of the rest of life as well. Industrial and information technologies had equal, but opposite, transformational effects on society. Now bioterials technologies have an even more dramatic impact.

Industrial Technologies Pushed Everything Up at the Center

In an earlier book, *The Shape of Things to Come: Seven Imperatives for Winning in the New World of Business,* I argued that the technologies of the industrial era were centralizing technologies that "pushed everything up at the center."

Industrial technologies created cities and countries and centralized factories and corporations. The economics of these technologies demanded central administration and control and the centralized management of the political, social, cultural, and even sacred institutions to complement and enhance the economic. The centralized command and control structure of the factory was borrowed as the management metaphor of the white-collar company, and the elevator made possible the skyscraper and the hierarchical organization. Information technologies, on the other hand, pushed everything out to the margin.

Information Technologies Pushed Everything Out to the Margins

Now largely housed in two-story buildings on small campuses through the world, the successful modern organization relies on the Internet, e-mail, fax, and video conferencing to adroitly manage a rapidly changing commercial *space* in the global economy. Today's leading companies are no longer concentrated in the money, production, or technology centers of New York, Detroit, or California (or the comparable parts of other industrialized nations), but are increasingly found in places like Charlotte, North Carolina; Nashville, Tennessee; Redmond, Washington; and North Sioux City, South Dakota. Countries formerly on the fringes of power are now in the ascendant. China's economy will shortly rival that of the United States in absolute size, and places like Singapore, Argentina, Brazil, Poland, and the Czech Republic, despite recent setbacks, seem poised to join the more economically successful nations.

Likewise, the devolution of power to the margins of society has been equally dramatic in the arts, government, and social institutions, fueled by inexpensive and powerful information technologies. These technologies have changed the balance of power in politics and culture; educational and social expressions now reach to the remotest village. Where technology and economics lead, the political, social, and cultural transformations follow. Although the social and political ramifications of bioterials are harder to discern at this early juncture, the economic transformations are already coming into focus.

Bioterials, Transforming Everything from the Inside Out

Although industrial technologies pushed everything up at the center, and information technologies reversed it all by pushing everything back out to the margins, *bioterials will transform everything systemically, from the inside out.* This is already becoming apparent from the new "laws" of bioterials economics that are just now emerging.

In earlier eras, scientific discoveries had important impacts on many areas of economic activity to the extent that they enabled the reorganization of production in more efficient ways, but eventually these efficiencies ran up against physical production constraints. In the Industrial Age, for example, all businesses reached a point where their productive capacity (outputs) point began to level off and eventually cease with the addition of more economic inputs (labor, capital, raw materials)—in other words, the law of diminishing returns to inputs. This law was predicated on the practical size limit of the production function and the inability to modify the characteristics or availability of raw materials. Bioterials technologies, however, will *systemically infiltrate* the production process of firms across the global economic spectrum. By conquering matter, these innovations will reorder the input-output equation across all industries that produce or use consumable goods.

Moore's Law captured much of the essence of the underlying economics of the Information Age. It described the rapidly declining costs of semiconductors and their concomitant increase in power and functionality in very short periods of time. The manifestation of Moore's Law was the eventual invasion of the microprocessor into most products and services. Moore's Law eventually made every company an information company. The new laws of bioeconomics will make every company a bioterials company.

Every Company a Bioterials Company

As we arrived in the last decade of the twentieth century, astute business observers contended that all companies had become information companies. By that they meant that virtually every company had come to rely on information as its primary source of value-added activity. This was often demonstrated by the fact that the largest component of the final selling price of most products and services was accounted for by information in one form or another (R&D, engineering, sales and service, communications, and even inventory and logistics whose major cost components are information).

This book is written for managers not just in today's bioterials firms, but in all companies. A major contention of this book is *that by the middle of the twenty-first century, all companies will be bioterials companies.* That is to say, all companies will produce, ship, consume, or in some other way, rely on bioterials products and processes.

To comprehend the full impact of these technologies, we need to understand, as explored in the several chapters, the activities of the researchers, scientists, and business futurists that are "re-architecting" the cellular and subatomic universe.

2

Conquering Matter

Explorations
in the Cellular
and
Subatomic Universe

We are about to embark on a new century and a new millennium. Predicting the events of the next millennium is a foolish endeavor. Even attempting to imagine the events that will shape the next 100 years seems full of peril. The next 30, though, are already coming into focus.

Early in the next century, in fact, we will see discoveries that are more global in their impact than the Internet, more important to our lives than fire, the wheel, and the car, smarter and faster than the world's biggest supercomputer, and more powerful than the combined strength of all the world's armies. The source of this wonderful new technology is all around us. It is in our bodies, the most complex pharmacy known to man; in the vast storehouse of energy and sustenance locked in the rest of the living world, plants, and animals, and in the vast factories of goods and services embodied in the inorganic materials of the planet. The new Bioterials Age is about to unlock the doors to this rich treasure chest of organic and inorganic materials. The development and exploitation of these technologies will define and dominate much of our economic, social, and political agendas for a good part of the next century.

Biology Trumps Physics and Chemistry

While the twentieth century was the century of physics and chemistry, the twenty-first century will be the century of biology. While almost magical in the riches they provide, physics and chemistry are about to be eclipsed, trumped if you will, by the far superior treasures of biology. The understanding and harvesting of biology's riches will fuel the economies of the world through much of the first half of, if not the entire next 100 years.

Since the invention of the steam engine and the successor technologies of the Industrial Age, the world has been consumed in an era of discovery and exploitation of the laws of physics and chemistry. From Newton to Einstein, the "superstars" of the scientific world have helped us understand and eventually exploit the physical world. The alluring and most economically productive of the sciences, physics and chemistry, have created for us a world of prosperity and relative ease.

By conquering energy, the technologies of the Industrial Age made the world a very small place. The steam engine gave way to electricity and gasoline, and eventually to the jet engine and the rocket fuel that took man to the Moon (still the greatest achievement of industrial technologies). The most enduring impression of the first astronauts to stand on the Moon, and many who watched with them via television, was not the Moon itself, but the view of the Earth as a very small planet.

In the last half of the twentieth century, physics and chemistry created the computer chip, the marvel of the Information Age. Almost single-handedly, the chip has "rewired" every aspect of our lives, from the mundane to the extraordinary, from the secular to the sacred. The chip became the heart of a worldwide communications infrastructure that converted us into what Marshall McLuhan proclaimed in 1963, as a "Global Village."

The last half of the twentieth century was witness to unparalleled achievements of the Information Age, as it shrank the world and conquered time. Today, as Information Age technologies arrive at an intersection with the bioterials technologies of the next century, we will see quite clearly that *biology trumps electronics,* in scope, speed, and impact. Bioterials combines all the power of earlier technologies and accelerates them beyond anything known before.

Bioterials: Global Scope, World Scale

The adoption and use of bioterials will be the most global event in history. They will be used more widely, faster, and more effectively than any previous technology. Their very nature, scope, and importance dictate that bioterials technologies are the most globalizing force known to mankind. No other scientific development—not agricultural, industrial, or even information technologies—is as immediately and so dramatically important to the world as bioterials.

The Industrial Age was a phenomenon created primarily in those countries that became the western democracies. The technologies of the era shaped not only the economics of the west, but its culture and social structures as well. These technologies were slower to be adopted in large parts of the rest of the world, and even today have not been adopted extensively in some areas such as rural China and Africa.

The Information Age transformed the industrial west, but was broader in its global reach. Despite the political will marshaled to stop them, they spilled over the borders of the west and penetrated and reshaped the economics, politics, and culture of much of what we now call the Second World. Those areas are often labeled "newly industrializing countries" or "economies in transition," and include the former communist countries of Europe and dictatorships of South America.

The world prior to the Industrial Revolution was essentially rural and the livelihood of most people depended on subsistence agriculture. There were a few cities and those areas called countries were essentially defined by the accident of geography (for example, islands such as Japan) or by strong linguistic or ethnic forces. The centralizing power of industrial technologies created two massive movements: *urbanization* to bring labor into convenient central locations and *nationalization* for purposes of economic control over trade, protection from foreign competition, and the central control of people, capital, and raw materials.

The Industrial Age also divided the world into the three economic divisions we have come to label the First World (North America, Western Europe, Japan, and Australia/New Zealand), the Second, or Developing, World (Eastern Europe, South America, and the more developed parts of Asia), and the Third World (China, Africa, and Central America). These designations relate primarily to economic measures such as GDP, per capita income, and the like. But they can also be equated to the differing adoption rates of industrial technologies.

What we now call the First, Developed, or Industrial World was the inventor and the first adopter of industrial technologies. Although the use of industrial technologies was widely diffused throughout these western democracies, the important technological developments originated in just a few countries: the United States, the United Kingdom, and Germany. Today, with less than 10 percent of the world's population, the industrial countries enjoy 70 percent of its wealth.

These same countries were among the leading developers and early adopters of Information Age technologies. Other countries, such as Japan and Korea, were critical in the commercialization of these technologies, permitting greatly reduced prices and thus accelerated diffusion. Today, these "information economies" are being joined by those such as Brazil and India as large producers of software, one of the key technologies of the Information Age.

The so-called Second World was slower to adopt industrial technologies, less astute in their application (primarily due to political considerations such as the belief in centralized government planning and control), and consequently fell far behind in the standard of living. Moreover, although slower to adopt information technologies than the west, the countries of the Second World allowed the gradual leakage of these technologies (first television, then the telephone, fax, and computer) across their borders. They are, however, after a slower start, now rapidly diffusing information technologies throughout their economies. Throughout the lower cone of South America, for example, PC and other business-oriented computer technologies are beginning to rival the widespread use of such products in western democracies.

These technologies are helping to dramatically improve their economies. Perhaps more importantly, though, information technologies became the pipelines of political change. They allowed political dissidents for the first time to communicate, plot, and organize, eventually resulting in the overthrow of their communist or right-wing dictatorships.

Today, the Second World has about 30 percent of the world's population and about 20 percent of its wealth. Although the Information Age impacted this less developed world late in the century, those countries, in the main, were busy through much of the twentieth century catching up with the Industrial Age. While many of those countries struggle with adopting industrial technologies, they are, at the end of the century, also facing the rapid diffusion of information technologies. They have, should they choose to use it, the experience of the more developed nations in choosing patterns of adoption and use of information technologies. Most seem clearly anxious to harvest the benefits as quickly as possible.

The Third World (rural Asia, India, and Africa), today accounting for some 60 percent of the world's population and less than 10 percent of its wealth, has been the slowest to adopt either industrial or information technologies. The very nature of bioterials technologies, though, suggests that they will not escape this wave of technological change. Much of the so-called agbio research has the Third World as its prime target. Thus, while few industrial or information technologies have penetrated far into the Third World, the bioterials revolution will go farther globally and, as we shall see, faster than any set of technologies before them.

Bioterials Technologies: Spontaneous

The impact of the Industrial Age, like the technologies it spawned, took three and a half centuries to mature and create the part of the world we now call industrial. But that modern industrial world rapidly became information-driven with the invention of the transistor (that became the computer chip) just 50 years ago. And, the broader impacts of electronic technologies were faster, geographically broader, and more encompassing than anything industrial technologies could portend. Or, perhaps we just had more time, generations in fact, to assimilate them. The Bioterials Age will afford us no such luxury. It will mature in one generation.

Using the hindsight of history, we can see the force with which Industrial Age technologies transformed us: from the printing press to the jet engine, industrial technologies propelled the western world to new heights of progress in virtually all fields of endeavor. The eruption of political, cultural, and social changes in the western world rivaled the impressive gains in economics and industrial progress. Even if punctuated at times with an occasional period of trauma, the transition from rural, agrarian life, to an industrial society was essentially evolutionary, as it took place over some 350 years.

Information Age technologies were dormant for nearly 100 years, from the invention of the telegraph and telephone in the late 1800s, until the invention of the transistor in 1947. The transistor, which "morphed" into the computer chip, dramatically spurred the economic, social, and cultural growth of industrial countries for the past half century. While Information Age technologies revolutionized the economics of the developed and, to some extent, the developing world, they also rapidly transformed much of our social, cultural, and political lives as well.

The Bioterials Era will, by comparison, be totally global, and in historic terms, almost instantaneous. And its wide-ranging effects are already being felt in agriculture, health care, and industrial applications. The era will reach its global maturity in just 20, or at most, 30 years.

By the late 1990s it was popular, at least among Internet aficionados, to talk about life, in electronic terms, as being lived at least several times the speed of industrial life. In fact, some even argued that it was similar to a dog's life, seven times faster than man's. The speed of change in the bioterials era will dizzy even the most seasoned "net-head." The more apt comparison for the Bioterials Age is that everything will speed up to resemble the life cycle of the fruit fly. Long the staple of freshman genetic classes, the fruit fly reproduces as many as 15 generations in a single semester.

Bioterials: Systemic

While industrial and information technologies have had a huge and enduring impact on much of the world, bioterials portend even greater changes. Industrial and information technologies "acted on" us, and we, in turn, manipulated them. The nature of bioterials technologies is quite different. They work from the inside out.

The essence of bioterials research is the manipulation of the "architectures" of cells and atoms. By modifying the "architectural skeleton," so to speak, bioterials technologies act *systemically— through us, rather than on us.* With earlier technologies, we learned to do things; and we did things to things. While those technologies may have changed our lives, they didn't change us. Bioterials are different because, in the extreme, they will fundamentally alter humans and the nature of the world around us. Furthermore, the impact of their research has, as pointed out in Chapter 4, more impact on more industries than any other previous technology. They will begin by altering the economies of the world, and end by altering our vision of who we are as people.

While primarily information companies (in computers, telecommunications, consumer electronics, software, etc.) have fueled economic expansion since the early 1950s, biotech and new materials companies are quickly becoming the new economic engines of growth and innovation.

Like the embryonic information companies that began to populate the business landscape of the 1950s, small innovative biotech companies are springing up around the world, with some 2400 companies in the United States and the European Union (EU) alone. Similar growth is taking place in Asia and other parts of the world. In addition, in the areas of agriculture and pharmaceuticals, large established companies, such as DuPont, Monsanto, Merck, and Pfizer, are either transforming themselves into biotech firms or developing close financial relationships with the small entrepreneurial firms breaking new technical ground. Biotech companies will, in the next 50 years, completely revolutionize agriculture, medicine, and industrial activities.

Imagining the Unimaginable

As described in Figure 2-1, bioterials researchers in private, government, and university labs are already working on a wide range of products that will transform matter. The list makes us begin to imagine the unimaginable—a world radically different from our own, and yet, perhaps, only years away. But the time interval between development and testing the commercial viability of these developments in the marketplace is dropping dramatically, even in the pharmaceutical, medical, and agricultural areas, where new products and processes must today undergo years of rigorous testing before commercial use is allowed.

In the United States several forces are causing the development and commercialization process of new biotech products to shorten dramatically, including pressure from patients for faster availability of new therapies and the more rapid approvals in other countries. In addition, the enormous cost of research and of the development of a range of faster testing devices is collapsing development times from years to days. How quickly some of these biotech developments will be in widespread use is open for debate, because the success of any particular bioterials product is still very much a "big bet."

Despite the uncertainties, indicators of economic change are already apparent. Figure 2-2 provides a quick overview of the economic forces marshaling for change. Of course, not all the companies or products will make it. The ratios of winners to losers are low. The biotech industry combines the winner-take-all characteristics of computer operating system software with the uncertainty of the roulette wheel.

But the payoff to the winners will be spectacular, and even more than in the Industrial and Information Ages, the winners in the Bioterials Age will revolutionize the economic laws that rule our lives. While the research focus of bioterials is at the microscopic level, the impacts are "writ large" on the global economic landscape.

Bioterials scientists are working on technologies that will give us:

- Creation of life in a lab.

- Predetermination of the sex of children and their genetic makeup.

- Pharmagenomics, which directs and tailors drugs to individual genotypes.

- The ability to "program" out of human genes the propensities to contract various diseases and illnesses.

- Genetically derived therapies for the prevention and cure of most cancers, heart disease, AIDs, and other diseases, including new strains of vaccine-resistant ones such as malaria.

- Repair of damaged brain cells and spinal cords.

- Production of proteins that fight infections or treat problems such as growth deficiency.

- Mass production in a lab of at least six U.S. Federal Drug Administration (FDA) approved monoclonal antibodies, which, when injected into a patient, hone in on the antigens that populate the surface of cancer cells.

- The ability to clone, or duplicate, mammals including humans.

Figure 2-1. Transforming matter.

- Control of aging and obesity.

- Animals that grow replacement organs for 50 percent of humans who die before getting a transplant organ from a human donor.

- Inexpensive "transgenic" vegetables that will produce vaccines capable of inoculating the world's poor against diseases that have ravaged them for centuries.

- A tree that will grow in a few years instead of 50 or 100, fundamentally changing the economics of everything wooden.

- A natural plant that will produce a substitute for the raw materials in plastic, potentially impacting the entire oil and petrochemical industries.

- The world's strongest fiber and the world's most powerful adhesive produced by insect and animal "factories."

- A biological, protein-based computer thousands of times faster that today's fastest.

- BioElectronic noses, tongues, ears, and heads to test industrial and consumer goods and provide new levels of real-time health care assessment.

- BioSynthetic skin, blood, and bone, as well as the "precusor" human master cell that can be directed to grow new bone and cartilage.

- New materials for products and packaging that repair themselves and adapt to their environment.

- New materials that swell and flex like muscles to replace human muscle and machine power in factories.

- New materials that repel any ink, paint, or stain.

- New materials that shape and reshape themselves for a huge variety of industrial, consumer, and health care applications.

- New energy sources that are efficient, pollution free, and almost free.

- New paints that capture and store the energy of the Sun in cold weather, and repel its heat in hot weather, reducing energy costs and pollution associated with heating and cooling.

- A "smart mouse" that points the way to eliminating aging in humans.

Figure 2-1. (*Continued*)

Some leading economic indicators suggest that the conversion to the Bioterials Age is already underway:

- There are some 2000 biotechnology organizations (private and public) in the United States and more than 1000 in the EU, and nearly another 1000 around the world. With a year-over-year revenue increase of some 45 percent in 1996, biotech is the fastest growing business segment in the EU. There are similar growth rates in many other parts of the world.

- Market capitalization, the amount of money invested in the U.S. biotechnology industry, increased 12 percent in 1997, from $83 to $93 billion. Nearly $500 million of private capital was invested in EU companies in 1997, and some $30 billion in the United States in pharmaceutical biotechnology firms alone.

- Huge, global commodity chemical suppliers, such as DuPont, Novartis, and Monsanto, are re-inventing themselves as biotech firms.

- Today, there are more people employed in biotech in the United States than in the machine tool industry, a key sector in the development of the industrial economy.

- The top five biotech firms spend an amazing $100,000 per year per employee in R&D, and most spend some 15 to 30 percent of revenues per year on R&D compared with today's so-called hi-tech industry that spends 10 to 12 percent per year, or industrial firms that typically spend less than 5 percent.

- Over 100 million people worldwide have been helped by the more than 65 biotechnology drug products and vaccines.

- There are more than 295 biotechnology drug products and vaccines currently in human clinical trials and hundreds more in early development in the United States. These medicines are designed to treat various cancers, Alzheimer's, heart disease, multiple sclerosis, AIDS, obesity, and other conditions.

- Biotechnology is responsible for hundreds of medical diagnostic tests that keep the blood supply safe from the AIDS virus and detect other conditions early enough to be successfully treated.

Figure 2-2. Leading economic indicators of the Bioterials Age.

- Many increasingly popular home pregnancy tests are based on biotechnology diagnostic products.

- The payoff for the $25 billion invested by the U.S. Government in fusion power is possible in the first half of the next century as scientists have recently made major breakthroughs in better understanding the nature of the materials under study.

- In some cases, as much as one-third of the meat, fruit, and vegetables consumers are already enjoying are biotechnology foods such as vine-ripened, longer lasting tomatoes, better-tasting carrots and peppers, corn and soybeans with superior growth characteristics, and drought- and disease-resistant plants of all kinds. Biologically re-engineered animals are making meat, fish, poultry, and diary products healthier, cheaper, and more efficient. Hundreds of biopesticides and other agricultural products are also being used to improve the food supply and to reduce our dependence on conventional chemical pesticides.

- Environmental biotechnology products make it possible to more efficiently clean up hazardous waste without the use of caustic chemicals, and even produce commercially useful by-products.

- Revolutionary new bioterials production processes that will produce everyday products such as new fibers, plastics, adhesives, and new metals at a fraction of the cost of current manufacturing technologies.

- Industrial biotechnology applications have led to cleaner processes with lower production of wastes and lower energy consumption, in such industrial sectors as chemicals, pulp and paper, textiles, food and fuels, metals and minerals, and energy. For example, much of the denim produced in the United States is finished using biotechnology enzymes.

- DNA testing, a biotech process—popularized by the O. J. Simpson and Monica Lewinsky cases—has dramatically improved criminal investigation and forensic medicine.

Figure 2-2. (*Continued*)

3

BioEconomics

The New Laws
of Bioterials

A technology as pervasive as biotech could not help but attract a lot of attention. A number of popular books and articles have already begun to describe biotech science and technologies, their potential impact on the environment and health care, and importantly, the ethical dilemmas that will accompany biotech development. Among others, both *Time Magazine* and *Business Week* have declared the next 100 years the biotech century.

No one, though, has looked at the compelling economic impact of not just biotech, but of the material sciences as well. Although economics is often called the dismal science, nothing could be more exciting than the economics of the next century. Bioterials technologies have the potential to create a whole new set of commercial dynamics in medicine and agriculture. They will touch off a new industrial renaissance that will increase the functionality and decrease the cost of virtually all manufactured goods. Bioterials will completely alter the nature of human interaction with the environment and will end diseases that afflict humans, plants, and animals. These new technologies will feed and clothe a population that Malthus could never have dreamed possible.

The economics of the last century were driven first by the mechanical might of the Industrial Age and then by the electronic expansion of the Information Age. In the next 15 years, bioterials will be recognized as more important than the Internet or, in fact, the entire information revolution. Before describing in greater detail the economic laws of bioterials in subsequent chapters, it is important to understand how technology drives economics.

The forces governing economic development trends over very long periods can be traced to a single concept—technological innovation. Year-to-year fluctuations in economic growth are a function of investment and employment. It is technology, though, which allows capital and labor to be employed in new and more productive ways. Thus, it is technology that has generated the secular increase in economic growth and living standards witnessed in the industrial world over the last two centuries. The economist Joseph Schumpeter was nearly unique among his peers in this century in understanding that the maturity and consequent wide application of major technologies (for example, the car, the telephone, the computer) changes markets and economies far beyond incremental improvements in machines and workers.

Schumpeter's concept of technology was broader than most. Rather than the current more popular concepts of the term, which tend to focus on computers and electronics and other "hi-tech" innovations, he defined technology as a process or product that enables a new method of "doing things" (for example, Total Quality Management or double entry accounting). New and improved methods of doing things improve the underlying economics of companies, industries, and markets. Such a conceptual framework suggests a view of economic development as fundamentally shaped by successive waves of "creative destruction," in which scientific or organizational breakthroughs redefine the structure of production across the economy. In fact, creative destruction by technologies has been the basis of the increasing well-being of western civilization.

Two important economic laws dictated both the growth and limits of the Industrial Age. The first, "Increasing Returns to Scale," epitomized the benefits of centralization and mass production. The workings of this law were the driving force behind the phenomenal riches created during this era. On the other hand, the law of "Decreasing Returns to Scope" suggested not only that there were limits to size and growth, but that industrial technologies brought with them many negative economic, environmental, and political manifestations.

Although the laws underpinning industrial technologies are still with us, they have been largely eclipsed by the laws of the Information Age. The economic laws of networking in the Information Age created new levels of economic wealth beyond anything that could have been envisioned during the Industrial Age. Just like industrial technologies, though, they brought their own set of political and social issues.

From the Farm to the Factory

Irrigation, fertilizer, and crop rotation turned the brown earth green and created enough food to feed a billion people by 1800. Later the tractor would help feed millions, then billions, more. Most people, no longer needed on the farm or as specialized independent crafts people, left the farm and village and joined thousands of others making things in factories in large and growing cities. The steam engine, gasoline, and electricity helped clothe, shelter, and transport those people, and provided luxuries heretofore reserved for royalty to the common man in many parts of the world.

The Industrial Age: Harnessing Energy

A broad view of economic development of the industrialized world reveals two waves of "creative destruction" in the twentieth century. The first was characterized by the employment of energy or power sources to substitute for the muscle power of humans. The use of steam, gasoline, and eventually electric power enabled an assembly-line production technology that exploited the benefits of task specialization. Such methodologies generated rapid declines in the relative price of finished goods, bringing many products that were once restricted to the very wealthy, such as automobiles, to the general population.

The inflection point for much of this transformation and rapid economic growth was the commercial marketing of electric power in the 1880s. (See Figure 3-1.) It was not electricity alone that ushered in the Industrial Age. It was also the innovators who saw the capacity to create the modern production assembly line through new means of power distribution. The mechanical belts and pulley equipment, characteristic of factories in the steam era, placed significant physical and technical restrictions on production. Electricity and

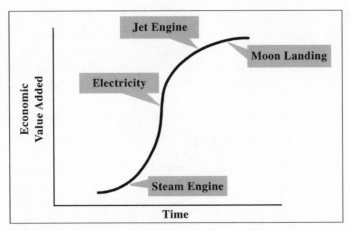

Figure 3-1. Strategic inflection points of the Industrial Age.

more modern production equipment helped alleviate, but not eliminate, many of these problems.

When steam replaced muscle power, and then electricity replaced steam, it was, in economic terms, merely an "input substitution"— established processes got cheaper and faster. The real gains reaped from a new energy source, however, were organizational. Electricity, for example, required companies to rethink their entire business process, redesign machinery and equipment, modify labor skills, and move people out of the factory and into the office. Because such transformations were gradual, and internal to organizations, they tended to be less visible than the outward manifestations.

But it was electricity that gave us the streetcar and the elevator, two essential technologies that created the hierarchical, industrial corporation. Electric power for the streetcar brought office workers to central office locations. The elevator permitted the vertical movement of people and the sharing of information from the lowest to the highest levels of the organization, now housed together in huge skyscrapers.

Thus, the invisible reorganizing power of energy, particularly electricity, along with its more visible power to move people and machinery, created the fundamental economic laws of the Industrial Age, expanding our horizons, but limiting our potential to achieve them. Two fundamental and in some sense opposing principles underlay the economics of industrial technologies: increasing returns to scale and decreasing returns to scope.

Increasing Returns to Scale. The most basic economic law of industrial technologies is the *increasing return to scale*. This principle holds that expanding the size of productive capacity lowers unit costs of production by enabling the cost advantages of assembly-line production. Although conventional wisdom today, its "discovery" early in the Industrial Age fueled much of the centralizing actions of businesses and governments alike. Similarly, the larger the political unit, the lower the costs and the greater the benefits. Both proved to be true, subject to the second law of the era.

Decreasing Returns to Scope. The second law of the Industrial Age holds that, for any manufacturing technique, the productive capacity created by widening its scope and adding more labor and/or capital inputs will eventually diminish and ultimately cease to be cost effective. This occurs for one of two reasons: the management cost of coordinating production becomes prohibitive or the unit costs of raw materials begin to increase to the point where they are not justified by their profit-making potential.

From the Office to the Lab?

The invention of the transistor at Bell Labs in 1947 revolutionized all communications devices—radio, TV, the "wireline" telephone system, and the mainframe computer. It was the inflection point of the Information Age, which had been lying dormant since the invention of the telegraph and the telephone in the late 1800s. (See Figure 3-2.) It also led to the creation of many new devices—the cell phone, CD player, VCR, PC, and palm-sized electronic organizer. Most importantly, it created networks that allowed not just the speeded up, *stand alone,* information power of these devices, but the cheap, instant, and *interactive* communications between these devices and the people that use them.

The transistor and its successor technologies in microprocessors touched off the rapid expansion of telecommunications and data networks that enabled the great economic transformation that continues today. Rapid declines in the cost of collecting, processing, and distributing information allowed companies to improve production processes, lower management costs, and increase responsiveness to changes in demand for their products. The *Economist* recently labeled the impact (primarily the decreasing costs) of such network-

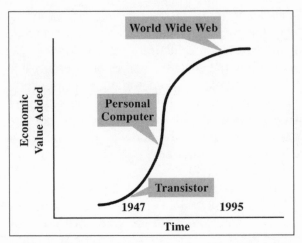

Figure 3-2. Strategic inflection points of the Information Age.

ing power as "the death of distance." They could just as easily have added "the death of time," as these networks made all information exchange in the world instant, as well as cheap.

As was the case with electricity in the Industrial Age, exploiting the full power of rapid information processing took several decades. Indeed, in the early 1950s, many observers believed either that computers had very little commercial value or that they would displace large numbers of workers and lead to mass unemployment. The economic record has disproved the pessimists, as output and employment have grown rapidly (albeit with considerable cyclical turbulence in the 1970s and early 1980s) and computer technologies have deeply permeated virtually every sector of the economy.

Early in the information revolution, computers were used to automate what were once labor-intensive tasks such as accounting and billing, telephone switching, etc., thus reducing many costs. These improvements were incremental in the sense that they computerized existing processes. It was only when computer technology began to change manufacturing processes in the late 1970s that the new laws of networking took hold. Computers began to facilitate communication across functions within and between firms. With marketers, engineers, and manufacturing managers from many related firms working together more closely, on a real-time basis, production and distribution could be adjusted to better meet the needs of customers.

In individual factories, advanced manufacturing techniques allowed "mass customization"—the production of individually customized goods at the cost of mass-produced goods. The most vivid example of this phenomenon was in the auto industry, where Japanese firms pioneered the use of such technologies to reduce product development times, increase the quality and variety of models, and reduce costs.

The Information Age: Harnessing the Power of Networks

U.S. firms followed, and the quality and variety of models available today in almost every product category, compared to just 25 years ago, is truly astonishing. Perhaps the most striking example comes from the computer industry itself, where it is now possible for an individual to custom design and buy a computer online. Even more spectacular is the explosion of new electronic appliances including cars and cell phones with GPS (Global Positioning Systems), electronic books, palm-sized computers, downloadable CDs, kitchen countertop WebTVs, "smart picture frames," and many more.

More recently, companies have been taking advantage of the Internet to keep in closer contact with suppliers and customers, resulting in better inventory management and the ability to customize mass-produced products for particular market groups. The effects of such improvements are beginning to manifest themselves in increased productivity. Like the Industrial Age, the economics of the networked economy are driven by two fundamental laws, only this time they worked in concert: continuous decreases in the cost of information and its increasing value when shared in a network.

Continuous Declines in Information Costs. Since at least the 1960s, the raw cost of computer processing power has declined by roughly 50 percent every 18 months. This phenomenon is known as Moore's Law in honor of Gordon Moore, the Intel co-founder who first observed it. And even at the end of the century, nearly 50 years after the invention of the transistor, the cost declines and the functionality increases of information technology show no sign of abating. (See Figure 3-3 for a historical perspective on the decline in information costs.)

Increasing Returns to Network Participants. The increased interconnection of computer networks and integration with traditional telecom-

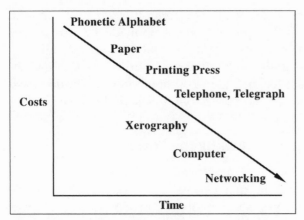

Figure 3-3. Decline in the cost of producing, storing, manipulating, and transmitting information.

munications networks has increased the value of being connected. Put simply, the benefits resulting from being attached to a network increase proportionately faster as the number of network users grows. In fact, each new addition to a network geometrically increases the value to all current participants. In the Information Age, therefore, the returns to scope (the wider the technology applications are used, for example, standard computer software) increase, opposite of what occurred in the Industrial Age.

Nowhere is the impact of this law more evident than the explosion of users—both buyers and sellers—on the Internet. Each new customer on the Internet increases the value to sellers, and each new seller on the Internet increases its value to buyers. Until the early 1990s, the Internet had few users and few features—essentially e-mail and file transfer. The maturing of information devices (their greatly reduced price and wide availability) and creation of the World Wide Web, by the mid-1990s spurred the rapid migration of commercial enterprises and users to the Web. Its full economic potential—for consumer and business-to-business commerce—is only now being realized and its economic benefits are growing proportionately.

The economics of bioterials are poised to dwarf the euphoria about electronic commerce.

The computer chip, software, and digital technologies pushed people out of the factories (now largely "manned" by robots), and into the office. Work became the creation, manipulation, and sale of information or services to an increasingly wealthy and growing population—6 billion people by 2000.

Now, the discovery of recombinant DNA, cloning, and the restructuring of the subatomic architectures of many materials, promises to feed, clothe, and shelter some 10 billion people by 2050. Although the nature of work in the Bioterials Age seems somewhat unclear (will we all work in labs?), the underlying laws of bioterials that will govern the world of work are already becoming very clear.

Bioterials: Endless Replication—The New Economic Paradigm

Biotechnologies display all of the characteristics of innovations capable of revolutionizing the structure and organization of diverse sectors of the economy in the next century. In a 1989 report, the Organization for Economic Cooperation and Development (OECD) identified four essential characteristics of a new technological and economic paradigm: An entirely new range of products accompanied by an improvement in many products and processes; a reduction in the cost of many products and services; social, political, and environmental acceptability; pervasive effects throughout the economic system. Without question, bioterials more than qualifies as a new economic paradigm.

To appreciate this potential, it's important to understand the history of biotechnology. (Although the scientific developments leading up to the commercialization is the subject of a later chapter, a brief overview at this point is useful.) The modern biotechnology industry was born a quarter century ago when scientists successfully spliced DNA from two distinct organisms to form an organism. The ability to replicate or recombine itself (for example, "recombinant") is at the heart of this technology. Such "recombinant DNA" was revolutionary in the sense that humans were now capable of altering matter at a cellular level to suit their needs. Capable of endless replications, cells could be viewed as "factories" whose outputs could be controlled by human modification of their inputs—the DNA that determines their characteristics.

The widest commercial application of recombinant DNA has thus far been in the pharmaceutical sector. There the focus is on discovering and developing methods to prevent, diagnose, treat, and cure the dozens of life-threatening and serious diseases and conditions for which satisfactory medical therapies or preventive agents currently do not exist. Genetic modification has the potential of turning the traditional medical paradigm on its head. Instead of waiting for something to go wrong and then trying to fix it, we are already beginning to gain the capacity to detect problems before they begin. Biotechnologies in the main are proactive, aiming to take corrective action at the cellular level before problems occur, thus reducing the dollar, physical, and emotional cost of staying healthy.

A second sector that has already reaped many benefits from biotechnology is agriculture. The traditional agricultural production model starts with seeds and fertilizer, adds considerable quantities of fungicides for weed control and pesticides for insect control (which in some cases have their own adverse effects), resulting in a crop. Combining the superior aspects of particular varieties (cross-breeding) with better fertilizers has succeeded, to some extent, in reducing crops lost to pests and increasing yields. Unfortunately, it is a very slow process.

It takes many generations to appreciably increase pest resistance, and even the best fertilizers fall victim to "decreasing returns" when used too heavily. Increasing the amounts of fertilizer eventually results in steadily decreasing crop yields—in other words, there can be too much of a good thing. Thus, the traditional approach of improving plants and animals over several generations (mimicking what nature has been doing throughout time) has proven valuable but slow. Furthermore, adding artificial stimulants such as fertilizers and "problem inhibitors," such as pesticides and fungicides, has allowed only incremental improvements to be made to agriculture.

Biotechnology, on the other hand, allows agricultural production to literally leap out of the incremental improvements of chemical applications and slow cross-breeding improvements. By modifying the cellular structure of seeds themselves, biotechnology can accomplish in one generation—improvements that once took a dozen. It reduces generational improvements to a single growing season while simultaneously increasing the quality, quantity, and geographic scope of production. Much the same can be said of the improvements in agricultural animals.

Most of the early commercial activity (as much as 90 percent) in biotechnology and new materials science is focused in health care and agriculture. Therefore, it is tempting to conclude that the economic effects of bioterials, although profound, will be very limited in scope, since these two sectors account for only about 15 percent of total economic activity. Such a conclusion ignores the potential impact of bioterials in industrial production. Early observers of electricity and computers erroneously predicted a limited impact. Likewise, it would be easy to limit our understanding of the capacity of bioterials to modify organic materials at a cellular and atomic level solely for the benefit of agriculture and health care.

The ability to modify matter at its most basic level has the potential to reshape the way we think about production, in terms of both the cost of raw materials and the actual production process as well. Although efforts to lower production process costs have been going on for years, firms have less control over the costs of raw materials. The economic gains that have occurred were in the area of better coordination and more efficient use of these materials.

Now, however, the scientific advances in bioterials technologies promise to change the very nature of the raw materials used in manufacturing and even new sources of energy. For instance, pulp and paper manufacturers depend heavily on wood, the availability of which is determined by the amount of forested land (which is decreasing) and the growth rate of trees (a once unchangeable biological process). Recombinant DNA opens the possibility of greatly speeding up the rate at which trees grow, and perhaps increasing the quality and durability of the wood they yield. Clearly this would fundamentally alter the rules of production in any industry for which wood products—paper, furniture, housing, and others—were an important part. In some cases as well, the new materials may even manufacture themselves into finished products.

The timber industry is but one example among thousands of potential ways in which basic control over raw materials can alter the production function to lower costs and improve quality. In addition to the input side, virtually unlimited potential exists with respect to environmental remediation of toxic by-products. The action of genetically modified bacterial agents actually transforms waste into harmless (or, in some cases, commercially useful) materials. And scientists have only begun to scratch the surface of cellular modification. It has been estimated that less than 1 percent of *single-cell* organisms have been genetically documented, to say nothing of multicellular organisms.

The Atom and the Gene

The words "atom" and "gene" suggest the vast potential of this new economic era. Both words connote tremendous power. Earlier in the twentieth century the word atom conjured up a positive, exciting world in the popular imagination; later in the century it has taken on some negative connotations associated with bombs and the supposed perils of nuclear power. In the new century it will again be thought of in a more positive way. Although the word atom has been with us in popular speech for some time, the word gene is relatively new. In the new economic era, these words are the equivalent of the computer chip in technology terms, but with many thousand times the importance.

The word *gene* is from Greek and Latin and is used in a number of forms to convey many ideas such as creation, beginning, or origin (as in *Genesis,* the first chapter of the Old Testament); pervasive, leader or all encompassing as in *general;* basic or root as in *generic;* rapid multiplication, as in *generator;* and succession, as in *generation.* The Romans and Greeks also applied the term to things feminine as the giver of life.

Despite its rather ancient heritage, the word itself is a product of the early twentieth century. The use of the term gene was first suggested by the biologist, William Johannsen, writing in the *American Naturalist,* in 1911. He argued, "I have proposed the term 'gene' . . . to be used in the science of genetics. The 'gene' is nothing but a very applicable little word, easily combined with others." A very applicable little word indeed! The gene contains the very mother-load of economics for the next century. It wasn't until late in the century, after the Watson-Crick discovery of the structure of DNA in the early 1950s, that the word found its way into public discourse.

Even more fundamental than the gene is the atom. The word again comes from Latin and Greek but was most widely popularized by the French. The ancients first used it to mean a "cut" from a strong stalk. The Greek philosopher Democritus (the philosopher from whose name we get the term democracy) was a major proponent of the word, arguing that the atom was the smallest unit of measure and the basis upon which the universe was formed (thus the basis for a democratic society). And perhaps presaging the speed at which the new economic era would proceed, they also used the term to represent the smallest unit of time (there were some 1880 atoms in an hour).

In the 1600s the French adopted the term *atome* to mean something so infinitesimally small as to defy further division. Its first use in English was in the scientific literature in the late 1400s but didn't come into general public use until the early 1900s. Arthur Conan Doyle, in his popular *The Return of Sherlock Holmes,* had his famous character describing a crime scene clue in which "the bust . . . had been smashed to atoms where it stood."

There were many names in science that knew the atomic world and brilliantly theorized about it, such as Planck, Bohr, Heisenberg, Feynman, and others. It was Albert Einstein, though, who brought the atom and physics dramatically into the public's imagination. Much of the wealth of today's society flows from the work of inspired physicists such as Einstein, Heisenberg, and others. Likewise in chemistry and biology, many minds over many generations added to our storehouse of knowledge of the cellular world, particularly in the twentieth century. It is from the scientists of the twenty-first century that the full commercial exploitation of this knowledge will emerge.

Hidden in this vast repository of subatomic structures and genetic codes lies the capacity to customize organic and inorganic materials and processes to virtually all human needs. The challenge of the next several decades will be to discover and exploit the secrets of the gene and the atom for everyone's advantage. In other words, to make every atom and every cell a factory. With such thinking, the enormous potential of the economic laws of bioterials comes into focus.

It would be foolish so early in an economic cycle to claim that all the economic laws of the period are known. After all, Gordon Moore didn't publicly articulate the Information Age law that bears his name until 1965, some 18 years after the invention of the transistor. And the law of increasing returns of networks, although originally described by Theodore Vail, an early AT&T CEO, in 1907, did not become well understood until after the invention of the World Wide Web. Nevertheless, certain economic imperatives, if not strictly laws of the new era, are becoming clear. The following chapters describe three new imperatives that will drive bioterials, and demonstrate that the Bioterials Age will prove to be not just a revolution of technologies, but of economics as well.

4

The First Law
of BioEconomics

The Daily Doubling
of Knowledge

The first law of BioEconomics holds that knowledge in the bioterials industry, at the height of its power, will double every day. The "store-house" of knowledge about bioterials has been increasing steadily since the mid-1970s, and should reach a speed of doubling every day early in the next century. Thus, the bioterials economic cycle will be short and almost vertical in trajectory, compared to the longer and more horizontal growth rates of the industrial and information eras, as illustrated in Figure 4-1.

The amount of knowledge about a particular field of endeavor is an elusive metric. If universities or governments develop such knowledge, it is widely disseminated and few efforts are made to value or track it. That is changing, however, particularly in the field of biotech, for both universities and governments are recognizing the huge windfalls that might accrue from their discoveries. If the research is done in private facilities, the knowledge is most often held confidentially in proprietary databases or commercial practices.

Although some attempts have been made to chart the full extent of the world's knowledge in a number of fields, no such effort is contemplated here. Several *proxies* for the accumulation of knowledge provide some insight into the state of the art of bioterials' knowledge and the speed at which it is growing. The best such

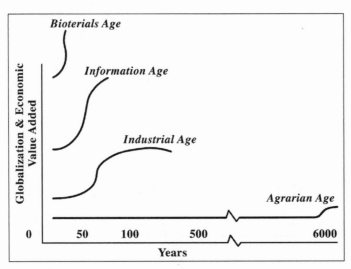

Figure 4-1. Economic eras.

proxy for bioterials is the patent system, where the growing knowledge base of bioterials is clearly evident.

Inventors of commercially viable products hope to reap profits
from their research and development efforts, so they seek ways to
prevent copycats from using that knowledge. One way to do this is
to try to keep the details about the underlying technology secret. In
most cases, this is difficult because potential competitors can often
learn these secrets by a careful analysis of the end product (in a process called reverse engineering).

The most common approach to protect the research is to acquire
a patent for the innovation. A successful patent forbids entities other
than the inventor from commercial exploitation of the innovation for
a fixed period of time (generally in the neighborhood of 20 years). If
funds are not available for full commercialization, the inventor may
also choose to license the technology to others.

The Role of Patents in the Doubling of Knowledge

Because innovations and discoveries in biotechnology have the
potential to open exponentially the range of commercial applica-

tions, it is in the economic and social interest to make these discoveries available for other researchers to build on. At the same time, making the results of research known to others raises the possibility of a copycat appropriating the research to design a product, thus "stealing" the economic benefits that rightly belong to the innovator. This would erode the incentive to do research in the first place.

The patent system is designed to encourage researchers and inventors to make their discoveries public by offering protection against copycats for a fixed period of time, generally 20 years. The patent defines the scope of protection; that is, what commercial applications are the sole domain of the innovator for the patent period. For a typical invention, such as the electric razor or Polaroid-type instant-developing camera, the scope of protection is self-explanatory. For biotechnology innovations, such as identifying a particular segment of DNA that governs the growth of an organism, the scope of protection is much more difficult to define.

Obviously, it is in the narrow economic interest of the inventor to seek the broadest scope of protection possible. The possibility that the innovation will facilitate other avenues of research means that it is in the overall interest of research to strike a balance in which the economic returns to the innovator are reasonable without blocking research in related areas. If the scope of protection is too broad, the spillover potential of innovations will be greatly diminished, possibly preventing valuable new products from seeing the light of day. If it is too narrow, innovators will be unwilling to use the patent system at all and will rely on secrecy and trade secrets, again reducing the potential for spillovers.

Courts have generally tried to limit the scope of protection for basic discoveries in biotechnology, asserting that patents can only be granted for inventions and not for natural laws and biological properties. Since there are precious few precedents for patent disputes involving biological processes, uncertainty abounds. Enough data exists, however, to get a sense of the accumulation of the knowledge stock of bioterials.

The primary criteria for patent approvals are: (1) commercial potential of the innovation and (2) "unusualness" of the innovation. Thus, the number of patent approvals is a reasonably good quantitative indicator of the increase in commercially useful knowledge. Because some innovations are kept secret, it is important to bear in mind that patent approvals probably understate slightly the total increase in commercial knowledge. Thus, for the purposes of under-standing the growth rate of scientific discoveries in biotechnology, however, it is important to keep in mind that patents represent just a "proxy" for new knowledge, but the best one available.

Trends in Biotechnology Patents Since 1977

The U.S. Patent and Trademark Office publishes data on the number of patent approvals for over 250 technology categories. The four cat-egories that comprise the most basic biotechnology innovations are shown in Table 4-1.

It is important to note that these categories do not include down-stream applications of biotechnology. For instance, there are dozens of separate categories for innovations pertaining to agriculture, chemical processes, environmental abatement, food additives, tex-tiles, and others that include some biotechnology-related patents. Because it is virtually impossible to isolate biotechnology-related patents in these latter categories, the current analysis limits itself to the four categories listed in Table 4-1.

Figure 4-2 shows the number of annual approvals for biotechnol-ogy related patents (the sum of the four categories listed in Table 4-1) since 1977 along with the time trend. To keep up with this growth, biotech examiners in the Patent and Trademark Office grew from 67 in 1988 to 184 in 1998.

The most striking result visible from Figure 4-2 is that the annual biotechnology patent approvals—not the cumulative total, but incre-mental additions to the stock of knowledge—have increased *almost sevenfold* in 20 years. This contrasts with all patent approvals that have increased by just 60 percent (from 130,553 in 1977 to 203,410 in 1997). In particular, the share of electricity-related industrial patent

Table 4-1. Patent Approvals

Number	Area
935	Recombinant DNA
800	Multicellular organisms
435	Molecular biology and microbiology
424	Drugs, bio-effecting, and body-treating compositions

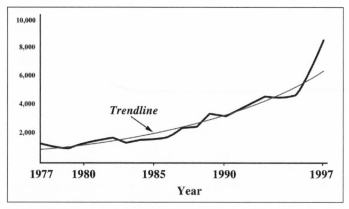

Figure 4-2. U.S. annual biotechnology patent approvals, 1977–1997. (SOURCE: U.S. Patent and Trademark Office and author's calculations.)

approvals is decreasing and that for information technologies has begun to level off.

There is a clear upward trend in biotechnology patent applications. In fact, over the entire period, approvals of biotechnology patents increased by an average of almost 10 percent annually, substantially faster than the vast majority of patent technology categories. The growth rate implies that the number of patent approvals doubled every 73 years on average. The chart also reveals that growth in patent approvals has accelerated since 1993. Is this a one-time statistical blip or a new phase in the biotechnology knowledge revolution? Qualitative and anecdotal evidence in corporate, university, and government laboratories suggest the latter, though it is too early to have irrefutable quantitative confirmation. The aggressive assertion of daily doubling times is based on this accelerated growth rate.

Trends in "Knowledge Doubling Times" Since 1977

A richer analysis of patent approvals would track the *rate at which patent approvals increase over time.* Using simple statistical techniques, one can estimate a forward-looking growth rate of patent approvals for any given year. To get a picture of the increasing velocity of biotechnology patent approvals, that growth rate is converted into the number of years required to double annual patent approvals. Data available at the time of writing only allowed an analysis through 1995, and estimates for the 1990s become less and less statistically robust, since they are based on fewer and fewer observations.

Figure 4-3 shows the results of this forward-looking analysis for biotechnology patents in the four categories noted in Table 4-1. The results are striking. Commercial biotechnology knowledge has been increasing exponentially in recent years. After holding steady for over a decade, doubling rates declined rapidly in the 1990s, and by 1995 the forward-looking doubling time was less than 2 years. The slight increase in doubling times during the latter half of the 1980s was most likely caused by a large backlog of applications combined with a shortage of trained patent examiners. Thus, some of the decrease in the early 1990s may be a "catch-up" effect from delays in processing earlier applications. It cannot explain the continued decline in subsequent years, however. Should the growth rates of new knowledge achieved by the mid-1990s persist, the stock of bioterials knowledge will double monthly by 2005, weekly by 2010, and daily in 2016.

However, these estimates don't take into account the stimulating effect of the completion of the human genome project. If, as projected, this is the "inflection point" for biotechnology (not just for the science, but attracting vast new pools of capital that stimulate the search for

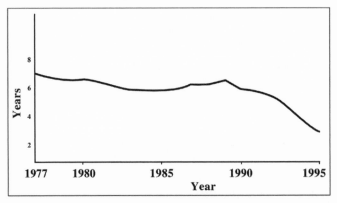

Figure 4-3. Average years to double annual approvals of biotechnology patents, 1977–1995. (SOURCE: U.S. Patent and Trademark Office and author's calculations.)

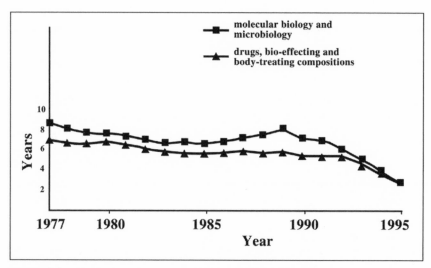

Figure 4-4. Average years to double annual biotechnology patent approvals, 1977–1995. (SOURCE: U.S. Patent and Trademark Office and author's calculations.)

new commercial applications), the rate of daily doubling could be reached in 2005. As will be noted in the final chapter, however, such a knowledge explosion will put tremendous strain on the patent approval apparatus of the United States and many other countries.

This pattern contrasts sharply with the doubling rate for all patents, which hovered around 20 years during the late 1970s and early 1980s, but increased steadily thereafter to reach 40 years during the 1990s. An increase in doubling times has even manifested itself in information technology–related patents in recent years, with the doubling rate increasing sharply from 6 to 8 years from 1992 to 1995 after remaining fairly stable at 6 years for the prior 15 years. This

Table 4-2. Number of Biotechnology Patent Approvals in Selected Years, 1977–1997

	Drugs	Microbiology	Multicellular organisms	Recombinant DNA
1977	660	591	0	14
1982	730	711	1	111
1987	958	1099	19	204
1992	1691	1965	52	356
1997	3372	4178	318	506

SOURCE: U.S. Patent and Trademark Office.

adds quantitative evidence that the Information Age is over, at least from the perspective of technological innovation.

The clear message of Figure 4-2 forms the basis for articulation of the first law of bioterials, the *Daily Doubling of Knowledge,* as it demonstrates the forward-looking doubling times for the four biotechnology categories. Additional confirmation comes from microbiology and drug patents that show an even stronger trend than the overall total because they are the most numerous. (See Figure 4-4 and Table 4-2.)

5

The Second Law of BioEconomics

The Global Scope of Bioterials Is Inversely Proportional to Its Subatomic Scale

The daily doubling of bioterials knowledge is but the first indicator of its huge potential. The next is the widespread diffusion of this knowledge—what economists call *spillover*—into other industries. While other new technologies, such as the automobile and the computer, have had widespread use in other areas, the *systemic* nature of bioterials portends the greatest technology spillover in history. While spillover benefits accrue in many mature economic sectors to some degree, the potential in bioterials is so large and diverse as to defy description. Indeed the inability to conceive of all possible productive uses of a given advance in knowledge is a concise way of defining spillovers. However, it seems fair to postulate now that the global scope of bioterials will be inversely proportional to its subatomic scale.

It was noted earlier that a limitation on economic growth and profitability in the Industrial Age was decreasing returns to inputs—essentially, the productive capacity created by adding inputs eventually diminishes and ultimately ceases to be cost effective. This law is predicated on an immutable production function and inability to modify the costs and characteristics of raw materials.

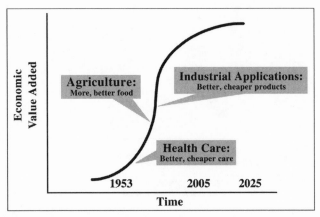

Figure 5-1. Systemic infiltration of bioterials.

To the extent that bioterials can modify the input-output relationship or reduce raw materials costs, firms may begin to see *constant or even increasing returns to inputs.* Across a sufficient number of industries, this could significantly accelerate productivity and per-capita GDP growth rates above their twentieth century average of 2 percent per year. Such broad stimulation of economic growth from one area of endeavor to others is what economists refer to as spillovers. Biotechnology has the potential to create the most important spillovers in history, starting primarily in health care, moving next to agriculture, and finally impacting major industrial sectors. The increasing movement of these spillovers across sectors of the economy is shown graphically in Figure 5-1.

Technology Spillovers

In economic jargon, spillovers refer to profits or other benefits from a particular product or technology that do not accrue to the owner of the technology. The textbook example of a spillover is the case of the honey producer who locates adjacent to an apple orchard. Locating next to the orchard has no adverse effects on the honey maker's profit, yet the output of the apple orchard increases due to enhanced pollination.

Much more important than such geographic spillovers are those related to the knowledge generated from research and development.

For any given discovery, it is impossible for the innovating person or firm to predict all of its ultimate uses. The primary reason is that complementary discoveries (either contemporaneously or in the future) can reveal new applications. An ancient example is the controlled use of fire. The "innovators" correctly identified at least one practical application—heating. But its usefulness for cooking meat was only identified later. Its ability to power machinery and vehicles could not have been imagined at the time because the requisite complementary technologies did not become known until much later.

Almost all R&D has a tendency to produce benefits that extend beyond the organization performing the research. This generally happens because the innovation has applicability across several industries or the organization or individual performing the work is unable to capture all economic benefits.

Perhaps the most-cited popular example of the use of a new technology across many industries is Teflon. Invented in the 1920s, it found its first application in materials for the U.S. space program but its commercial benefits were mostly reaped in cookware. As to the case of the reach for all the economic value being beyond the grasp of the inventor, recall that neither the inventors of the transistor, nor Steve Jobs (Apple Computers), nor even Bill Gates (Microsoft) could capture all the benefits of their pioneering work (although Gates has come close).

Figure 5-2 provides a way to better understand the dynamics of spillovers and the resultant economic benefits. Assume that a firm undertakes R&D motivated by a specific economic return such as an improved product or a cost-reducing production technique. This R&D (which may be supplemented from knowledge borrowed from the results of academic research) increases that firm's stock of knowledge, but it also can have the unintended effect of increasing the stock of knowledge in other companies. This happens through two main channels.

First, the discovery itself can "leak" to other companies, even if the innovation is patented. For example, the firm that developed the new idea might chose to license it to other companies. In addition, however, the patent also may provide ideas for other firms to improve products or production processes without infringing on the developer's patent rights. Even if the discovery is kept secret, migration of technical personnel from firm to firm may also cause inadvertent diffusion of knowledge.

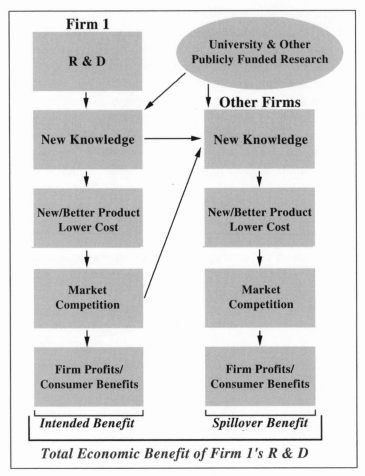

Figure 5-2. Dynamics of knowledge spillovers.

The second channel of knowledge diffusion occurs when the idea developer introduces the innovation to the market. Simply observing the finished product or performing reverse engineering can provide new product and production ideas to both competing firms and firms in entirely different industries.

As Figure 5-2 indicates, this spillover of new knowledge vastly enlarges the total economic benefit of the original research. The important thing to note here is that this knowledge diffusion *need not adversely affect* the profitability of the firm undertaking the research. This stems from the fact that knowledge is in principle infinitely extensible, meaning that its use by any number of firms does not prevent the innovating firm from exploiting it. It is this feature of knowledge that raises the possibility of "increasing returns" to knowledge inputs. Innovations permanently raise not only the profitability of research-performing firms, but major innovations often raise the rate of economic growth for the economy as a whole.

The question raised by Figure 5-2 is the relative magnitude of the unintended "spillover" benefits of R&D relative to the intended benefits. Quantitative economic analyses consistently show that the value of unintended spillover benefits to other firms is at least one-half the value of the returns accruing to the innovating firm, but often are equal in size to, or sometimes greater than, the intended benefits. Thus, the size of the boxes in Figure 5-2 provides a fairly accurate indication of relative magnitudes.

Information Age Spillover: The Computer

A modern example of the vast economic benefits generated by research spillovers is the development of the computer and, in particular, the PC. The developers of the earliest computers correctly foresaw the computer's application in mathematics and science because of its ability to manipulate numbers rapidly and accurately. However, most failed to predict the eventual importance of computers in office management, entertainment, communication, and manufacturing processes. This does not indicate their short-sightedness; rather, it confirms the general rule that the benefits of a given innovation, in addition to fulfilling an already-identified purpose, have the potential to create entirely new markets for products and services.

In fact, the spillover of microprocessor and personal computer technologies was at the heart of the current 8-year economic expansion in the United States (beginning in 1991 and continuing until the time of this writing, it is the second longest in U.S. history). Spending on telecommunications and computer products and services to spur productivity reached nearly $650 billion by 1998, almost 8 percent of GDP. The computer and telecommunications sector itself became the second largest industry in the economy (health care being the largest), surpassing the auto, heavy manufacturing, and construction industries. Analysts also maintain that these microprocessor-based technologies reduced inflation by a full percentage point during the period. Despite the impressive gains in productivity across the economy now being stimulated by computing and telecommunications technology, bioterials holds the promise of even more.

Classifying Spillovers

Basic Research

Economists generally classify research activities into three broad categories defined by the potential for spillovers, as shown in Table 5-1. Basic research is generally carried out in university or other academic settings where study and experiment are not primarily guided by commercial objectives. Even though it is not motivated by commercial applications, basic research generates the knowledge on which all such applications ultimately *depend*. For this reason, spillovers from basic research are extremely large, and correspondingly the incentive

Table 5-1. The Stages of Research and Development

Stage of research	Description	Potential for spillover	Private benefit/social benefit (private investment incentive)	Percent of overall privately funded R&D (approximate)
Basic research	Discovery of properties and characteristics of building blocks	Very large	Low	5
Applied research	Further understanding of key characteristics important to a specific commercial application	Some	Moderate	30
Product development	Development of prototype and profitable production technique	Small	High	65

for profit-making businesses to fund and perform their own basic research is small indeed.

Applied Research

Applied research builds on basic scientific discoveries, but the key contrast with basic research is that a specific commercial application has been targeted. This narrows somewhat the focus of research and hence reduces the potential spillovers. The final link on the R&D chain is the development of an actual prototype and a cost-effective production technique such that the product can be brought to market. Since the product is specifically designed to accomplish a well-defined set of tasks, the possibility of adapting the product's technology to other productive uses decreases substantially. Because of these incentive effects, individual companies spend the vast majority of their research dollars—over 90 percent—on applied research or product development.

Product Development

Product development is research that is devoted to the development of the actual commercial product. It is by far the largest area of R&D, and plays an important role in creating spillovers. While the earlier forms of R&D can simulate the imagination of scientists and researchers from other disciplines, it is often the technologies' manifestations in terms of product functionality that captures the imagination.

Unprecedented Bioterials Spillovers

The web of research currently being woven by university researchers, small and large business laboratories, and governments around the globe is rapidly revealing the characteristics, properties, and recurrent patterns of the basic building blocks of bioterials. The construction and understanding of such atomic and genetic maps will facilitate an unprecedented explosion in commercial applications that today can scarcely be imagined.

The patterns of chemical properties embodied in the periodic table of the elements fueled the birth and rapid expansion of chemical engineering a century ago. In much the same way, the "map" of the human genome, and the full understanding of the architecture of the atom, will be the inflection points for rapid growth in knowledge and commercial applications of bioterials.

Obviously, the potential spillovers from a given innovation depend on how "basic" the innovation is. Looking again to history, the economic spillovers from the discovery of fire are clearly much larger than those resulting from computers. In fact, computers themselves depend on fire—the coal- and oil-powered generators that provide a large fraction of the world's electricity. There are two primary reasons why biotechnology knowledge spillovers will be on a scale heretofore unimaginable. First is the sheer volume of research activity. As noted in Chapter 1, annual biotech R&D spending estimates range from $7.7 to $10 billion in the United States alone (and growing rapidly), accounting for a whopping 36 percent (on average) of biotech firms' sales. This does not include the many billions more in public funds that support complementary research in government labs and universities.

Second, much of this research takes the form of basic research or applied development, meaning that the vast majority of spillovers have yet to manifest themselves. This contrasts sharply with Information Age research, which is now highly concentrated in applied product development, yet another sign of the maturity of that sector. In addition, because biotechnology research targets the fundamental understanding of matter itself, spillovers can and will accrue to any enterprise that uses matter—which is to say every single enterprise in the world economy.

A telling example of how biotechnology-related research can turn around a sector is the case of textiles and apparel in the United States. Long battered by competition from low-wage countries, particularly in East Asia, the American textile industry has often been cited as one of the casualties of the move toward freer world trade. However, closer investigation of the sector reveals some interesting results. First, research intensity in the sector, though small compared to others, has doubled relative to sectoral GDP since 1990, in large part driven by the quest for biotechnology-based improvements in durability and comfort. This effort has already paid off handsomely—not only has the sector grown quite rapidly in absolute size, but productivity—that is, the efficiency with which it uses inputs and the quality of its end products, has increased.

Every Cell and Atom a Factory?

Because biotechnology research seeks to understand matter and modify it to suit the needs of human production and consumption, it is unique in its potential to modify the production function of a wide range of firms. Broadly speaking, the cost of production in any firm comprises four main elements—workers to provide manual and intellectual input, capital equipment to assist employees in their task, raw materials to which value is added, and energy to carry out the manufacturing process.

The costs of the latter two elements have long been essentially out of the control of individual firms; rather, they depend on trends in commodity markets, discovery and exploitation of new energy sources, and the like. In addition, they continue to account for a large proportion of production costs. With an excess of 50 percent of production costs locked up in raw materials and energy for the large majority of manufacturing industries, clearly any innovation that put firms in more control of these costs holds the promise of large savings.

Biotechnology holds great promise to enable reductions in the cost of energy and materials and/or improvements in their quality—in fact all biotech-related research is motivated to some degree by precisely this goal. The example of faster-growing trees changing the production function of the timber industry cited earlier in the text is one example, but there are many others. In health care, production of insulin has long been constrained by the high cost of extraction—an example of a product for which raw materials account for nearly the entire production cost. Biotechnology research has made possible the production of synthetic insulin from genetically modified pigs, thus reducing the cost of the primary raw material for treatment of diabetes.

Bioterials Spillovers:
An Atom Deep and a World Wide

While some spillovers are already apparent, it is clear that the ultimate economic returns to bioterials research are difficult to identify and predict in advance because of the vast potential of knowledge spillovers yet to come. Since few characteristics and regularities are yet known about the basic building blocks, the economic benefits from them have yet to be realized.

Though there are areas in which biotech research has already yielded commercially viable products, notably in pharmaceutical, agricultural, and environmental applications, they represent the tip of an iceberg whose size cannot yet be determined. As resources committed to basic biotechnology R&D increase, the commercial fruits of this research will eventually increase exponentially more rapidly, as applied researchers build on the knowledge of patterns and regularities in atomic and genetic behavior that came before. Such knowledge should pay out against a broad range of industries. As noted previously, such a situation strongly suggests that, as research progresses, the commercially viable knowledge it generates will increase.

Major Target Markets for Bioterials Products

Pharmaceutical applications are expected to dominate sales of biotech products for at least the next decade (see Table 5-2), in large part because the medical side of biotech is the best developed in terms of research and the state of knowledge. This trend is also evident in the breakdown of market areas currently being pursued by bioterials biotech companies. (See Table 5-3.)

Since bioterials is not an "industry" per se, but rather an enabler of more efficient processes across a wide variety of sectors, it is impor-

Table 5-2. Sales of U.S. Biotechnology Products by Product Type, Actual 1996 and Projected 2006, in Billions of 1996 Dollars

	1996 (actual)	2006 (projected)
Medical products:	9.4	28.6
Therapeutic	7.6	24.5
Diagnostic	1.8	4.1
Nonmedical products:	0.8	3.8
Agriculture	0.3	1.7
Specialty chemicals	0.3	1.6
Nonmedical diagnostic	0.2	0.5
Total	10.2	32.4

SOURCE: J. Paugh and J. Lafrance, The U.S. Biotechnology Industry, U.S. Department of Commerce, Office of Technology Policy, July 1997.

Table 5-3. Market Areas in Which U.S. Biotechnology Firms Are Active in Product Development, 1996

	Number of companies	Percent of total
Medical:		
Therapeutics	448	41.8
Diagnostics	346	32.3
Immunological products	146	13.6
Vaccines	105	9.8
Drug delivery systems	94	8.8
Chemical:		
Reagents	224	20.9
Specialty chemicals	159	14.8
Agricultural:		
Fermentation/production	116	10.8
Plant agriculture	106	9.9
Environmental remediation	93	8.7

SOURCE: J. Paugh and J. Lafrance, The U.S. Biotechnology Industry, U.S. Department of Commerce, Office of Technology Policy, July 1997, based on data from the Institute for Biotechnology Information.

tant to look beyond the traditional market analysis that focuses on sales as a measure of economic importance. An examination of the innovations which have remodeled the economy in the past—electricity and electronic networks—reveal some interesting observations. They actually account for a surprisingly small share of overall output.

Electric utilities account for no more than 2.5 percent of the GDP and electronic equipment for 2.1 percent. In fairness, this vastly understates the impact these technologies have had on the economy because their effects have permeated nearly all industries. Such widespread use will be true for bioterials products as well. One example is the ability of new pharmaceutical products, most often incorporating biotechnology processes, to reduce overall health care expenditures by obviating the need for more expensive hospital care. A recent Manufacturers Alliance (MAPI) report estimates current savings at $36 billion and growing—far greater than the $9 billion actually spent on biotechnology-related medical products.

Table 5-4 demonstrates the size of industrial sectors whose activities are already being revolutionized by biotechnology. Clearly $10 billion in current sales vastly understates the potential impact on the economy, as bioterials will undoubtedly impact *nearly one-third of the U.S. economy.*

Table 5-4. Size and Relative Importance of U.S. Private
Industries Most Likely to Be Affected by Biotechnology and
Bioterials, 1996

	Billions of dollars	Percent of private-sector GDP
Biotechnology:		
Health services	445.5	6.6
Chemicals and allied products	155.8	2.3
Environmental services	140.0	2.1
Agriculture and forestry	130.4	2.0
Mining	98.7	1.5
Bioterials manufacturing	1309.1	19.6
Total	2279.5	34.1

SOURCE: U.S. Department of Commerce, Bureau of Economic Analysis.
NOTES: Environmental services data are extrapolated from a 1990 benchmark of
1.7 percent of the GDP estimated by the OECD. Health services does not include
public-sector health care expenditures, which amounted to approximately $330
billion in 1996.

However, a full market analysis of the biotechnology sector is
exceedingly difficult at this point in time, since researchers are only
beginning to scratch the surface of biological process modification
and its potential application to commercial activities. Development
of commercially viable products is currently most well developed in
the health, chemical, agricultural, mining, and environmental remediation sectors, which currently account for nearly 15 percent of total
output. Bioterials are at a much more primitive stage of development, but they have the potential to revolutionize the raw materials
used by a wide spectrum of manufacturers.

Biotechnology R&D differs significantly from other kinds of research
because the end results are much more difficult to identify and predict
in advance. Unlike traditional fields of research, such as electronics
engineering, few characteristics and regularities are yet known about
the entities to be studied. As resources committed to biotechnology
R&D increase, the commercial fruits of this research will eventually
increase proportionately faster as projects build on new knowledge.
Economists have already begun to detect evidence of such knowledge
spillovers in specific geographic regions that have high concentrations
of biotechnology researchers. In the United States, biotechs have
tended to cluster in the west (California, Colorado, and Washington

State), the northeast (Connecticut, Massachusetts, New York, New Jersey, Pennsylvania, and Maryland), the midwest (Illinois, Indiana, Ohio, and Wisconsin), the central south (Virginia and North Carolina), and the south (Florida and Texas). In Asia, Japan dominates all other countries, while in Europe, the United Kingdom is by far the biggest player. Such clustering is important, as companies seek to leverage scientific expertise in academia and business. Such a clustering is occurring in the Boston area, for example. Figure 5-3 shows the clustering of biotechnology firms in North America while Figure 5-4 shows those clusters in Asia, Figure 5-5 those in Africa and the Middle East, and Figure 5-6 those in South America.

Mapping the Human Genome and the Periodic Table of the Elements

The birth of modern chemistry and the rapid development of the commercial applications referred to generically as chemical engineering offers a fascinating and revealing analogy to the coming biotechnology revolution. As far back as the eighteenth century, scientists realized that all matter is made up of combinations of basic building blocks called *elements*. Through experiments, they realized that these building blocks would react with one another under certain conditions to produce substances with completely different properties. For example, the combination of hydrogen and oxygen, both highly flammable gases, yields water, a liquid effective in extinguishing many types of fires.

This fundamental theory of chemical reactions was pretty well worked out in its entirety by the early nineteenth century, well before the discovery of most elements. The number of known elements grew rapidly; by 1830, 55 of the 92 naturally occurring elements had been discovered and their basic properties described and documented. But it was impossible to describe the properties of all compounds that might form from the combination of two or more elements due to the sheer number of permutations. Such a task would be impossible without some sort of classification scheme by which elements could be placed in logical groups as a function of their chemical properties.

Classifying the elements according to their reactive properties was thus the major research challenge facing chemists in the middle

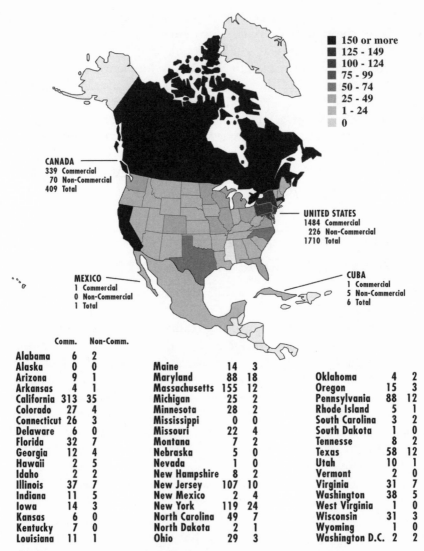

Figure 5-3. Concentration of biotechnology in North America. (SOURCE: *J. Combs and Y.R. Alston (eds.)*, The Biotechnology Directory, *New York: Stockton Press, 1997.*)

decades of the nineteenth century. As early as 1829, German chemist Johann Wolfgang Döbereiner noted chemical similarities between bromine, chlorine, and iodine, and touched off a fervent search for other patterns in chemical reactions. The milestone event was the publication of Mendeleyev's periodic table of the elements in 1869,

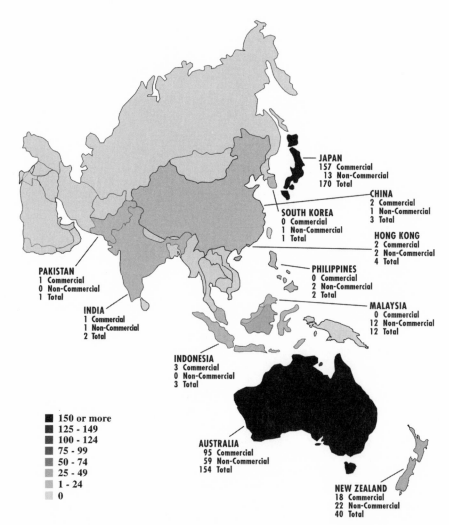

Figure 5-4. Concentration of biotechnology in Asia. (SOURCE: *J. Combs and Y.R. Alston (eds.),* The Biotechnology Directory, *New York: Stockton Press, 1997.*)

which grouped elements into categories displaying similar properties based on periodic changes in valence patterns. His theory was validated when several newly discovered elements fit exactly the properties his table predicted.

This discovery, with periodic refinements, paved the way for rapid commercial exploitation of chemical reactions and continues to serve as a roadmap for applied research and development. Knowing pat-

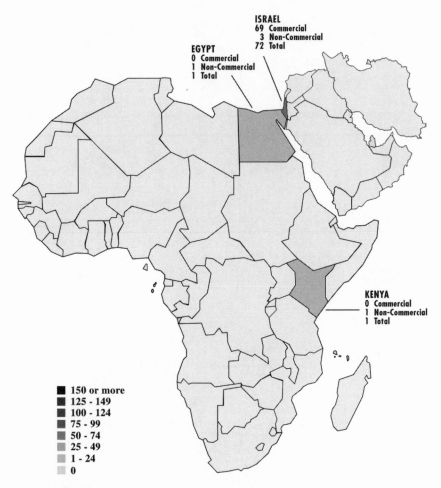

Figure 5-5. Concentration of biotechnology in Africa and the Middle East. (SOURCE: *J. Combs and Y.R. Alston (eds.),* The Biotechnology Directory, *New York: Stockton Press, 1997.*)

terns of chemical behavior vastly simplified applied research and commercial applications, and the rapid growth of chemical engineering in the early part of the twentieth century is a testament to this knowledge. Today, the chemical industry has grown to become one of the largest manufacturing industry groups, producing over 70,000 products that generate nearly $400 billion in sales. More importantly, because so many products depend on chemicals, it is a key determinant of the overall well-being of the economy.

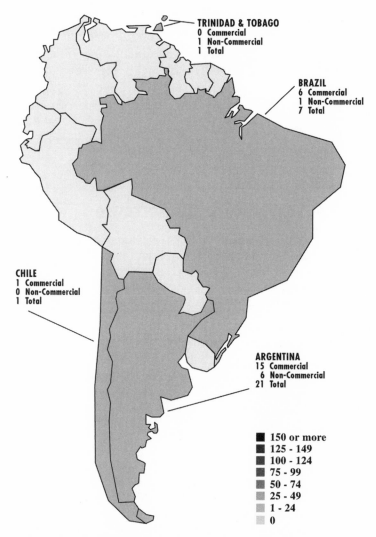

TRINIDAD & TOBAGO
0 Commercial
1 Non-Commercial
1 Total

BRAZIL
6 Commercial
1 Non-Commercial
7 Total

CHILE
1 Commercial
0 Non-Commercial
1 Total

ARGENTINA
15 Commercial
6 Non-Commercial
21 Total

■ 150 or more
■ 125 - 149
■ 100 - 124
■ 75 - 99
■ 50 - 74
■ 25 - 49
■ 1 - 24
■ 0

Figure 5-6. Concentration of biotechnology in South America. (SOURCE: *J. Combs and Y.R. Alston (eds.), The Biotechnology Directory, New York: Stockton Press, 1997.*)

The same pattern is clearly emerging in modern biotechnology—except on a much more rapid timetable. The fundamental theory of biotechnology is already quite well-developed—scientists understand that DNA governs the cellular processes of all living things and that changes in the structure of DNA cause changes (sometimes dramatic) in an organism's characteristics. Some parts of the DNA of some organisms have been analyzed and their properties documented, but not yet enough to establish a roadmap to guide applied research and product development. The biotechnology revolution is thus at the point where chemistry was just before the development of the periodic table. The discovery and documentation of genetic regularities across organisms—the biological analog to the periodic table of the elements—will spark a new wave of bioengineering. It will be the inflection point of the bioterials era.

Bio-Materials: Scale, Scope, Importance

The human genome project will ultimately provide a genetic map of human DNA and thus help applied researchers develop biotechnology products to diagnose and treat diseases and even prevent diseases from occurring in the first place. Analogous efforts for other organic substances with substantial economic value (such as wood and hydrocarbons) must be encouraged to provide guidance to applied research in bioterials, environmental abatement, agriculture, and any number of applications not yet identified.

Some things are already quite clear: we know, for example, that it is technically possible, via recombinant DNA technologies, for humans to genetically modify biological processes. However, because so little is yet known about the fundamental properties of these processes (that is, which parts of DNA strands control what processes in the thousands of known species), commercially viable applications of the underlying technology are, with the exception of pharmaceutical and agricultural applications, in their infancy. The best we can do at this point is to look to the industries, people, and businesses where bioterials are having their initial impact. Chapters 8, 9, and 10 do so, with examinations of the impacts of biotechnology on health care (primarily pharmaceuticals) and agriculture, respectively. However, the speed at which this will occur has not yet been examined. The next chapter proposes the third law of bioterials, which holds that the full commercial exploitation of these technologies will be half that of information technologies and 18 times faster than that of industrial technologies.

6

The Third Law of BioEconomics

Accelerating Vertical Growth Rates

The first two laws of the Bioterials Age—the daily doubling of knowledge and the global scope and scale of that knowledge, set the stage for the third, and perhaps most important, law of BioEconomics: accelerating vertical growth rates. This growth rate includes all aspects of the economy—geographic, across industries, and even into the basic social and cultural organization of human life. In the Information Age, business analysts warned that companies had to adjust to constant change. This was dictated by the governing law of the era, Moore's Law, which implied constant growth rates. The rate of change in the Bioterials Age, however, will be constantly accelerating.

Growth Rates: From Horizontal to Vertical

The economic growth trajectory of the bioterials economy will be almost vertical. Figure 6-1 shows estimated worldwide per capita GDP in constant 1990 dollars from 6000 B.C. (the approximate beginning of organized non-nomadic agricultural activities) to A.D. 2025. The shape of the curve is indeed astonishing. For nearly eight centuries, material human well-being expressed in monetary terms was essentially unchanged (with an ever so slight dip during the Dark

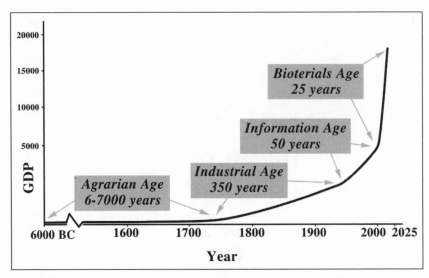

Figure 6-1. Estimated world per capita GDP in constant 1990 dollars, 6000 B.C.–A.D. 2025. (SOURCE: *J. Bradford De Long*, Estimating World GDP, One Million B.C.–Present, *http://econ161.berkeley.edu*)

Ages of 1200–1400), hovering around $120 per person annually. The Bioterials Age is blinding in contrast. It will most likely add more dollars to average material well-being in a quarter century than were added since the beginning of history—including the Information Age!

In the Industrial Age, per capita GDP increased extremely rapidly by previous historical standards; in the two centuries up to 1950 it grew from about $180 to $1622. There are two critical points to note about this increase. First, the vast majority occurred after 1850, a full century after the time when historians generally agree that the seeds of the Industrial Age were planted. Second (and not evident in Figure 6-1), this increase was confined to a relatively small number of geographic regions—Western Europe, followed by North America, and only later in the nineteenth century in Japan. Thus, while the Industrial Age was far-reaching by historical standards, it was fairly limited in both scale and scope relative to what was to follow. Furthermore, companies, indeed entire societies, had the luxury of time to adopt and adapt to the new technologies.

The Information Age saw a then-unprecedented further acceleration in per capita GDP increases. Since 1950, per capita GDP has increased fourfold to reach an estimated $6539 by the year 2000. The same two caveats about the Industrial Age are evident here, albeit to a much lesser extent. There is a slight, but clear, acceleration in the increase in per capita GDP beginning in 1975. This confirms what we already know anecdotally. While the core information technologies (the transistor, microprocessor, and software) were developed in the late 1940s, it was not until at least three decades later that they matured and began to permeate entire economies. This lag allowed precious time for companies to react to the new technologies and adapt their production strategy accordingly.

In addition, the economic benefits of the Information Age did encompass a number of regions outside of Europe, North America, and Japan (including many Southeast Asian and Latin American countries), but have yet to significantly touch India, China, and Africa—home to half the world's population.

Juliet Was Just 13!: Pushing the Limits of Human Longevity

Wherefore art thou Romeo? This legendary Shakespearean line is all the more poignant when we realize that Juliet, at age 13, had already reached "middle age" before experiencing the excitement of a first love, because average life expectancy at the time was only about 25 years. The fragility and brevity of an individual life, threatened by countless unknown and untreatable maladies, was such an established and accepted reality of existence that social and cultural traditions—including early marriage and high fertility rates—developed as a compensating factor.

In our own age, "youth" is now considered to span a longer time than most of Shakespeare's contemporaries could hope to live. Life expectancy, like material well-being, shows an accelerating upward trend (Figure 6-2). Virtually constant at around 25 years of age from the beginning of the Agricultural Age to the early part of the Industrial Age, it increased markedly from 1800 to 1950, largely due to medical innovations which mitigated the scourge of infectious diseases and reduced infant mortality. This trend continued later in the twentieth century as medical technology was diffused through much of the developing world. But, as with economic growth, the Bioterials Age promises to add more years to human life expectancy in the next half century than were added throughout all prior human his-

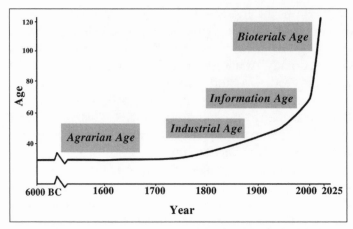

Figure 6-2. Estimated average worldwide life expectancy at birth, 6000 B.C.–A.D. 2025.

tory! Such a rapid change will only accelerate the dramatic demographic shifts (most notably the aging of the population).

The corollary of the coming unprecedented increase in life span is continued growth in the world's population. Figure 6-3 shows estimated world population at 25-year intervals from 1000 to 2150. In a now familiar trend, its growth was incremental and virtually invisible until the beginning of the Industrial Age. A sharp acceleration occurred

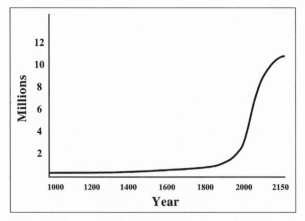

Figure 6-3. Estimated world population, 1000–2150. (SOURCE: *J. D. Durand,* Historical Estimates of World Population, *Philadelphia: Population Studies Center, University of Pennsylvania, 1974.)*

beginning in the 1950s, largely due to the worldwide diffusion of vaccines, antibiotics, and other previously developed medical products. But this trend toward sharp increases is expected to continue apace at least until 2100.

The reason population will continue to grow is not so much a function of reducing infant mortality—this challenge has in large part been medically addressed, even though political and resource constraints have in some cases hindered diffusion of requisite health care in certain geographic areas. Rather, bioterials are acting on the other end of the life span—offering the possibility of genetically arresting key parts of the aging process to extend the potential human life span well beyond the commonly accepted limit of 120 years. It is interesting to note that the projections illustrated in Figure 6-3 are based on a *deceleration* of fertility rates in the vast majority of developing countries toward the low levels of today's industrial countries. By extending the individual life span, bioterials technologies will counteract the expected declines in fertility to some extent and are thus, in part, responsible for the continuation of the population explosion. However, as will be described in Chapter 10, they will also give us the tools to make that population the best fed in history.

Temporal Compression, Global Diffusion

The temporal compression of the Bioterials Age relative to earlier periods in terms of years is only half the story. Perhaps more importantly, the impact of bioterials technologies will be heavily frontloaded: in fact, scientific discovery and commercial exploitation will occur almost simultaneously.

The evolution from discovery of a key enabling technology to widespread social and business impact of that technology is so oft repeated that it tempts us to accept it as a law of nature. Few would argue with the following stylized explanation:

1. Discovery or invention of a key enabling technology concept (such as mechanical power or the semiconductor) leads to a flurry of applied research and product development for a limited number of commercial applications.

2. After some period of time (decades in the Industrial Age, years in the Information Age), the first commercially viable products (usu-

ally catering to well-defined and limited applications) appear on the market.

3. After a further period of years, as use of initial products stimulates ideas for other applications, the actual technology "revolution" occurs, as the technology rapidly and deeply penetrates the economy, usually bringing about tremendous social changes as well.

Thus, the revolutionary aspect of technology has historically been "back-loaded," which explains the shape of the curves in Figures 6-1, 6-2, and 6-3. However, the Bioterials Age will turn this once-sacred paradigm on its head. The explosive economic and social impact of bioterials will not wait for the twilight of the age 25 years hence. The initial bioterials product development (step 2 in the 3-part process in the preceding list) is not confined to a narrow set of applications, but spans everything from the food we eat to the clothes we wear and nearly everything in between. As shown in Figure 6-4, the typical "fanning out" of commercial applications for the technology (which once took years or even decades) is now happening simultaneously. Thus, not only will the bioterials revolution be the most time-compressed in history, but *its economic and social impact will be front-loaded in this compressed time span.* Companies no longer

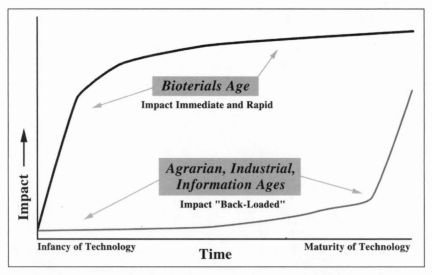

Figure 6-4. Economic and social impact of new technologies: The new front-loaded paradigm.

have the luxury of time to base strategic decisions on a "wait and see" attitude toward bioterials technology.

Drug Discovery: From Decades to Days— From Semesters to Seconds

The time compression of discovery and product development is already evident in the area of pharmaceutical products. Capitalizing on the free fall in the cost of data and knowledge sharing and automated research enabled by the Information Age, academic and commercial scientists are dramatically reducing the time required to discover, develop, and test therapeutic drugs. Network computing has enabled unprecedented collaborative research efforts among institutions around the globe, and indexed online knowledge bases of the effects of biochemical agents on results of clinical trials have reduced wasteful duplication of research. No longer must professors and corporate researchers schedule leaves of absence from their home institutions to collaborate with their peers on a daily real-time basis. The logistics cost of global collaboration have been reduced essentially to zero.

There are numerous examples of the time compression of all stages of drug development. Zymark, a Hopkinton, Massachusetts-based company heavily involved in robotic and automated analysis of potentially useful molecules and compounds, has dramatically shortened the initial discovery process. Seemingly mundane innovations, such as standardizing Petri dishes and test tubes, have enabled robots to carry out chemical analysis, once done by lab technicians, on a broader and much more rapid scale. This has helped them to reduce the throughput of assays (the chemical and biological samples to be analyzed) from months to days. In another example, robotics and automation have increased Celera's (a biotechnology firm founded by noted genome researcher Craig Venter) capacity to analyze 150,000 plasma preparations per day, orders of magnitude higher than an individual lab technician's capacity of 10 per hour.

Ramping Up the "GeneFactory"

The metaphor "GeneFactory" captures the "mass production" of analysis of genetic sequences which is possible with the marriage of biotechnology knowledge with vast computer processing power. The information intensity of genetic research is large indeed—a single gene structure can contain up to 70 million sequences. However, the ability to analyze and compare sequences is far greater. Venter's company Celera employs the world's most powerful nonmilitary supercomputer to compare gene sequences. Its 1200 interconnected DEC Alpha processors can compare 250 *billion* sequences per day. This sheer power, combined with a DNA sequencer (called the ABI Prism 3700) that is 100 times more sensitive than anything previously available, will virtually guarantee a continued shortening of the drug discovery process.

Automation and computer modeling have also shortened the testing phase of development. The quintessential example is BioNumerik, a San Antonio, Texas, firm named the best biotech firm of the year in 1999 by *Red Herring* magazine. It specializes in computer-aided simulations of drug experiments, which could reduce the time required to carry out clinical trials from 6 to 2 years.

It is thus eminently clear that the "re-engineering" of pharmaceutical research has temporally compressed *every stage* of the drug development process. During the discovery phase, more potentially useful substances are being isolated, increasing the ultimate throughput of commercial products. In the screening and testing phase, multiple clinical trials can be monitored simultaneously, and in some cases be replaced by computer simulation, providing more complete information with which to improve the effectiveness of the drug under development. And finally, re-engineering enables a net reduction in time from discovery to commercialization. This creates the direct benefit of additional corporate earnings—the reward for being "first past the post" in terms of product introduction—as well as the much larger indirect benefits of improved quality of life for the beneficiaries of those products.

Major Drug Deals: Accelerating Diffusion of Pharmaceutical Products

The already numerous biotechnology-based pharmaceutical products confirms the notion that understanding the basic technology and active commercial product development are occurring simultaneously. But beyond that, trends in policies governing testing and regulatory approval are further compressing the time between product development and launch.

Because of concerns about potential adverse side effects of pharmaceutical products, the United States and most other nations require drug developers to carry out comprehensive testing, both through biochemical analysis and animal and human clinical trials. Once this is completed, the developing firm submits a request for approval to the appropriate regulatory body. In the past, if a firm wished to market its products in multiple jurisdictions, it would have to file separate requests often requiring time-consuming (and often duplicative) analysis. Furthermore, backlogs and a lack of resources at regulatory approval agencies often meant that applications could languish for several years after all clinical trials had been completed. These two trends combined to substantially lengthen the drug development cycle during the 1980s.

A Fast and Global FDA?

Significant progress on compressing time frames has been made on both fronts. In the United States, a new drug approval system based on user fees was implemented in 1992, and succeeded in cutting the average time between submission and approval from 30 to 18 months in 1997. This period is expected to decline even further to 6 months by 2002.

With respect to the duplicative and time-consuming efforts involved in filing and following up on applications in multiple jurisdictions, the International Conference on Harmonisation has been working since 1991 to streamline the drug approval process in North America, Western Europe, and Japan. Its ongoing discussions among regulatory agencies in those regions have resulted in a growing number of standardized guidelines for clinical testing, meaning that clinical trials no longer need to be custom-tailored to a particular country's regulatory requirements. However, not all parts of the process have yet been standardized. Looking ahead, the Conference hopes eventually to adopt a truly standardized process, in which drug companies apply just once for approval for commercial distribution of pharmaceutical products in virtually the entire industrial world. Furthermore, it is highly likely that the rest of the developing world will follow suit, enabling global penetration of medicines faster.

No Time to Blink

The Bioterials Age leaves no such luxury of time to adapt to technological shifts. Relative to previous historical periods, economic growth will be essentially vertical in slope, but only the companies who understand how to exploit bioterials technologies *now* will be a part of this unprecedented economic opportunity. Developments and discoveries pertaining to bioterials are moving so rapidly that companies can no longer afford to be reactive. They must dare to look beyond the Information Age and comprehend the innumerable ways in which bioterials will change the way they do business.

7

New Materials

Every Atom a Factory

*We have labeled civilizations by the
main materials they used: The Stone
Age, The Bronze Age and the Iron
Age . . . a civilization is both
developed and limited by the materials
at its disposal. Today, man lives on the
boundary between the Iron Age and a
New Materials Age.*

DR. GEORGE P. THOMSON,
NOBLE LAUREATE, PHYSICS

For most of the last 100 years, material science has been the back-water of engineering research. Like Rodney Dangerfield, the scientists who toiled there couldn't get any respect. Their "science" was largely concerned with trying to make existing materials fit new uses. Or, they worked at such pedestrian tasks as better ways to weld two metals together.

Today, though, these materials engineers are at the cutting edge of science. They have completely turned the process of discovery on its head. Joined by leading physicists, chemists, and a whole host of engineering minds from a number of other areas, such as electronics, and even biologists and medical researchers, they are reshaping everything about the science and commercial use of inorganic matter.

And in the process, they've all but erased the sharp distinction between the organic and inorganic worlds. Many synthetic bioterials come from a natural, organic process. Tercel, for example, a modern, "miracle" fabric, comes from bacteria. It may be manufactured like other inorganic fibers, but it is from an organic source. Many other examples appear daily. In fact, the whole science of matter has been expanded, primarily from concern about natural materials, such as metals, to include new composites, polymers, ceramics, and photonic, porous and adhesive materials with strikingly impressive attributes. And they are even developing "smart" materials that sense, think, form, and reform themselves or react to the environment around them.

In the past, materials science worked at the level of whole natural materials. Their chief pursuit was to find uses for the materials given the properties that they inherently possessed. Today, materials scientists, at the cutting edge of improving the material world around us, start with the application—such as metals that shape and reshape themselves for surgeons or packages and paints that take advantage of the changing environments they encounter—then design the atomic structure of new materials to fit the job.

Conquering Matter

New materials scientists, along with their scientific cousins, the engineers and physicists working at the subatomic level, and the biologists working at the molecular level, are, collectively, doing nothing less than conquering matter. In early May of 1999, scientists at Stanford University's Linear Accelerator Center, followed a few weeks later by a comparable Japanese group at Nagoya University, announced the opening of a "B-factory" for studying the "quarks" of matter (the smallest subatomic particles yet discovered) and their antimatter counterparts. By pushing the limits of our understanding of the smallest pieces of matter, they are leading the way to conquering it.

And in the process, they are making every atom and every cell a factory—factories capable of producing a rich new storehouse of cost-effective goods and energy.

Although the engineers working on new materials worry about the practical uses for new materials, the theoretical physicists are probing the very depths of the world below the atom. Some, like Lydia Lee Sohn, a Princeton University professor, are breaking new ground in the area of "mesoscopic" systems that conduct hundreds of microamps of electricity through a single atom. (See "A Material Girl.")

A Material Girl

It's a material world
and I'm a material girl
MADONNA
Material Girl

The smaller, the better.

That's the approach Dr. Lydia Lee Sohn, Princeton University's "material girl," takes in her ground-breaking research on "mesoscopic" systems, circuits that can conduct hundreds of microamps of electricity through just a single atom.

With that much power in that little space, the speed of the state-of-the-art Pentium 300-MHz microprocessor could be increased by a factor of about 1000. Sohn sees countless other applications for her work as well, in fields such as medicine, chemistry, and biology.

"There are properties of these atomic devices where, beyond a certain size, you could control the motion of a single electron," the very young Assistant Professor of Physics says. What's preventing people from using them now is you'd have to work at very low temperatures. At atomic levels, you could use them at room temperature.

"It's remarkable," she goes on. "The technology is moving so fast. The first transistor was just invented in 1947." She wasn't even born until more than 15 years later, on October 26, 1966, in Manhattan. "For me, it isn't just the science itself," she says. "It's just truth. There's nothing subjective about it. It's very concrete. What I make now is devices," Sohn says.

That conviction has taken her a long way in a short time. Even she's a little taken aback by the whirl of events sometimes. She was class valedictorian at Parisappany Hills High in 1984, and set off for Harvard that fall. Her first technical paper was published just a year later.

In 1988 Sohn graduated magna cum laude, with a BA in Chemistry and Physics. Four years later, Sohn received her Harvard PhD in Physics at the ripe old age of 25.

A NATO postdoctoral fellowship found her in Delft, Holland, the following year. She then worked 2 years at the Bell Labs in Murray Hill,
New Jersey, as a postdoctoral fellow in physics. Her prolific writing
continued: In just 3 years, 1993 to 1995, Sohn published 12 papers. She
also gave no fewer than 22 major lectures and conference presentations
over the same span.

Sohn began work at Princeton in 1995, and has remained there ever
since. Her own sense, interestingly enough, was that one of the earliest
advocates of molecular machines and nanotechnology, *Engines Of Creation* author Eric Drexler, had missed the mark. "He had a vision, but
his approach was too way out there at the beginning. There's some
basis of projecting things and some basis of dreaming things. I'd like to
stay with things that can be proven."

Sohn has a real appreciation for the women scientists who came
before her, for the Marie Curies and Rosalind Franklins who blazed
even earlier trails.

"I can now appreciate how much they've gone through. I've benefited from a lot that the older generation has done." She's almost always
the youngest member in any group of physicists. "I do suffer from that,
it's both hard and fun," she says. "It's okay, but it is lonely at times,"
she goes on. "What's nice is that in this field of mesocopics everyone's
pretty encouraging, because it's so hard. There's no need to be cut-
throat."

At Princeton, one of her favorite mentors was Biology Professor
Arnold J. Levine, who has since moved on to become president of
Rockefeller University in New York City. Sohn sees Levine's field as a
possible future destination for her own work in mesoscopics.

"I think a lot is going to merge with biology," she says. "A lot of it is
trying to interface the mesoscopic world with molecular biology,
because you're on the same length scale. Mesoscopics can't just live
with physics. It has to collaborate . . . You could think of wild and crazy
ways to use the material."

Sohn has shown a great talent for doing that her entire life.

Sohn's work, and the work of other theoretical physicists just like
her around the world, is leading the way to the development of new
materials for all aspects of the material world. The result will be new,
better, and cheaper energy sources, vastly improved raw materials
for the production and distribution of goods and services, and even
a renaissance in manufacturing technologies themselves.

From Trial and Error to "Architecting" Matter

For much of history, materials scientists have taken the materials they had at hand as a "given." These early materials scientists gave little thought to creating new materials. To them the discovery process was a sometime fortuitous, mostly haphazard, always backbreaking, and an endless search through thousands of existing materials.

Chemists, on the other hand, had a slight edge. Working with the benefit of the periodic table of the elements, they mixed known chemicals together to see what new chemicals they'd get.

Thomas Edison tested some 1800 different gases in his light bulb before he found one that worked. Charles Goodyear, untrained in chemistry, but convinced that something would make rubber usable did much the same. He had strong feelings he could "do something" with that strange new elastic material made from the sap of South American trees. To make it practical, that something would have to keep it from going soft and gooey in the heat or from cracking in the cold, its natural tendencies. He tried combining rubber with every substance he could lay his hands on, even chicken fat. When he spilled a rubber-sulfur mixture on a hot stove by accident, he "discovered" his solution. Goodyear didn't know it, but the sulfur bonded the rubber molecules into an elastic network—most importantly, a temperature-resistant elastic network. Goodyear knew what he wanted, but he didn't know how to achieve it except in a haphazard, trial-and-error sequence.

Now, with their dynamic new approach, modern bioterials scientists turn the discovery of new matter on its head. Today, world-class materials scientists define a particular use or functional attribute and then, knowing the properties of individual atomic elements and the manner in which they are likely to combine with each other, set about fabricating a new material by "architecting" it with a new atomic structure.

Traditionally, materials scientists were the scientific equivalent of construction workers, simply executing the natural world's predetermined "atomic plan." Their more adventuresome cousins in chemistry, working at the molecular level, used bulk "mixmasters" (relatively speaking, even if they were combining minute amounts), pouring chemicals from one beaker into another or using some similar method.

Now, both chemists and materials scientists are "atomic architects," redesigning the atoms of individual elements that are built into molecules of a desired shape to fit a specific function or need.

Material scientists often use a "three-legged stool" metaphor to define their endeavors: the atomic structure of the material, the inter-relationship of the atomic components, and the manner in which they are combined, that is, how they are treated (heated, cooled, etc.) as they are "re-architected."

Goodyear's rubber mixture, for example, had the right materials, but they needed the hot stove to form the beneficial union. Much of bioterials work must be done at very small sizes, or at extreme temperatures, though once constructed, they can be returned to a normal state with fantastic new properties.

It's a Small-*er* World After All

At one time philosophers and scientists alike declared that the atom was the smallest unit of matter, the basic building block for everything else in the world.

Today, of course, we know they were wrong. "Splitting" the atom became one of the most celebrated scientific achievements of the twentieth century. Discoveries of subatomic particles subsequently poured forth. Despite those scientific breakthroughs, most of us still lived, until very recently, in a "macro" world, dealing with most elements of matter in their largest forms. Through much of the twentieth century, what we knew best, and thought were the wonders of the age, were materials such as steel and gasoline.

In the Information Age, we took a quantum step downward into the "micro" level, and the world got incredibly smaller. The term micro itself turned up everywhere, attached to everything from the tiny chips (microprocessors) that powered the entire era to the giant companies (Microsoft) that defined its economics.

Within a very few years, however, anything micro will seem rather large, as the "nano" world erupts into public consciousness. And it gets even smaller than that. The Bioterials Age will challenge our understanding of how small is small.

A micron, the size of the pathway of an electron on a computer chip, is *one-millionth of a meter.* These chip pathways have only recently crossed the "submicron" barrier, where they are now less than a full micron. But a "nano," the current state of the art for work in bioterials, is *one-thousandth of a micron.*

Ultimately, bioterial researchers focus on a world even much smaller than that. Atoms, the basic units that scientists manipulate when working with bioterials today, measure about an angstrom, *one-tenth of a nanometer.* The new atomic world of bioterials, then, is one-ten thousandth of the electronic world we've come to know so well. And at such infinitely small sizes, everything moves faster.

In the Information Age, everything moved at the speed of electricity. Late in the twentieth century, fiber-optic technologies helped prepare us for the transition to the bioterials era by moving us up to the speed of light. Today materials scientists model new materials in quantum theory at nano, pico, and even femto seconds. With bioterials, the smaller and faster everything gets, the broader and more pervasive the impact.

Nano Scale, Macro Scope

The scope of the bioterial scientists' world is as broad as the scale of their work is small. Like some fast spreading primal ooze, bioterials research is creeping ever outward to absorb a growing number of fields of scientific endeavor. It is breaking down the traditionally rigid divisions in the academy and in industrial R&D labs alike. In fact, the interdisciplinary nature of bioterials is one of its hallmarks, incorporating biology, engineering, physics, and chemistry, and much more.

At the National Nanofabrication Facility at Cornell University, for example, researchers from disciplines across the campus collaborate at this world-renowned facility. In a similar, though smaller, operation at the University of Washington in Seattle, the university notes that representatives of 12 different departments are, or will be, involved. This interdisciplinary research is mandatory because the implications are so broad.

New Tools...

To do work in the "nanoworld," scientists have developed special tools, such as the Scanning Tunnel Microscope (they should have called it the Nanoscope!) and LEEPS (low-energy electron point source). LEEPS is a microscopic imaging technique that guides scientists when manipulating things as small as a piece of DNA. It has been critical to the work being conducted on DNA-based computing.

Unlike its predecessor, the powerful Scanning Tunnel Microscope doesn't see things at all, but is, rather, a distance-sensing device that uses a computer to render an image of the data. Its tip is only an atom wide, a very sharp point indeed. Such new tools have had a dramatic effect in hastening the speed and efficacy of research in bioterials.

Just as important in speeding up the discoveries, though, is the role played by computers and information networking that are rapidly diffusing this new science to university, government, and commercial R&D labs around the globe.

Even with extremely exacting tools like the Scanning Tunnel Microscope, the science would not have progressed as far and as fast without the tools of the Information Age. Ironically, just as bioterials is about to replace information as the engine of the economy in the twenty-first century, and as bioterials technologies transform electronic technologies, computers and telecommunications are hastening the transition.

One of the most intriguing areas of bioterials focus is in creating new materials for computers, which it turns out, despite their lightning speed, are much too slow for this new world. The materials in today's fastest computer do not permit it to compute anywhere near as fast as the computing speeds of the new materials just now being created—including biological ones. Scientists are experimenting with a whole new range of materials including organic proteins and even DNA itself. (See "The Biological Computer.")

The Biological Computer

Scientists are speculating that biology holds the key to overcoming some of the innate limitations of today's most sophisticated PCs. The desktop digital computer excels in computational work, but lags in other areas, and natural materials may close the gap between machine brains and their natural equivalents. A protein-based, "biological computer" would replace the solid-state transistors with molecules that alternate between two states, the familiar 0 and 1. Since these molecules are 1/1000th the size of their silicon equivalents, the computer would be 1000 times faster.

A completely molecular-based computer is some distance away, but a hybrid seems feasible within 10 years. Robert Birge of Syracuse University is looking at a protein, bacteriorhodopsin, which contains chromophore, a chemical that causes profound changes in the protein when it is struck by light. The protein shows dramatic increases in data storage—about 300 times current capacity—because it stores information in three dimensions rather than two. Also, it can store images whole, which facilitates the associative thinking needed for neural networks. A given image is compared with several stored in memory, each in close proximity to the other, and the closest one chosen. This makes artificial intelligence easier, because it breaks down the linear logic of the digital computer.

Birge sees the hybrid digital-biological computer containing several different memory/processor devices, operating cooperatively with each other in a parallel architecture. The digital device we already have would perform computations, while a cube of bacteriorhodopsin would provide a large storage facility, another cube would provide large random-access memory, and a film of bacteriorhodopsin would provide associative memory. Users could easily detach a small cube of bacteriorhodopsin and carry it with them.

... and New Tool Users
for the Nanoworld

But not every one has been convinced that work in the nanoworld has been worth the effort, and many disagreed on the proper approach and procedures. Some scientists even felt nanofabrication would never work. Others, like Christine Peterson and her husband Eric Drexler, devoted their lives to making it a reality. (See "The Very Small World of Christine Peterson and Eric Drexler.")

The Very Small World
of Christine Peterson and Eric Drexler

Christine L. Peterson and her husband K. Eric Drexler live in a very small world. A very, very, very small world.

Peterson is Executive Director of the Foresight Institute, a nonprofit organization in Palo Alto, California, working to maximize the benefits and minimize the drawbacks of emerging technologies. Drexler is a former professor at MIT and a major force behind the nanotechnology movement.

Peterson organizes the Foresight Conference on Molecular Technology Nanotechnology, the primary conference series on the subject. She co-wrote the 1991 book *Unbounding the Future: The Nanotechnology Revolution,* known as "the nanotechnology book you can give to your Mom," with Drexler and Gayle Pergamit.

Although Drexler doesn't give interviews, Peterson is far more accessible. Her best-known quote is: "If you're looking ahead long-term and what you see looks like science fiction, it might be wrong. But if it doesn't look like science fiction, it's *definitely* wrong."

Personally unassuming, but extremely bright and persuasive about his favorite subject, Drexler heads two major scientific associations that devote themselves to the advancement of nanotechnologies: the Foresight Institute and the Institute of Molecular Materials.

Drexler has the ability to follow a line of reasoning logically and thoroughly, delineating the implications as far as they go. The author of three books and numerous articles on nanotechnology, he has inspired many more.

Interestingly he has done little research himself, nor has he provided any major breakthroughs. He has, though, from the first, seen the promise of nanotechnology.

"Molecular nanotechnology will have broad applications," he told a U.S. Senate Subcommittee on Science, Technology and Space in 1992. "It will provide a general-purpose method for processing materials, molecule by molecule, much as computers provide a general-purpose method for processing information, bit by bit. It will by nature be highly efficient in both materials and energy use. Its products can include: clean efficient productive manufacturing systems; new molecular instruments for science and medicine; extremely compact, energy-efficient computers; stronger materials for lighter and more efficient vehicles; and inexpensive solar cells suitable for use in roofing and paving."

It almost seems as if Drexler saw the whole future, with all its possibilities, whole and entire in a blinding flash and has never wavered from it. In fact, he has prodded, persuaded, and pleaded for the money so that others would make it happen.

Even as a student at MIT, he attracted bright people to himself, acting as their leader, their organizing force. He was the center; he did the visionary, intellectual work, while they slugged it out in the lab.

But it wasn't nanotechnology that first captured his attention. When he arrived at MIT, he was fascinated with space exploration. He did a lot of research into a rocket with an external power source, one that might be located in the sky. He reasoned that so much of a contemporary rocket is fuel, putting the fuel somewhere else would save about 95 percent of the takeoff weight. This meant that rockets could be almost all payload, and wouldn't need nearly the energy to escape earth's gravity. The cost savings per rocket would be enormous. He knew, though, that finding this external place would be difficult. Before he could solve the puzzle, he discovered the nanoworld.

When he encountered the idea of nanotechnology, Drexler was converted on the spot. He recognized its possibilities immediately.

Today, Drexler uses two main models to describe the nanoworld that he so covets. On the one hand, he argues nature's superiority to human machines. A chromosome, he suggests, for example, can store information much more compactly than its computer equivalents. Thus, he holds up nature as a standard against which to measure the new devices that nanotechnology develops.

His second model is a kind of Tinkertoy set, with atoms as the basic elements. He has spent some time, for example, thinking of the atom as a bearing: it's not very smooth, so would it roll like a wheel, or would it bump, rendering it too rough to use as a bearing? He has found that the irregular surface of the atom doesn't matter because of the various physical forces (for example, magnetic) operating on an atom that prevent it from actually "rubbing" against its neighbors.

In addition, Drexler's nanoworld is populated with "assemblers," special agents putting these Tinkertoy elements together to form a range of new energy-saving, hard-working, inexpensive devices— devices that will transform our world by doing much of what we need cheaper, faster, and better.

For Drexler and eventually Christine Peterson, whom he met at MIT, nanotechnology promises an idealistic tomorrow, with humans and nature living in great harmony, an army of biomaterial-based servants doing much of the work that occupies us now. The cost (in money) would be almost negligible, and the cost (in environmental damage) even less. Medicines will cure sicknesses, although improved photovoltaics will provide energy without using up stored-up mineral resources. And food to feed the hunger masses would grow naturally in breadbox size machines supplied with only basic materials. Grass would become steak without the messy intermediate stage of a cow. Environmental pollution becomes a thing of the past.

Part of Drexler's rationale for this rosy vision is the core idea of the economics of nanotechnology: endless, effortless, inexpensive replication. This is at the heart of the new economics of the Bioterials Age: the ability of substances to reproduce themselves, to constantly and perfectly mutate—to clone themselves into perfect copies—so that the process, once begun, costs almost nothing to continue.

Accordingly, Drexler argues that nanotechnologies will take over so much of what humans currently do, at such a low cost, that he has begun to concern himself with the question of what people will do with themselves after the revolution. Given his driven nature, his joy in few pleasures other than work, he is an unlikely "poster boy" for the Bioterials Age.

Drexler's detractors, such as Lydia Sohn, are numerous, but he battles ahead, unshakably true to his vision. Whether or not he is right, remains to be seen—in a very, very small world.

The skeptics cited Heisenberg's uncertainty principle, which actually applies directly to electrons, but points out that you can never know *exactly* the position of an electron. You can predict its behavior and state its position as long as you qualify it with a percentage (for example, a 60 percent change that it will be here—much like predicting the weather), but you can't say precisely where the electron is at any specific instant. If you can't know the exact position of an electron, can you really say where it is?

Similarly, in classical atomic theory, atoms are known to smash into each other, causing heat. Such movement would seem to prevent small-scale, extremely precise work. But researchers have found that placing them in strong magnetic force fields or using extreme cold can stabilize atoms. Neither of the objections has proved to be a major obstacle. In fact, the organic world led the way to understanding the inorganic.

Modeling the Organic World

The inorganic world of nanofabrication and new materials models itself very much on biotechnology. Biologists typically work at the molecular level. To "repair" a DNA molecule, biotechnologists compare the defective portion of a DNA molecule with the undamaged model (a protein sequence with a series of amino acids and chromosomal structure). Then a new amino acid, nucleotide, is spliced into the existing molecule at a particular point, replacing the offending one. It is minute, exacting work.

Materials scientists work at the atomic level, rearranging the atomic structures of materials to create new and better ones. Theoretical physicists explore the intricacies of the subatomic. Regardless of the depth of analysis—cell, atom, or subatomic—the distinction between the organic and the inorganic collapses.

Erasing the Line Between the Organic and Inorganic Worlds

When matter gets down to its atomic base, it is immaterial whether or not it is organic or inorganic. In the Bioterials Age, the line between the inorganic and the organic world inexorably disappears. In nature, inorganic materials like bone, teeth and shells are grown, with organic materials providing the latticework whose surface affects the shape of the inorganic growth. Scientists mimic this natural combination of the organic and the inorganic in their own work of creating new forms of matter.

For chemists specializing in cellular chemistry, the notion that the cell is alive is meaningless. The techniques used by subatomic physicists is much the same. Even much of the terminology is the same. As in biology, scientists working with inorganic matter often describe such engineered molecules as "replicating" themselves. And they speak of "growing" layers of new materials on substrates.

Much of the work in this area is on the leading edge of theory. The leap, however, from laboratory to production, is not an easy one. Many amazing "breakthroughs" are slow to make it from the pages of *Popular Science* onto the shelves of Home Depot. Trying to reproduce in the factory what worked in the lab often proves difficult. Although much of the focus of new materials is on lower costs, sometimes, in the early stages, costs are prohibitive.

But in other areas, new materials are already proving their worth, with applications from the medical to the military. Although both these areas are of great importance, new materials will have their biggest impact on commerce.

Smart Sensors

One of the most promising and exciting fields of bioterials research is "smart" sensors. They are called smart because they include the ability to sense, then learn or remember as they go along. So, for example, a consumer is "alerted" by the changing colors of the packaging holding a perishable item in the refrigerator, as the "use by" date approaches. For an airline, ceramic "actuators" change their shape in an airplane wing to reduce vibration, or simply to improve airflow at different airspeeds. Some new construction materials actually sense the seismic vibration of an earthquake and dampen it.

In the case of health care, the immediate applications already on the horizon are almost endless. Consider that healing profoundly damaged or burned skin is almost impossible because the regrowth that is necessary for healing doesn't take place. The damaged area may be just too large. New cells can do no more than fill in a little around the perimeter, forming a scar tissue at the edge of the wound, rather than filling in the "hole" to heal it. If an artificial latticework—this new material is already in the labs—can be established, something that the new cells will accept and recognize as their own, new cell growth will build on it and fill in the void. Ideally, the latticework disintegrates over time, leaving only natural cells. Interestingly, the "metaphor" for this new latticework material is coral because of its porous structure.

Another promising use for smart materials is in materials that can change but "remember" their size or shape. For example, such materials are being proposed for underwater pipes. Welding such pipes together underwater is very difficult and, hence, expensive. By cooling the pipe material, it temporarily shrinks. Being smart, it "remembers" its original size. Thus, the pipe is cooled and stays small while delivered to the site. Once fitted, the water warms the pipe and it enlarges itself, forming a tight fit, and eliminating the need for complicated and expensive underwater welding.

In another application, surgeons wishing to "scrape" the insides of clogged arteries need specially shaped tools to do the job correctly. The correct shapes for scraping though, are not appropriate for inserting in the blood vessel as they can damage the delicate membranes. Using new smart metal, the surgeons can "tell" these special tools to remain straight during insertion and retraction but to assume the proper scraping form during the procedure.

New Fibers

We don't spend much time thinking about them, but fibers, of all shapes sizes, structures, colors, and combinations, dominate our world. They clothe us, feed us, help us see in the dark, let us talk to others around the world for almost free, and generally tie our world together.

As an excellent example of how the natural, biological, and artificial worlds intermix, DuPont developed a new polyester that is stretchy, silky, and breathable. This fiber, called 3GT, is not based on petroleum distillates, but the excrement of bacteria, a milky liquid that can be spun into 3GT. In their labs, researchers have long had a chemical version of this fiber. And they know that certain bacteria could convert the chemical glycerol into 3GT, but both were too expensive. So, scientists engineered a new kind of bacteria that would take ordinary glucose—corn syrup—and make 3GT. DuPont doesn't have a commercial product yet, but they have bought Pioneer Hi-Bred, a major supplier of corn, and they are looking at building a factory close to a cornfield.

These actions are especially meaningful coming from DuPont, the inventor of nylon, which was perhaps the first act of modern materials management. The company is also a leader in the development of biosilks. Biosilks are essentially fibers developed from living organisms such as spiders. Research is under way at universities, such as Cornell, and companies, such as DuPont, to alter the genetic code of spiders to produce nonsticky web silk. The spider web silk is a polymer that is five to ten times stronger than steel, and can be extended up to 20 percent of its length without breaking. In the case of spider silk, numerous applications are already on the drawing board, including improved sutures for surgery, stronger artificial ligaments, strings for parachutes, even for use in suspension bridges.

One of the most beneficial uses of fibers support is the special way they let light transmit messages through "optical" cables. The fiber-optic cable is a very thin, hollow tube that is coated to keep the laser light inside the cable, even when the cable is bent. The wavelength of light, peak-to-peak, is about 500 nanometers, one-half of a micron, rendering atoms invisible to even the most powerful, light-based microscopes. Because light travels quickly through these fibers without degrading, it is a very efficient way to transmit messages. Further, by varying the wavelength of the message, the same fiber optic tube can carry many messages at the same time.

For a number of years, there was an imminent danger telephone companies were running out of capacity to carry the ever-increasing amount of telephone traffic (voice, fax, and much of the data of the Internet). Fiber optics solved all that.

Now, the problem lies at the end of the line. The computer-based devices that send the light at one end and receive it at the other are electronic, and they are much slower than the speed of light through the fiber cable. The signals must be converted from optical to electronic, involving considerable processing time. And, because the resulting electronic signal is weak, it also involves amplifying the information. All this takes time and energy.

Fortunately, the day is not far off when this system—an "optoelectronic" system because it combines optics and electronics—will be replaced by one that is totally photonic—consisting solely of light through fiber. Because it would make many devices superfluous, photonic computers would be greatly miniaturized and, hence, faster.

But many problems remain before this promise becomes reality. In the first place, the computer chip itself (rather than a device on the chip) must generate a light signal. Unfortunately, silicon, the basic material of the chip, doesn't readily emit light. Scientists know that if most of the silicon is etched away from a chip, leaving thin silicon wires only a few nanometers wide, the silicon will glow.

These silicon wires are very fragile. And the spaces between these wires, because the wires are so brittle, may need to be filled to protect them. In the future, it may be possible to do away with some wiring in optical computers as signals can be transmitted from one device to another without any medium to transmit them, creating a chip-to-chip communication system.

Within the chip itself, miniaturized fiber-optic cables will be used to guide the signals around the chip at a very rapid pace—20 to 80 billion times per second. To make all this work, researchers are "growing" an inexpensive but very complex crystalline structure—an organic polymer known as a magnetic modulator. Such new materials will convert the world of computing and communications from the relatively slow darkness of electronics to the blinding light speed of optics.

New Polymers

The optical computer may also hold the key to another problem facing the next generation of computers: storage. We are currently drowning in the information that our various electronic machines are producing. Current computer technologies can barely keep up with this tremendous flow of words, data, video, and images.

Today's best methodology involves magnetics: disk or tape. The magnetic polarity at any point is positive or negative, a "bit" of information. To store more data, the size allotted to each bit is decreased, including decreasing the boundaries between bits. Using lasers to read information can increase the amount of information stored. The laser is more precise and smaller, thereby increasing the amount of data that can be stored. This type of hybrid system, called "magnetoptics," holds great promise for information storage in the near future.

Further off, a truly optic storage system may be the solution. It may be possible that holograms, holding whole pages of information, can be stored in an inorganic block of ferroelectric oxide crystals. For this medium, a laser translates a document into a "picture" in an electric field inside the crystal. Another laser can reproduce this picture, different angles of incidence producing different pages of stored information. This information is stable, rewriteable, and is found quickly—all-important features for a computer storage device. But crystals are expensive.

To develop a less expensive alternative, scientists are building a polymer (a long protein-like string of individual elements—plastics, elastics, and many fibers are polymers) that contains all the features they want by adding individual elements, each tied to a particular feature. Researchers are also looking at a "natural" alternative, a protein that comes from bacteria (technically bacteria are inorganic substances) that grows in extremely salty water. Because the salt content varies, so does the oxygen, and the bacteria must live in an environment that switches from high to low oxygen. To do this, the bacteria switch from oxygen for respiration to photosynthesis.

This is a chemical change caused by light that performs the role of a light-operated switch. A film formed with this protein can be irradiated and its chemical properties switched, storing a holographic image. The pictures that ensue when a laser is pointed at the film are not as clear as scientists need, but they have great hope for the future as they re-architect the properties of the medium.

It is already possible to use two lasers to read material, the lasers crossing at a particular point. This point does not reveal a holographic image, but it is three-dimensional. The data is written and read in a single operation, increasing the speed of the computer, and it may provide a storage device with a capacity 300 times greater than the ones currently available. These devices show particular ability to recognize patterns and think associatively, abilities that make artificial intelligence much closer to reality.

Smart Materials

Smart materials, much like smart sensors, are substances that learn. Rather than doing a specific task in response to a given stimuli—welding car doors together when a sensor says the panels are in front of the machine—a smart material modifies its behavior over time. It alters its behavior by knowing, for example, when it is about to fail. Other materials, not quite so smart, but more intelligent than those used presently, replace a whole set of mechanically inclined materials.

Some researchers are building smart new materials that mimic human biological processes such as hearing (an "electronic ear"), smelling (an "electronic nose"), tasting (an "electronic tongue"), and even an "electronic head." For example, engineers and biologists at the University of Texas, Austin, have collaborated to produce an "electronic tongue" that can detect and measure various chemicals in liquids. The electronic tongue, and these other simulated organs, are expected to have wide application in industrial and health area markets. Another example in development is an artificial muscle that contracts when an electric current passes through it. Developed initially for health care applications, it could potentially replace an industrial motor in a factory. (See "The Electronic Tongue.")

The Electronic Tongue

Many years ago, textbooks for chemists had precise instructions for testing the chemical composition of unknown compounds: "stick your tongue in the beaker of liquid and taste it!" The textbooks would go on to tell the chemists what different types of chemicals tasted like. While chemists have long since developed better methods of determining the properties of unknown substances, the need for precise identification of different tastes and the detection of things, such as toxins and bacteria, remains constant in many industries.

An integrated team of scientists and engineers at the University of Texas at Austin may just have the answer. They have developed what they call an "electronic tongue" to do real-time tasting and detection of the chemical composition of fluids. With the help of biologists, they have "mapped the taste geography" of a human tongue (there are some 100,000 taste buds, each with a specific job and a unique location on the tongue) and replicated it on the surface of a computer chip. The chemical "taste buds" are micromachined into the surface of the chip, and change color when they are in contact with different chemicals in fluids. The electronic tongue can detect about 100 different combinations of sweet, sour, salty, and bitter. The results are videotaped by a digital camera that observes the action.

The electronic tongue is expected to have application in health care for testing blood and urine and in the food industry for consistency of tastes and also the presence of bacteria. In addition, it is expected to join a wide array of other types of "sensors" in industrial, commercial, and consumer applications for efficacy, safety, and security applications.

These electronic organs are referred to as *smart materials,* as they are single-component systems. Other devices contain more components, and they are more properly called *smart systems.* In some cases, these smart systems actually self-assemble in certain environment conditions. Such systems are finding use in military applications but are promising for industrial uses as well. Many of these smart systems involve sensors, which in turn actuate a smart material. For example, it may soon be possible to implant an insulin sensor in a diabetic. As the sugar level rises in the person's blood, a sensor registers the change and releases insulin. Further out, scientists hope the smart material encapsulating the insulin itself will react to sugar in the blood, expanding its weblike structure and releasing the insulin, a smart material that needs no sensor.

Ceramics

Quartz crystals have been around for some time. They are the basic elements in radio transmitters and loudspeakers and have found a new use in digital watches. The quartz releases an electric charge when it is squeezed. As such, it converts mechanical action to electrical and vice versa.

nds of ceramics have been found to have these same
..cs if they are supercooled, especially if they are placed in a
strong magnetic field to align their polarities. This action is much the
same as iron: iron isn't "magnetic" unless a strong magnet takes the
positive and negative polarities of individual molecules and lines
them up in the same direction.

These new ceramic devices can be used as vibration dampers by
installing two of them and having the second establish a secondary
vibration that is 180 degrees out of phase with the first. These could
be used to quiet automotive springs and airplane bodies, which produce most of the "noise" often heard during flight.

Other ceramic materials also change their shapes as electricity is
applied to them. They have already found a use in the backing for
mirrors that focus telescopes, allowing astronomers to adjust the
focus on telescopes in response to atmospheric disturbances. These
materials may also allow airplane designers to change the shape of
wings and ailerons, creating a plane without external moving parts.

A modified version of these same ceramics has been shown to
respond with a mechanical action—a constriction—when light is
shone on it. These may be used as loudspeakers at the end of a fiber-
optic cable, without the complications of electronic systems that currently do the job. This material has also been turned into a smart
materials inchworm that walks—albeit slowly—when a laser is
flashed on it.

Ceramics production is projected to be some $30 billion a year by
2010. Already there are some 3500 to 4000 engineers around the
world working on various ceramic activities.

Materials with a Memory

A new variety of shape memory alloys are being developed that,
when cooled, deform into a shape that is smaller than normal. But
they "remember" their original shape and snap back when heated.
One application is surgical instruments that assume a benign shape
when inserted into the body, a new shape to perform the procedure
when "told," and then the benign shape again to be pulled out.

The alignment of the atomic structure is actually skewed during
this process and then returned to its original shape. This process can
be repeated again and again. Japanese researchers are using wires

made from one of these materials as the muscles for robot hands, and the robot has achieved sufficient dexterity to pick up a cup of water.

Another liquid material has the ability to freeze instantly when an electrical charge passes through it. This may be used in the clutch of a car, so that the plates of the clutch, always subject to wear and tear, never have to come in contact with each other. Instead, a bond (engagement) can be effected instantly by passing a current through the liquid and connecting the engine and the drive wheels.

The Endless Energy Machines

The material sciences are also focused on the age-old dream of a new substance that becomes a continuous energy machine. In fact, the U.S. government alone has spent nearly $50 billion since 1980 in search of newer, more efficient ways to harness energy. Industrial scientists, meanwhile, are working with thermoelectric materials that are used in a wide variety of "environmentally friendly" applications, including small-scale power generation, refrigeration, cooling computers and lasers, and even space exploration. With a fast-growing world population hungry for energy of all kinds, this is certainly one of the major long-term global problems. And material science is working on long-term solutions.

In the shorter term, one of the major efforts is electric power for automobiles. The problem here is not the power but the power storage: batteries. Present-day electric batteries are heavy and expensive. Further, the batteries can be recharged a limited number of times, creating an environmental problem when they are discarded. Currently, the range on a set of batteries is about 100 miles, after which they must be recharged, which takes somewhere between 2 and 6 hours. This may work for a "commuter" car in a family that also has a regular internal combustion engine car for long-distance trips, although it will not replace the automobile as we currently know it.

Researchers are working on various alternatives to the lead-acid batteries that will provide more power for a longer time, need less time to recharge, and pose no environmental problems when disposed. At present, there are no clear solutions. Different alternatives have desirable qualities, but either cost, danger (some of them tend to explode), or environmental damage limit their usefulness.

More promising perhaps is the fuel cell technology that combines hydrogen and oxygen on board the automobile itself, creating electricity on board rather than storing it in a battery. The hydrogen and oxygen are carried separately in individual fuel cells, since the hydrogen is potentially explosive when combined with oxygen and a spark. They are each passed through a solution and over electrodes, which pick up electrons and pass them to an electric motor. Only water vapor is produced as an emission.

A similar process uses either methanol or natural gas, each of which is readily available. Like the hydrogen-oxygen fuel cell, the process is chemical, so it is more efficient than a combustion engine. But methanol and natural gas produce a dirtier emission than hydrogen-oxygen. Prototype buses are currently using the purer, hydrogen-based engines, because buses are large and they have the room to store the rather large fuel cells. The manufacturer of these buses is concentrating on methanol for their automotive variants.

A larger question, probably, is the one of solar energy production. The sun delivers enough energy to the earth to provide all of our foreseeable needs, if only we could make efficient use of it. At present, we use silicon-based computer chips and the photovoltaic effect to convert sunlight into electric energy. In fact, solar energy manufacturers use the less-than-perfect chips that the computer industry discards.

The first such chip converted 6 percent of the ambient sun into electricity, which is low but beats nature. Silicon has a theoretical limit of about 29 percent partly because it responds only to a segment of light's wavelength, due partly to energy losses in the conversion process and partly to scattering. Because of silicon's properties, the wafer used must be grown in a crystalline tube and then cut into fairly thick slices—a few hundred micrometers—for it to perform as a photovoltaic.

Thinner variations are possible in other types of silicon. The efficiencies aren't as great, but the cost is lower because less material is used and the method for growing it is less expensive. These silicones can be fine-tuned to capture different parts of the light's wavelength. Collectors may eventually include a variety of photovoltaics, each tuned to a different segment of the light spectrum, with some of them being especially effective in the diffuse sunlight of cloudy days. So different climatic regions may use different types of photovoltaics.

What's Not There: Porous Materials

A variation of material science is the study of what's not there, as opposed to what is: porous materials. Zeolites have a natural crystalline structure such that a gram of zeolite has a surface area of 900 square meters. Normally filled with water, these zeolites have been used for years by the petrochemical industry. Because of their extremely acidic nature, they "crack" large hydrocarbons to make more useful by-products, such as ethylene and benzene, yet the zeolites are environmentally safe. Their apertures are called *micropores,* each one a few angstroms wide.

Scientists are interested in larger-pored substances, though nature usually tries to collapse these wide-aperture materials into more compact shapes. Using a combination of organic and inorganic substances, scientists have developed materials with mesopores: holes that are about 100 angstroms across, larger than the molecules themselves. In fact, the mixture acts differently than the constituents would by themselves, depending on the exact composition and the manner in which they are combined.

This is, in fact, a process similar to the process that nature uses to create shells. With such large holes, these artificial zeolites will separate larger molecules than natural zeolites can. They are also used to create nanometer-wide wires, which are supported by zeolites, a stronger combination than the wires by themselves.

Strangely enough, these zeolites are not significantly less dense than normal materials. Their holes are arranged in channels, rather than being distributed evenly throughout the material. Most materials have a density of between 50 and 75 percent. Scientists have taken some materials with a density of only about 1 percent and formed solids with them—such as liquid smoke—by raising both temperature and pressure to the point where the difference between a liquid and a gas disappears. The result is a semitransparent solid called an *aerogel.*

This process is difficult, making aerogels expensive. Other researchers have used less-rarified techniques and produced materials with a 2 percent density—for all practical purposes the same— which show great promise as insulators between double-glazed windows or for passive solar panels.

Diamonds Are Forever

At the opposite end of the density spectrum are diamonds, the hardest, most dense material known to exist. Diamonds are formed deep inside the earth under conditions of extreme temperatures and pressure—about 80,000 atmospheres—though they do not explode when some catastrophic event propels them to the earth's surface.

Diamonds have an extremely rigid structure. Since the 1950s, scientists have been able to create artificial diamonds by reproducing the extreme pressures and temperatures that formed them inside the earth.

Diamonds are almost pure carbon. Their closest chemical equivalent is graphite, so the first attempts to create artificial diamonds put graphite under extreme pressure. It seemed the natural thing to do. But this yielded nothing. To get the results they wanted, they successfully compressed metal, not carbon, mimicking the natural process of the earth's core. Scientists believe the metal acts like a catalyst giving the carbon atoms a positive charge and helping each atom form, with four other carbon atoms, the tetrahedron structure that gives diamonds their formidable strength. The artificial diamonds don't resemble the diamonds in a ring, but are more like dust and used mainly as abrasives. A new low-pressure method of developing artificial diamonds has been developed recently. It grows crystals on a substrate, at speeds of up to one millimeter per hour, and is useful mainly in developing diamonds as coatings that are extremely resistant to wear.

Diamonds are also excellent insulators. Surprisingly, they also show potential as semiconductors when mixed with a metal such as boron. They provide real performance advantages over silicon because the speed of the electrons in the chip is faster, the distances around the chip can be decreased because of the improved insulators, and they can tolerate higher voltages and temperatures. The problem is that the diamond must be perfectly formed to work. That level of perfection isn't available yet, though it gets closer every day.

Designing Matter

There is increasing public awareness of new developments in biology. Much less is known about new materials research, although it represents a sizeable part of the economy. Extractive materials today represent about 8 percent of the GDP in the United States. The inclusion of all other materials would push the number well above 10 percent. It is clear that new materials will have less impact on everyday life than will biotech. However, new materials will have a profound effect on the cost and quality of almost every physical good. And, there are large and growing synergies between the two fields. Much of the work of new materials scientists is inspired by nature. As nature moves to increasing complexity, so to do our needs for new materials. In an ever more complex future, though, we will increasingly be able to "design" much of our material world, both organic and inorganic.

8

Designer Genes
Re-Engineering the Body

Some people think the most powerful person at Columbia is the president of the university. The most powerful person at Columbia is the person who decides who gets a heart for a transplant. Biotechnology, by producing an endless supply of new hearts, will make the president the most powerful person at Columbia once again.

DR. "JEFF" QIAN, FORMER BIOTECH
RESEARCHER AT COLUMBIA UNIVERSITY

One hundred years ago, in 1899, Charles Duell, the U.S. Commissioner of Patents, wrote to President McKinley to suggest the closing of the patent office because he believed that everything that could be invented had already been invented.

British scientist Sir John Maddox, in his 1996 book, *What Remains to Be Discovered,* makes no similar mistake. He looks back over several centuries of amazing scientific discoveries and takes quite the opposite perspective.

His question: "What's next?" His answer: Quite a bit.

Many of the questions Maddox believes science will answer in the

115

next century relate to biology or human processes: How did life start some 4 billion years ago? How did the human species, genetically quite similar to apes, start evolving (some 4 million years ago) on a path that led humans to walking erect and talking? What is thinking and how does it work?

Despite what's left to be discovered, biotech has already made almost unbelievable strides. In fact, researchers in cell and tissue technology have made such substantive strides in the past few years that they can propagate, protect, and modify cell and tissue function or response for a wide variety of medical applications. Through the combination of new pharmacological substances, biomaterials products (either natural or synthetic) for specific functions (for example, with selective permeability for use as "resorbable" scaffolds, modified surfaces for promoting adhesion, and "self-assembly" systems for drug or vaccine delivery) and nanofabrication and microsurgical techniques, multifunctional teams of biologists, engineers, and materials scientists are addressing the pathologies of every organ system. Among other "products," they are creating biosynthetic skins, cell therapies, and replacements that preserve lineage (phenotype) and genotype and bioartificial organs.

Biotech scientists have already identified the genetic code of humans that link diseases to single damaged genes (of the 40,000 known diseases, about 3000 of them are genetically related).

Among them:

- The gene involved in Parkinson's disease.

- The gene involved in a fatal childhood neurological disorder involving faulty cholesterol metabolism.

- The gene involved in a cardiovascular syndrome, which can result in abnormal heart rhythm and sudden death.

- The gene involved in an age-related macular degeneration, the leading cause of blindness in older Americans.

Among other major advances:

- Neuroimaging techniques that enable researchers for the first time to visualize the human brain in action.

- Identification of the length of telemeters, the structures at the end of chromosomes, that determine whether or not cells divide, which is invaluable knowledge leading to greater understanding about cancer and aging.

- Identification of proteins that inhibit angiogenesis and thereby block tumor growth, helping to create new therapeutic strategies against cancer.

- Identification of cancer and other disease-preventing mechanisms in plants and animals.

- Discovery of the three proteins that enable the malaria parasite to develop in the mosquito, and consequentially pointing the way to the development of antimalaria drugs.

- A new antidiarrhea vaccine for diarrhea caused by rotaviruses, a major health problem for children around the world.

- Techniques for the customized delivery of drugs to specific parts of the body.

- Antipain and anticancer treatments harvested from marine animals such as snails, corals, and sharks.

- Important techniques for the "growing" of replacement human body parts in animals such as cows and pigs, the first being a finger joint.

- Computer chips that "read" genetic makeup . . . and much, much more.

Is there anything left to discover? Plenty!

Over the next few years, pharmaceutical research will, conservatively, increase the drug target areas (about 500 currently) to some 25,000 new ones. If only 25 percent prove to have genuine potential, it would represent a 14-fold improvement over today's efforts. Will they be successful? If the amount being spent on research is any indication, they clearly will be.

The R&D dollars chasing these genetic targets is growing dramatically. In 1998, spending by U.S. companies increased more than 10 percent to some $21 billion. The top 20 pharmaceutical companies have more than doubled their nominal spending in the past 7 years. This year, European companies will spend some $14 billion.

In addition to the $39 billion in private R&D monies spent around the world, government research and health budgets, under severe pressure in most areas, will nonetheless increase more than 8 percent in the United States, along with increases by other governments such as Italy, South Korea, and Canada.

Government and private research efforts, as part of South Korea's "Biotech 2000" program, have invested about $1.5 billion in research in the last 4 years. Although the economic difficulties of the past few years may impact the final level of spending, the government's portion is to increase some 80 percent this year, while private interests will increase their spending a more modest 30 percent! Canada's biotech, somewhat hampered by general economic conditions, are nonetheless proceeding apace. Their efforts are examined in the next chapter.

Today major strides are being made in biotech research. A key discovery (the structure of DNA) occurred just 45 years ago, and a key "strategic inflection" point in the commercialization process took place in the mid-1980s. Significant new advances have been piling up since. In historic terms, the key discoveries have all occurred in a very brief span of time.

Biotech, in a few short years, has become the true "hi tech" of our times. Despite the excitement surrounding many of the most recent discoveries, it's important to remember that it took several million years for biotech to become the "overnight sensation" of the 1990s.

Biotech: 7000-Year-Old "Overnight" Sensation

Biotech's origin stretches back to the farmers some 5000 years before Christ, who happened to notice that certain varieties of crops, such as corn, grew better in some conditions than others. Unknowingly, they began what would become the most important industry in history some 7000 years later. They were simply experimenting with developing better plants. They, like us today, were simply trying to improve their lot.

Following up on the success of hybrid plants, farmers about 1000 B.C. (their information networks weren't as fast as ours are today!) began cross-breeding female horses with male donkeys to create a new animal, the mule, that combined the best of both breeds. Mules were known for their superior endurance, intelligence, and long life. Little did the breeders know that these sure-footed animals were the first genetically engineered species in history. Cloning, so controversial in today's world, is but the latest step in this evolutionary process that started more than 3000 years ago.

Brew masters and cheese makers, using the action of bacteria and yeasts, were also early biotech engineers, experimenting with products found in nature to create new foods and beverages. Likewise, we know today that many of the most effective drugs and cures for a wide variety of ailments come from plant, animal, and even inorganic materials. The early "medicine man" was the expert biologist of his day, concocting potent herbal remedies for treating the sick. Although some mythologies portray such practitioners as a wild shaman, each day brings new discoveries about the substances found in nature that have long historical traditions in disease treatment or prevention.

Efforts aimed at using and improving plants and animals continued throughout the centuries. For much of this time, those efforts were widely applauded. The efforts aimed at "improving" the gene pool of humans, though, that came to be known as *eugenics,* was not so universally accepted. Eugenics enjoyed a brief spate of popularity in the United States, favored by many of the rich and famous. Hitler's actions to "cleanse" the German populace pretty much ended the eugenics movement in the middle of this century.

More recently, public attention was again drawn to genetic improvements with the spate of announcements on cloning, starting with tadpoles, by Robert Briggs and Thomas King in 1953. It was followed in the late 1970s with the cloning of three mice. The first larger mammals were cloned in the 1980s. However, this was only a "partial" cloning as the cells were harvested from both sexes of sheep and cows and "sexually" fertilized. The most important event thus far, of course, was the spectacular achievement by Ian Wilmut of the asexual cloning of a sheep, "Dolly," in 1996. Again, though, not everyone was thrilled with the news.

One area that has escaped widespread negative press is the use of many of these techniques to assist parents with having children. The first "in vitro" (outside the womb in a test tube) fertilization of a human egg occurred in 1978. Thousands more have followed "Baby Louise." Today, in vitro fertilizations are commonplace, and the science of human reproduction has taken dramatic leaps forward. In 1998, medical researchers announced the ability to select the sex of an unborn child.

Counting Calories and Conquering Cancer

Perhaps a simpler way to understand the potential of cell manipulation is to look at the issues of obesity and cancer, which are widely recognized as two of western society's major health problems and consequently priority targets of medical research.

Whether it's nature or nurture that leads to being overweight is also still up for debate. But concern about fat has become a national obsession. Understanding obesity has required an enormous amount of time and money by biotech scientists. Some recent activities, though, are beginning to look promising, as the genetic origins of obesity come into focus. The only research activity that exceeds efforts to combat fat is directed at conquering cancer. Cause and effect in both areas are coming into sharper focus under the intense research efforts of biotechnology.

Only recently has obesity been found to be influenced by genes. In fact, at least 130 different genes! As a result, at least 62 weight-reducing drugs are in various stages of development by pharmaceutical companies. Some of these drugs will be designed to go after cells that monitor and control a variety of secretions in the stomach, esophagus, brain, and other organs where numerous chemicals and enzymes are stored that affect body responses such as hunger.

And in regard to cancer, the single largest area of clinical research, major work progresses with monoclonal antibodies and other gene therapies in a frantic effort to find ways to block EGF (endothelial growth factor) which tumors use to induce cells to divide. "The Answer to Cancer?" describes the exciting work under way to find a cure for this killer.

The Answer to Cancer?

About 1.2 million cases of cancer will be diagnosed in the United States this year. Unfortunately, for some 60 percent of those stricken, there is no effective therapy.

Those who have any hope of treatment currently have three unpleasant choices: they can face a surgeon's knife (often repeatedly), they can have their bodies subjected to powerful radiation (with harsh side effects), or they can be bombarded with a variety of strong chemicals. When one procedure doesn't work, patients may end up with a combination of these treatments, with mixed results.

Within the next few years, these difficult approaches will be supplanted by several genetic cures that get to the heart of the cancer and eradicate it. No dream, these procedures are quickly becoming a reality.

After two decades of promising research, there are now over 350 innovative biotech cancer therapies in clinical trials, 57 of those in the final phase 3. Major drug companies have already signed deals for over 50 treatments for breast cancer alone.

Among the most promising treatments so far:

- Tumor Necrosis Therapy (TNT) from Techniclone, uses a genetic "smart bomb," which is injected into the blood stream and finds its way to the cancer tumor, delivering precise radiation treatment to the inside of the tumor, killing it from the inside and leaving the surrounding tissue intact. Other companies have developed similar genetic delivery systems, but using viruses or proteins that kill cells or makes them vulnerable to the body's normal immune system.

- An anti-angiogenesis drug, being developed separately on three different continents, shrink-wraps the tumor and starves it of oxygen, causing it to suffocate and die.

- Another treatment currently in trials interferes with the cancer cell's life cycle and causes it to commit suicide.

- A kind of "vaccine" will be made from a patient's own tumors, stimulating the immune system to seek out and kill only cancer cells.

- Some scientists envision a point where they will be able to catch the cancer while it is still in a microscopic cell state, killing it before it can do the slightest damage to the body.

Discovering DNA:
The Building Block of Life

By today's standards, biological science took a long time to successfully reveal the mysteries of DNA. And many scientists, particularly from Europe in the early years, played key roles in the development of molecular biology. Experimenting on the hybridization of common garden peas, the Austrian monk and botanist Gregor Mendel in the 1860s developed the first mathematical laws of heredity. The

Swiss physician Fritz Miescher discovered DNA, or deoxyribonucleic acid, the building block of life, as early as 1868.

Despite the important early work of Mendel and Miescher, the science of genetics only truly began to develop in the 1930s with the work of a young German physicist named Max Delbruck. Delbruck was fascinated by the similarity of genetics to quantum mechanics. Quantum mechanics had already introduced physics to the concept of discreteness (the notion of jumps) and had also forced physicists to recognize the role played by chance. Biologists at that time had already found that genes are discrete, indivisible particles that can randomly jump from a stable to an excited or "mutant" state. To Delbruck, this was very similar to molecular actions in quantum mechanics. Delbruck began to grapple with the question "What is a gene and what is it made of?" This was a natural progression for a physicist, who knew that quantum mechanics had already answered the question "What is a molecule and what is it made of?"

Delbruck was excited by the idea of discovering the mysteries that he felt certain were locked inside the tiny gene. In 1937, at the dawn of the Nazi era, Delbruck accepted an invitation from the Rockefeller Foundation to come to the United States and continue his research in gene reduplication, later winning a Nobel Prize for his work.

But it was Erwin Schrodinger, another German physicist whose tiny book *What Is Life?*, published in 1944 near the end of World War II, who distinctly defined the link between genetics and quantum mechanics. This little book, ignored at first by scientists, eventually opened the door to a new science of molecular biology.

As Sir John Maddox suggests in his book that science will continue its pursuit to unveil the mystery of the origin of life. American scientist Stanley Miller's startling experiment in 1953 demonstrated that several of the principal component chemicals of life could be formed when an electric discharge (simulating lightning) was passed through a flask containing simply air and ocean water. Although to date no one has managed to take Dr. Miller's effort further, his remarkable experiment is included even today in many textbooks.

An experiment conducted in 1998 by Dr. Gunther Wachtershauser, an organic chemist at Munich Technical University, attempted to reconstruct the chemical events that may have led to the first living cells. Wachtershauser combined certain elements under extremely high temperatures. The results, published in the journal *Science* in April 1999, showed that peptides (short protein chains) can form naturally under conditions that might have existed 4 billion years ago. Miller disagrees with the high-temperature approach and argues that his experiment revealed that these components of life could be formed under normal conditions that exist today.

Beyond these efforts to determine the origin of life, as the century draws to a close, scientists in California are awaiting the green light from the Ethics Committee of the American Association for the Advancement of Science to attempt to create a live cell from inorganic chemicals. If successful, the project could result in creating a totally synthetic organism within a few years.

In 1953 at the Cavendish Laboratory in Cambridge, England, following Schrodinger's lead, two young scientists, James Watson and Francis Crick, made the most astonishing discovery of all. (See "The Headliners: Watson & Wilmut.") By using x-ray crystallography, a measurement technique developed by the British father and son team of Henry and Lawson Bragg, Watson and Crick defined the exact structure of DNA. They called it the rule of complementarity, because their model revealed that the DNA molecule chains contained sequences that were strongly interconnected and always complemented each other (that is, A always opposite T and T always opposite A). Although they no doubt worked long and hard at the discovery, the actual breakthrough occurred while the two were playing a "game" with DNA residues resulting from crystallography x-ray analysis. These two obscure scientists had discovered, almost by accident, a fairly simple solution to DNA structure.

The Headliners:
Watson & Wilmut

The two most powerful figures of twentieth century biotech couldn't be much different. One an American, the other a Scot, both attended Cambridge University. And both created headlines with one masterstroke of genius. The resemblance ends there.

In 1953, the brilliant and brash 24-year-old American, a geneticist named Dr. James Dewey Watson, playing a "game" with Englishman Francis Crick at Cambridge University, discovered the double-helical structure of DNA. The world of science has never been the same since. Nine years later, Watson and Crick shared the Nobel Prize for their work with colleague Maurice Wilkins.

In 1997, a soft-spoken embryologist named Dr. Ian Wilmut announced that his team at Scotland's Roslin Institute (owned by PPL Therapeutics, but recently bought by the "fountain of youth" company Geron Corporation) had successfully cloned an adult mammal, a sheep named Dolly. Media from around the world sped to Roslin, and Wilmut quickly became one of the most famous, and controversial, scientists in the world.

Watson and Crick's discovery created an entirely new field: biotechnology. Wilmut's created both the realization and fear that we could soon cross a final frontier—humans could be cloned.

For the Birds

Watson, born April 6, 1928, in Chicago, was the only son of James and Jean Watson. The elder Watson was a businessman who, his son says, wasn't terribly successful. But he did have a passion for bird watching that young James Watson soon came to share.

By the time he was 8 years old, Watson already had his first book on birds. The Watson home, in fact, was chock-full of books. Soon, Watson's interest in birds made him aware of science—though he was not always in awe of its practitioners.

After just 2 years in high school, Watson was accepted into an experimental 4-year college at the University of Chicago to study zoology. It was 1943 and Watson was a 15-year-old college freshman.

At university, his boyhood interest in bird watching soon grew into a serious desire to study genetics. In 1947, he received his B.S. in zoology, and earned a fellowship to continue his studies at the University of Indiana in Bloomington. At Bloomington, he was influenced by geneticists H. J. Muller and T. M. Sonneborn and by microbiologist S. E. Luria. He earned his Ph.D. in zoology in 1950.

Postdoctoral work took him to Copenhagen in 1950 and 1951. In the spring of 1951, Watson went to a symposium in Naples, where he met Maurice Wilkins and, for the first time, saw a demonstration of the x-ray diffraction of crystalline DNA. This inspired Watson to change his research toward the structural chemistry of nucleic acids and proteins.

It was a fortunate shift for science, but in many ways a risky move for Watson. "DNA, you know, is Midas' gold," Wilkins said later. "Everybody who touches it goes mad." Watson didn't go mad. He went to Cambridge.

At Cambridge University in England, he met the 35-year-old Crick. In some ways they couldn't have been more different, yet they became ideal partners. Building upon work by Wilkins and x-ray diffraction expert Rosalind Franklin, Watson and Crick were able to delineate the molecular structure of DNA and explain the mechanism of its replication in early 1953.

The pair published their results in the prestigious British scientific journal *Nature,* and soon became scientific superstars.

Watson's hero, Linus Pauling, was also looking for the structure, but they had beaten him to the punch. Their collaborator, Rosalind Franklin, a feminist before her time, died of cancer in 1958. She did not share the Nobel Prize, which is not awarded posthumously. Many feel she has never received the credit she should have for the discovery.

Watson and Crick flipped a coin to decide whose name would go first on their shared byline. Ironically, the actual proof that the double helix existed wouldn't come until more than 30 years later. Only then did it become possible to crystallize synthetic parts of DNA and analyze them with x-ray crystallography.

From 1953 to 1955, Watson worked at CalTech. He and Crick joined forces again for a short time in England from 1955 to 1956, but reported personality clashes brought Watson to Harvard until 1968.

His 1968 Penguin book, *The Double Helix,* which painted an often-unflattering portrait of scientists, has been translated into over 20 languages and is still in print. "A goodly number of scientists are not only narrow-minded and dull but also just stupid," Watson wrote.

That same year, Watson was named Director of the Cold Spring Harbor Laboratory on Long Island, New York, one of the world's top research institutions. Watson, who still works there, is one of four Nobel laureates on staff.

In 1988, Watson was named the first Director of the Human Genome Project at the National Institutes of Health (NIH). This vast government project is set to map the entire genetic code by the year 2005, at a projected cost of $3 billion.

He stayed there until 1992, reportedly leaving due to conflicts with then NIH director Dr. Bernadine Healy. Watson didn't depart the Human Genome Project without slamming one of the brightest new kids on the DNA block, former NIH staffer Dr. Craig Venter, then of The Institute for Genomic Research.

In testimony before the U.S. Senate, Watson called Venter's idea of patenting a gene's exact sequence "sheer lunacy." Although Venter's lab is the only one in the world to have published the genetic sequence of more than one free-living organism, Watson stunned Venter by telling a U.S. Senate committee Venter's method "could be run by monkeys."

By 1995, though, Venter's later work was drawing great praise from Watson, who has never pretended to be a shrinking violet. "I never felt a part of the establishment," Watson told a 1992 University of California-San Francisco symposium. "Conventional wisdom is often wrong."

He remains one of genetic engineering's most outspoken, but powerful and prestigious advocates.

Animal (Gene) Crackers

Ian Wilmut was 9 years old when Watson and Crick became household names. He was born in the English town of Hampton Lucey in 1944. He grew up in Coventry and attended the University of Notthingham, graduating with an Honors Degree in Agricultural Science.

His mentor at Notthingham was G. Eric Lamming, a world-renowned expert in the science of reproduction. Wilmut says that from that point on, he knew that animal genetic engineering would be his life's work.

Like Watson, he then spent time at Cambridge, earning his Ph.D. in Animal Genetic Engineering. His thesis was on the deep-freeze preservation of boar semen. In 1973, he created the first calf ever produced from a frozen embryo. Wilmut fittingly named the calf "Frosty."

That same year, Wilmut was appointed Research Leader at the Animal Breeding Research Station in Scotland. The research institution is now called Roslin Institute and he has worked there ever since.

In 1990, Wilmut hired cell biologist Keith Campbell to help him with animal cloning studies. Their first success came in 1995, with the birth of two Welsh mountain sheep cloned from differentiated embryo cells. On July 5, 1996, they used the same process to create the first mammal cloned from adult cells, a Finn Dorset lamb called Dolly.

The sheep's namesake was curvaceous country singer Dolly Parton, who was chosen because Wilmut's experiment involved fusing a mammary gland cell from an adult ewe with an egg cell from another ewe. "There's no such thing as ba-aaaaad publicity," joked Parton, who was honored to have the world's most famous lamb named after her.

Dolly's birth (the sheep, that is) was a well-kept secret at Roslin until February of 1997, when the media was advised that *Nature,* the same journal that had broken the Watson/Crick discovery, was running a story about her. The announcement was a bombshell in both the scientific community and the popular press. It set off a debate among leaders in many different fields about the possibilities and implications of cloning.

At Roslin, this period became known as "Dollymania." Dolly quickly became the most photographed sheep of all time, and she was even invited to appear on an American talk show.

Wilmut, however, did not consider the idea of Harvard-trained physicist Richard Seed to clone humans for commercial purposes to be a laughing matter. He said that the idea of copying a person remained his greatest fear.

"There are still no reasons I would find it acceptable," Wilmut told MSNBC.

Instead, the bearded Wilmut hopes to continue his work with animals to enable scientists to study genetic diseases that, at present, are incurable. He talks of genetically producing proteins in the milk of farm animals that could be used to treat hemophilia, emphysema, or cystic fibrosis. Another biotechnology application could help curb the shortage of human donor organs, by altering pigs so that their tissue would become suitable for human transplant.

As the controversy continues to swirl and other researchers around the world come up with new cloned animals, Wilmut deals with it by taking long solitary walks in the Scottish countryside.

Watson and Wilmut made headlines more than 40 years apart. One loved to defy conventional wisdom and to tweak the noses of the establishment; the other preferred the quiet of farm and family.

But both set off scientific shock waves that will continue crashing for years to come.

Subsequently termed the "double helix," their solution explained for the first time the nature of DNA structure and gene replication. The discovery was unparalleled in science. Suddenly, DNA had become the most important molecule of life. Watson and Crick's model was to be recognized as one of the most important discoveries in history, rivaling the discovery of the atom or the invention of the computer chip.

Just as understanding the structure of the atom gave birth to quantum physics, Watson and Crick's definition of the structure of DNA has brought us into the age of molecular biology. And, although quantum physics provided the gateway to the development of atomic energy, molecular biology now offers us the potential for a kind of biological energy—energy that will fuel vast improvements in health, increases in knowledge, and the growth of wealth and prosperity.

As early as 1953 Watson and Crick probably never dreamed that their discovery would lead to a scientific revolution on such an unimaginable scale by the end of the century. How could they know that their little "game" would not just launch the enormous opportunities for gene modification in health care, but also become the catalyst for enormous strides in agriculture and eventually even industrial production technologies.

Today, though, the results are clear enough. As we enter the Bioterials Age, the interdependency of human, animal, and plant is becoming more and more apparent as research in biotechnology progresses on all fronts. By implanting human genes in animals, organs can be modified, even grown for transplantation into humans with a much-reduced risk of rejection. Scientists are testing the use of coral to grow bone cells; animal stem cells are being investigated as treatments for a variety of degenerative conditions and to eventually allow us to "grow our own" livers, bladders, skin, veins and arteries, and even limbs! Neurons, which may be grown in laboratories using tissue from human fetuses, hold promise to stimulate cell production of dopamine to treat Parkinson's disease. We seem to have come full circle, back to an earlier human who relied heavily on plants and animals, and as will be obvious, on minerals as well.

Watson and Wilmut, Mendel and Miescher, Delbruck, and Schrodinger captured the headlines through the century. Many others, though, have made impressive contributions to the understanding of the biological world. Like their colleagues in the subatomic world, described in Chapter 7, some have worked in relative obscurity, at least outside the heady world of science. Others, like Seymour Benzer, however, are starting to "fly" in the eyes of the media.

Seymour Benzer's "High Flying" Gene Applications

For more than 40 years, the science of biotech has been advanced by the work of Seymour Benzer, a molecular biologist whose laboratory at CalTech is devoted to genetic research using the fruit fly. A contemporary of Dulbreck and Crick, Benzer, now 76 years old, made the world's first detailed map of the interior of a gene in the 1950s. His work helped validate Watson and Crick's discovery of the double-helix structure of DNA. Fascinated by the endless diversity of human existence, Benzer looked to the simple fruit fly to test his theories.

Perhaps as a too-close observer of the human condition, he sought out flies that exhibited aberrant behavior for his research! Benzer firmly believes that key sequences in the genetic codes of both fruit fly and humans are very similar. Thus, he argues that there is a strong genetic parallel between the fruit fly and humans; that what we learn from the tiny fruit fly, whose brain is less than the size of the head of a pin, will one day be extended to explain the behavior of humans.

Benzer's team at CalTech has identified in the fruit fly a number of genes that seem to be involved in aspects of human nature. Genes involved in sleep disorders, memory problems, and neurodegenerative diseases, for example, are among his discoveries. To help prove his theory, Benzer named one of the genes "Methuselah" because he is convinced that it determines our life span. He then manipulated this gene in a male fruit fly to determine whether, in fact, the gene had any direct influence on longevity. The specimen lived 100 days, 40 days longer than the average life span of a fruit fly! His findings may have important implications in extending the human life span.

Recently dubbed "The Lord of the Flies" by the *New Yorker* magazine, Benzer's work has attracted a number of detractors. Among them are Richard Lewontin and Edward O. Wilson of Harvard University, two of the world's leading evolutionary biologists. These highly respected researchers argue nurture over nature, that man is essentially a creature of his culture, not his instinct. They believe that the genes of flies, worms, mice, or even humans have little to offer in defining, predicting, or changing human nature. Only time will tell us which of these opposing views will prevail.

Cloning: Hello Dolly!

With Watson and Crick's landmark discovery of the structure of DNA in 1953 as a basis, molecular science required another 43 years to produce Dolly, a cloned sheep born July 5, 1996, at the Roslin Institute in Edinburgh. But it was not until the following February 1997 that her creator announced her existence in *Nature* magazine, creating a media frenzy.

Dolly was created from the fusion of a nuclear-free unfertilized egg with a donor cell taken from the udder of a 6-year-old ewe. As if not "irreverent" enough to create life without sex, the "creator," Dr. Ian Wilmut, named her Dolly after Dolly Parton, in recognition of the fact that the cells had come from an udder.

The asexual reproductive technique used by Wilmut, cloning, is based on a nuclear transfer, a technique that scientists have been using for some years to copy animals from embryonic cells. Nuclear transfer involves combining a donor cell and an unfertilized recipient egg. In animals, a donor cell, complete with nucleus, is fused with the recipient egg. Once fusion takes place, some of the fused cells will start to develop like a normal embryo and produce offspring when implanted into the uterus of a surrogate mother. This was basically the methodology used to clone Dolly.

But the appearance of Dolly also tested and proved a more advanced method of cloning which used cultured cells to produce

embryos. In a technique reminiscent of Frankenstein, these nondupli-
cated or "quiescent" cells were manipulated in Wilmut's laboratory by
introducing electric current and other means to encourage the cells to
fuse and mimic the activity of sperm. Wilmut's work produced Dolly.
But the most astonishing result was that Dolly proved cultured cells
could now be used successfully to clone animals.

As a postscript, not only did Dolly exist as a full-grown adult
sheep, created from tissue of another adult sheep, but also she was
later able to reproduce herself. In March of 1999, Dolly delivered two
lambs in Scotland, impregnated by a ram named David.

The Long, Winding, Double-Helix Road to Dolly

The idea of cloning is not new. As early as the turn of the twentieth
century, scientists had learned to clone plants. Improving on centuries-
old techniques, they started cross-breeding species with one another.
They found they could produce hybrids—new species such as tan-
gelos from tangerines and oranges—that would look and taste better
than their individual components.

But it was not until the 1950s that we saw the beginning of the
breakthrough that led eventually to Dolly. It was Dr. Robert Briggs, an
embryologist who wanted to understand how genes are activated and
inactivated during development, who successfully transferred nuclei
from cells of frog embryos into 197 frogs' eggs. Of these, 35 became
embryos yielding 27 tadpoles. At the time, this was a groundbreaking
experiment in proving that early embryo cells could be cloned.

In the late 1960s, John Gurdon, a developmental biologist at
Oxford University, tried Briggs' experiment again. Using Briggs'
approach, Gurdon was able to prove that cells retained all the genetic
information needed to direct the development of an adult organism.
Gurdon also found that he could reduce the difficulty of cloning by
being more careful when handling the manipulation of cell nuclei to
prevent damage in the transfer stage.

It took almost another decade to produce the next significant breakthrough. The world was electrified in the summer of 1979 when Karl
Illmensee, a German researcher working in Geneva, announced that
he had cloned three mice. It was the first time that mammals had been
created from embryonic cells. Although it was a stunning achieve-

ment, Illmensee's cloning was much more limited in scope than Wilmut's later accomplishment with Dolly. Illmensee had used cells from very young mouse embryos, whereas Wilmut used cells from an adult to create an identical twin of an animal that had already been born and grown to full adulthood.

Although it didn't rival the intense media response to Dolly, Illmensee's announcement nevertheless caused a sensation. A front-page story in *The New York Times* ("First Cloning of Mammals Produces 3 Mice") pointed out that "Earlier reports that mammals and even a human being had been cloned have never been authenticated or taken seriously. This is the first such report to be accepted by the referees of a leading scientific journal." The next day, *U.S. News & World Report* wrote "Scientists are now within one step of what once was termed science-fiction fantasy: the cloning of a mammal." And a *Newsweek* reporter, Sharon Begley, asked the question of the ages, "Now that a mammal has been cloned, can a man be far behind?"

Others followed Illmensee's amazing accomplishment. In 1983, two colleagues of Illmensee, David Solter and James McGrath, paved the way for Dolly by developing a protocol for transferring nuclei from mouse to mouse. A young, low-paid scientist, named Steen Willadsen, working as a "Milk Board Fellow" at a Cambridge University research center, was the first to use nuclear-free unfertilized eggs to create an embryo.

Unlike traditional science that flows from university laboratories, cloning experiments are often conducted in agriculture departments, where researchers may be working surrounded by barnyard animals. These agrilabs were mostly supported by grants from commercial farm product producers. For example, in 1994, Neal First, working with a large grant from W.R. Grace and Company, discovered by chance that cell division triggered in a hibernation phase could yield multiple offspring, in this case, four calves. But the first actual births of a mammal from cultured cells were Wilmut's twin lambs, Megan and Morag, born at the Roslin Institute in 1995. Dolly was to be next.

Meanwhile, the prospect of cloning a human being raised provocative ethical, political, and religious issues worldwide. Legislation to make experimentation in human cloning illegal in the United States is pending in Congress. But experiments in cloning will not be confined to the United States. Scientists in Korea have already reported that they have taken the first steps toward a human clone in the laboratory.

To Clone or Not to Clone:
Is That Really the Question?

Today, some argue that cloning a human is best left undone. Others argue the benefits of producing a parts bank of healthy organs that can be available for transplant into the host, or "natural," organism, in this case, a human. Another major benefit would be to alter the genetic makeup of the clone to the extent that certain defects could be eliminated in future generations.

In another development, gene therapy is already being used to stop the growth of tumors in lab animals. Scientists at the University of North Carolina have recently learned to overcome hardy tumor cells' resistance to chemotherapy, a technique that has the potential to save many thousands of lives. Taken a step further, altering genes that resist cancer drugs would virtually stop the growth of tumors in a person for life.

A transgenic clone of a Dorset sheep in Scotland aptly named "Polly" already carries the human gene in the form of a human protein, factor IX, which was added to the cell that provided the lamb's genetic heritage. Polly raises the possibility of cloning selective herds of animals for human food consumption. The elimination of animal disease, such as Mad Cow Disease, encephalitis, salmonella, and other infections that have plagued food producers, may now be on the horizon.

Can cloning animals benefit humans in other ways? The answer to that question could justify an entire a book in itself. The potential benefits to humans of animal cloning are unlimited. Dolly clearly opened the door to replace diseased organs with those grown in animals. There is also the potential to heighten the human immune system using drugs created from tissue of cloned animals. Less spectacular and much less important than health care, but economically attractive, is the potential to reap the benefits of goods created from cloned animals such as the recently announced ability for genetically breeding sheep that can literally sheer their own wool.

Scientists are already working on the problem of using cloning to re-create extinct animals. Russian and Japanese scientists are scouring the Siberian Steppes in the hope of finding a frozen specimen of the Wooly Mammoth which roamed the earth from 1.8 million years ago to the end of the last ice age, about 11,000 years ago. Should they find one, viable DNA in tissue from the specimen could be used to create a cloned Wooly Mammoth using an elephant as the surrogate mother. The scientists are so confident of their eventual success that they have set aside a 160-square-kilometer "park" where they one day hope to raise, and breed, their re-created Wooly Mammoths.

Cloning: New Frontiers in Gene Medicine

Cloning from cultured cells in the laboratory now provides opportunities for a wide number of medical applications. Ian Wilmut, writing recently in *Scientific American,* suggests some of them.

He notes that scientists are examining the idea of producing universal human donor cells and storing them as permanent, stable human embryonic stem-cell lines from cloned embryos. Cells could then be differentiated and withdrawn as needed for implanting to correct or prevent specific human conditions such as baldness. This approach would be more cost effective than creating an embryo to treat a specific patient's condition.

Someone in need of a heart or kidney today must get on a list and wait for a donor. The needed organ must be a close match in every way—blood type, size, tissue structure, and genetic makeup—in order to reduce the incidence of rejection. The wait is often long and frustrating, and many die before the new organ arrives.

To simply use existing animal organs won't work, according to Wilmut. Animal organs transplanted "in situ" would be destroyed by the human immune response. Proteins in animal cells that have been modified by a certain enzyme trigger this response. On the other hand, if animal organs could be genetically altered to eliminate the enzyme, then the rejection response could be eliminated altogether. If animal organs could be genetically altered to mimic human diseases, however, the disease conditions could be studied and perhaps such organs could be transplanted in humans. Although this raises additional ethical questions, there is new hope for the use of genetically engineered organs grown in animals for transplantation to humans.

Another medical application of cloning that Wilmut proposes would involve replacing defective genes in cells to prevent passing them to offspring. Couples would need to be willing to produce an embryo that could be treated by advanced forms of gene therapy. Nuclei from modified embryonic cells would then be transferred to eggs, creating children entirely free of a given disease.

Despite its high profile, cloning is but one of many potential applications of gene technology in altering the human body for the better. Although it is clearly significant, advances in other areas of gene manipulation hold even more immediate promise for success in clinical medical applications.

Genes and the Broken Heart

Countless applications in clinical medicine that use gene technology have been under serious investigation for some time with substantial progress being made. There are at least a half dozen labs having success with *angiogenesis*.

Angiogenesis is an exciting application that could eventually replace risky bypass surgery and angioplasty, the current therapies of choice for blocked coronary arteries. With angiogenesis, cardiologists can now insert a growth-factor gene directly into the heart, prompting a response that tells the heart to grow its own blood vessels. Thus, the patient can actually grow his own bypass! Although still experimental, the procedure has been shown to improve blood distribution in the heart and allow convalescing patients to better tolerate stress. Angiogenesis, when it becomes widely available and accepted, will be the first example of gene therapy being used to correct a life-threatening human condition.

Results of new studies in mice by Dr. Judah Folkman at Children's Hospital in Boston could signal another approach. Dr. Folkman's research demonstrates that the same substances that inhibit the growth of blood vessels can turn off the blood supply to plaque deposits and, thus, stop their development. Folkman readily admits that more work needs to be done to establish a connection between blood-vessel formation and heart disease in humans.

Building the Better Body

Likewise, substantial progress has been made in using gene therapy in treating cancer and heart disease. Some dozen or more publicly traded companies, such as Entremed, Immiclone, and Techniclone, are conducting trials, asking questions such as: Could there be a connection in the biological processes of heart disease and cancer? What if we could stop the growth of tumors by cutting off their blood supply? Although doing his pioneering work in the formation of new blood vessels (angiogenesis), Dr. Folkman discovered two genetically engineered anti-angiogenic compounds (angiostatin and endostatin). In May 1998, Dr. Folkman startled the medical world when he announced that by combining two genetically engineered proteins, endostatin and angiostatin, he could stop the growth of tumors in mice by cutting off the blood supply to the tumor. This was an exciting discovery because it seemed to offer hope to millions of cancer patients.

But the optimism was short lived. Other laboratories were unable to duplicate the experiments. This had a negative impact on the shares of EntreMed, Inc., a small Rockville, Maryland, biotech company that licenses both endostatin and angiostatin. Also, the Bristol-Myers Squibb Company encountered difficulty producing angiostatin and pulled out of a joint effort with EntreMed to produce both of the drugs. But a bright spot remains for the use of endostatin and angiostatin. Scientists from the NCI (National Cancer Institute) recently went into Dr. Folkman's lab and successfully replicated his results with endostatin and angiostatin. They are now attempting to repeat the experiments in their own laboratories.

Dr. Folkman's research with gene-engineered compounds, such as endostatin and angiostatin, and his theory of inhibiting tumor growth in cancer and also the growth of plaque in the cardiovascular system hold promise for treating cancer and heart disease, the two leading killers of the western world. Additional research suggests there could be a biological link between heart disease and cancer and that compounds, which cut off blood supplies, could become the next generation of medical therapy.

Experimental gene research holds wide promise for building a better physical human being. Here is a small sample of the many exciting therapies that are either already in the pipeline or in various stages of experimentation:

- Identification of the gene that affects the level of a person's addiction to nicotine. The gene tells brain cells how to make the "transporter" that mops up the excess dopamine caused by nicotine. Scientists theorize that dopamine produces the illusion of "rush" in smokers. Scientists hope that this discovery will lead to their ability to tailor treatment for the addiction, to help people quit, and to eventually discover a way to modify the gene and thus control the addiction itself.

▪ Failed organs can now be actually rebuilt from cells grown in a laboratory. To date, bladders made in a laboratory have been successfully transplanted into six dogs.

▪ Stem cells found in animals are capable of regenerating brain and spinal cord cells and could lead to treatments for diseases such as Parkinson's, Alzheimer's, and stroke.

▪ Other stem cells taken from deceased human embryos and fetuses could allow people to grow their own organs and limbs. Neurons from transplanted fetal cells have been shown to prevent cysts from forming on damaged spines, produce insulin in diabetics, and increase production of dopamine in patients with Parkinson's disease.

A World Without Disease?

Infectious diseases have plagued humans since the dawn of time, and the battle against them is almost as old. Although vaccines have been around for hundreds of years, it is only recently that they've been based on genetic technologies.

Today's "miracle" vaccines result from an entirely new approach called "DNA vaccines." They first appeared in 1992 from work in the immunology laboratories of Chiron, an Emeryville, California, biotechnology company. These DNA vaccines are based on introducing DNA "snippets" directly into the body. The DNA snippets are designed to instruct a cell to produce an antigen. The antigen, in turn, produces a strong "T cell" response to guard against microbial invasion.

One of the most important of these DNA vaccines is for the treatment of AIDS, a disease that has eluded science for almost half a generation. Chiron, for example, is working on a DNA "vector" vaccine that uses a harmless virus that has been genetically altered to produce HIV antigens.

These advances in immunology are built on hundreds of years of scientific work: Edward Jenner's discovery of the smallpox vaccine in 1796; Louis Pasteur's discovery in the 1870s of immunizations for animal diseases including chicken cholera, anthrax, and rabies;

Albert Sabin's work in the 1930s in developing flu and yellow fever vaccines; and Jonas Salk's polio vaccine in the 1950s.

In 1996, Peter Doherty from Australia and Rolf Zinkernagel from Switzerland won a Nobel Prize for deciphering how the "cellular" immune system works. They found by using killer T cells to seek out body cells that have been infected by a pathogen (a disease-causing organism), these killer cells destroy the infected cells and stop the disease from spreading.

As we approach the twenty-first century, the science of immunology is on a fast track. Within 10 years, researchers say we could live in a world where vaccines are available to prevent hepatitis C, meningitis, otitis media, diarrhea, strep throat, malaria, and a host of other diseases, including a vaccine to prevent cancer with a single injection.

The Institute of Medicine under the National Academy of Science (NAS) is attempting to organize private research efforts by prioritizing vaccine development for the twenty-first century, listing vaccines the federal government wants on the market in the next 10 years. One goal is to develop vaccines that will both benefit poor countries and prevent the re-introduction of certain diseases to western industrialized nations. With stepped-up efforts to develop vaccines that address government guidelines, a new generation of vaccines is expected to emanate from gene technology.

As more and more diseases are conquered, we can expect a corresponding increase in human longevity, which was only 47 years at the beginning of the twentieth century, and is 76 years at its close.

The ultimate goal, of course, is a world without disease. Although U.S. children are routinely vaccinated for a variety of diseases, those in many parts of the world are not. Recognizing the logistical problems of vaccination in the Third World, Bill Gates, CEO of Microsoft, recently donated $100 million to help vaccinate children throughout the world.

"Mapping" the Human Genome

All of the efforts described in this chapter are important, but nothing compares to the "Holy Grail" of molecular biology, the Human Genome Project. When completed, the project will have sequenced the entire human genome, containing about 80,000 to 100,000 genes.

If 5 percent of the proteins encoded have therapeutic value and only 25 percent prove to hold genuine potential, this still would represent a 14-fold increase over current levels.

Like the explorers of the Renaissance, biotech scientists are travelling in uncharted territory. Their goal is to "map" the human gene structure for themselves and future explorers. Just like the competition between the major European powers of the fourteenth and fifteenth centuries, to go further and faster than the others, the effort to map the human genome has taken on the drama of a competitive race.

The Human Genome Project was launched as a U.S. government project in the early 1990s. The project is so massive in scope that it is often compared to the Manhattan Project or the Apollo Mission. The original completion date of the project was 2005, but has been moved up several years (according to the Genome Project's Web FAQs, it will be finished in 2003). With immense profits at stake, private industry entered the race.

Celera Genomics Corporation, a division of Perkin-Elmer, is making the most aggressive private effort. The company, under the direction of Craig Venter, is working feverishly to complete the sequencing of all the human genes. Venter, a creative and controversial scientist whose radical approach to the project uses RNA to tap into only those genes that are needed in a sequence, expects to better the government effort by several years. (See "Venter Vaults Ahead.") Incyte Genomics has announced that it, too, will produce a map within a year, and produce a genetic sequence database for each gene. Mapping of the human DNA relies on high-speed computers to decode and assemble DNA sequences. These sequences contain known and unknown strands of DNA, which have been bound to a computer chip and then been found to match via laser scans.

Venter Vaults Ahead

What's in a name? In the case of Dr. J. Craig Venter's warp-drive Celera Genomics Corporation, the name reveals a great deal about both the man and his biotechnology vision.

"The name 'Celera,' derived from the word 'celerity' which means swiftness of motion, mirrors the speed with which our new company intends to provide pharmaceutical companies and researchers the information contained in the complete human genome and to help enable the development of new therapies, targeted diagnostics and individualized medicine," Venter says.

Celera, formed in April of 1998, teamed life sciences manufacturer Perkin-Elmer with Venter's nonprofit TIGR (The Institute for Genomic Research) in an effort which he claimed would be able to map the entire human genome by 2001. Furthermore, Venter says that the endeavor would be finished at just one-tenth the cost of the $3 billion, federally funded 15-year Human Genome Project, whose target completion date to map the arrangement of the 3 million base pairs in the genome was not until 2005.

"These . . . sequencing projects will be undertaken using breakthrough DNA sequencing technology developed by Perkin-Elmer," Venter told a House Energy and Environment Subcommittee in June of 1998, "and a DNA sequencing strategy that was pioneered by my colleagues and me at TIGR, known as the whole-genome shotgun sequencing method."

The announcement caused a sensation in both the scientific and the popular press. The map of the genome is the key to the biotechnology revolution of the next century, providing advances that could turn many common diseases into nothing more than painful memories.

But could Venter do what he claimed? Was he taking scientific shortcuts with his method that would later prove disastrous? Or would he, as some have speculated, eventually be ranked with Copernicus, Isaac Newton, and Albert Einstein as one of the greatest scientific innovators of all time?

Few clues in his early life indicated Venter would be much of anything other than a pain in the neck. He was born in Salt Lake City in 1946, and as a child refused to take tests. He barely graduated from high school in San Francisco in 1964. Venter moved down the California coast to the Orange County community of Newport Beach. He worked nights in a department store so he could pursue his daytime "jobs": surfing and sailing.

His endless summer was anything but endless because Venter was drafted. The Navy originally recruited him for its swim team. But while he was in boot camp, President Lyndon B. Johnson's escalation of the Vietnam War ended the services' athletic teams.

The hospital corps required a shorter hitch than other parts of the Navy, so Venter joined them instead. He was sent to a hospital in Da Nang, where the former surfer quickly became a senior corpsman, treating hundreds of wounded and dying soldiers. He turned 21 during his tour of duty. His wife, TIGR President Claire Fraser, feels that Vietnam changed Venter by making him believe that every minute was precious. In those battlefield hospitals, he began to wonder why some soldiers died instantly from their wounds and some survived. What was life, anyway? How did it work?

To find the answers, he decided to study medicine. When Venter returned from the Vietnam War, he earned both his undergraduate and doctorate degrees in physiology and pharmacology from the University of California at San Diego in just 6 years. He and wife Fraser went to work first at the State University of New York at Buffalo and, in 1984, at the National Institute of Health.

Despite ample funding and publishing opportunities, Venter grew restless at NIH. Traditional sequencing methods forced him to labor 10 years on the gene for the adrenaline receptor in human brain cells. Venter didn't feel his work was enriching anyone's comprehension of life. "Like a lot of really innovative scientists, he isn't constrained by current thinking," says *Time* reporter Dick Thompson, who has written several stories on Venter. "That also makes him a difficult person to collaborate with. It's a trait that works for him and against him . . . He thinks outside the box, and acts outside the box."

In 1991, Venter published a paper in *Science* that described a critical innovation. "My colleagues and I developed a new strategy for identifying genes more rapidly and at much less expense than had previously been possible," he told the House Subcommittee in 1998. "With the new strategy (expressed sequence tags, or ESTs), we greatly exceeded the work of many previous years of effort in just a few months."

He formed TIGR as an independent, nonprofit research institute in 1992 to implement the programs he had envisaged for his lab at NIH. There were less than 2000 human genes known the year before he founded TIGR; within a few months the new company doubled that. The work of TIGR worried many of Venter's colleagues, including the first head of the Human Genome Project, Dr. James Watson.

"There was growing controversy surrounding the issue of U.S. government patenting ESTs that I discovered," Venter says. "I was frustrated that I would be unable to participate in the revolution in biology that we had helped start. I did not want to leave NIH, but after much soul-searching I felt it was the most appropriate option."

Perkin-Elmer purchased Applied Biosystems in 1993. Applied Biosystems had built sequencing hardware Venter used at NIH to develop the EST strategy. Connecticut-based Perkin-Elmer invested over $100 million in R&D in 1997 alone. By the spring of 1998, TIGR and Perkin-Elmer had joined to form Celera.

"The aim of our project is to produce a highly accurate, ordered sequence that spans more than 99.9 percent of the human genome,"

Venter says. "There is value in obtaining the sequence of the human genome as quickly as possible—not for the sequences themselves, but for the research opportunities it will create." Venter argued that the new private venture should work in concert with, and not in place of, the much larger government Human Genome Project.

His earlier partnership with ex-Harvard biophysicist William Haseltine's Human Genome Sciences (HGS) came to a very public end in 1997. HGS was a for-profit company that sought to turn scientific findings into marketable drugs, utilizing a staff of 300. TIGR's 175 faculty and staff members were involved in nonprofit research, the goal of which was to enhance knowledge, not revenue.

Using Venter's EST strategy, TIGR has now identified over half of the estimated 100,000 genes in the human genome. With this rapid progress have come increased calls from Venter's legion of critics, including some in the scientific community who regard him as the enemy. There were fears Venter might become a Bill Gates of biotechnology, controlling the information about the human genome as intellectual property much as Gates uses Microsoft's monopoly in operating systems to wield a stranglehold over various areas of the software business.

Others thought the Celera methodology shaky. "I predict that the proposed technical strategy for sampling human DNA sequences will encounter catastrophic problems, at the stage at which the tens of millions of individual tracts of DNA sequence must be assembled into a composite view of the human genome," Washington University geneticist Maynard V. Olson told the same House Subcommittee. "I predict that there will be over 100,000 'serious' gaps in the assembled sequence. A 'serious' gap, in this context, is one in which there is uncertainty even as to how to orient and align the islands of assembled sequence between the gaps." "Some of these (gaps) may occur in DNA regions with great biological significance," Dr. Francis S. Collins of the National Human Genome Research Institute says.

Venter supporters acknowledged that the genome map would contain holes, but that scientists would fill them in over time. Venter also offered to release this data into the public domain at least every 3 months, and release the complete human genome sequence at the project's end.

"Our actions will make the human genome unpatentable," Venter says. "I have been associated with intellectual property issues related to DNA sequences from the beginning and have great appreciation for the sensitivities of the concept. By making the sequence of the entire human genome available makes it virtually impossible for any single organization to own it as intellectual property."

Venter's goal is nothing less than delivering the sequence of the
entire human genome by 2001. The clock is ticking. But perhaps more
than anyone alive today, Venter has shown the ability to speed up the
time of DNA discovery. Perhaps more than anyone alive today, he is
uniquely qualified to steer us into the age of biotechnology.

Diseases, such as cystic fibrosis and muscular dystrophy, are
already targeted for therapeutic applications of new genes that will
be identified by this project. Beyond disease, the human genome
map will eventually create the ability to select personal attributes
such as IQ, physical appearance, and gender.

Ongoing R&D across the whole spectrum of molecular biology,
coupled with the mapping of the entire human genome, will spawn
a vast array of new therapies and techniques designed for the bet-
terment of humans. While improved health and more productive
agriculture have to be considered the ultimate goal of all this work,
economic gain is an important motivator.

The Unity of Plant, Animal, Human . . . *and* Mineral

One of the most dramatic insights of molecular biology is the fundamental relationship, the unity of virtually all life at the cellular level.
Although the interdependency of the species—humans, animals, and
plants—has long been recognized, this new evidence has sharpened
the focus and underscored the need for careful stewardship of biodiversity.

Even more intriguing is the growing awareness that at the atomic
level, all matter—organic and inorganic—is the same. Although
many biologists have been working to create new forms of life from
living cells, it has now been theoretically argued, if not yet proven,
that life can be created from individual atoms from *any* source. It is
almost as if science is about to prove the belief of the ancients that
we are one with the earth.

With the "sexual" cloning of tadpoles, the first steps toward the creation of human life had been taken. It is the science of *asexual
cloning,* or creating a group of identical cells from a single parent, that

is receiving the most attention. True cloning, both in science and the popular imagination, relies on a single DNA hybrid molecule that is replicated in a bacterial host cell to yield a clone or a group of clones.

Will a similar approach using inorganic matter be the key to creating life and matter itself? Only time will tell. But for the moment, the possibility of cloning a human being with all its complex and controversial ethical issues continues to be the center of scientific debate. Cloning, simply a branch of biotechnology science, represents perhaps the most intriguing mix of challenge, opportunity, and controversy.

This evolving unity of humans, animals, plants, and minerals will also fuel a new unity across a wide spectrum of business. While it is increasingly obvious that the technologies underlying AgBio and health care are merging, they are also beginning to merge with large segments of industrial technologies. Early in the new century, bioterials technologies will be at the heart of agriculture, food, health, and many manufacturing businesses. The economic impact of the merging of these businesses is enormous.

The economic impact of health-related molecular biology alone is likely to be substantial. An important indicator is the amount spent on research. In the past 7 years, the R&D budgets of the 20 largest U.S. pharmaceutical companies have more than doubled. If this trend continues for the next several years, annual R&D spending per company is expected to rise from an average of $1.2 billion to around $2.5 billion by the year 2005.

This sudden burst in health care related R&D spending is bringing about dramatic changes throughout that industry. Small biotech companies, many of whom lack the money necessary to market their products, are rapidly signing marketing and cross-licensing agreements with larger biotech and pharmaceutical companies.

As the next chapter will explore, these agreements are designed to free up capital for research and to expand product lines, turning "Big Pharma" into one of the most dynamic industries in the world.

9

Betting the "Pharma"

The BioMedical Complex

*Biotechnology is where the computer
industry was 30 years ago and like the
computer, biotechnology is going to
have a larger impact on your lives
than you can imagine over the next
20 years.*

BIOTECH NAVIGATOR
(*WWW.BIOTECHNAV.COM*), MID-1999

From Sci Fi to Reality

Much of the information about biotech (that part of bioterials concerned with biological technologies) reaching the public in the
1980s and the early 1990s sounded a lot like science fiction. But the
sci fi–sounding days of genetic engineering ended in 1996 with
the explosive news that the Scottish organization, PPL Therapeutics,
had successfully cloned a sheep. A public outcry followed as the
world wondered if human cloning was now right around the corner. Unfortunately, the debate has obscured the more useful side of
genetics and distracted most people from the real story of eradicat-
ing human ills through the biological sciences.

In a few short years, twentieth century health care methodologies will seem medieval and archaic. By the middle of the next century, today's medicine, which attempts to find a weapon that works against a given health threat, will be largely replaced by genetic approaches that reveal the actual sources and biomedical pathways of disease. The result is that doctors, in the main, will "architect" the genetic prevention of a disease rather than treating the disease itself. Skin, limbs, arteries, organs, and even entire bodies will likewise be "redesigned and manufactured" into superior forms.

Genetic medicine will eventually have a powerful impact on how much physical suffering we endure, how rapidly we age, how our tissues regenerate, and how long we live healthy lives. It will change how we view our bodies and raise a plethora of ethical issues that will affect everything from how our genetic information is used to whether parents should be able to choose the sex of their child.

Challenging the Definition of Life

The premise of this book is quite simple: We are at the end of the Information Age and about to enter the Bioterials Age. An important distinction between the two eras, however, is that although the computer was a tool that *changed how we did things,* biotechnology will *change who we are as people.* Biotechnology will challenge our definition of life itself!

Several other aspects of the growth and development of the biotech industry stand in stark contrast with earlier technology developments and the economies they begot. Industrial technologies, such as the development of the cotton gin and the steam engine, were largely the product of individual, "eccentric" inventors. Likewise, many of the first widely successful commercial PCs and operating system software are the products of individual developers, often working in small groups in the basements and garages of Silicon Valley.

There are no basements or garages for biotechnology, though. The biotechnology sector is a complex amalgam of huge and skilled global drug marketing companies commonly referred to as *Big Pharma,* government research efforts supported with massive budgets, innovative university labs, and small but highly sophisticated research-oriented companies often called simply the *biotechs*. Surrounded by massive computing power, endless gigabytes of digital storage, and a global communications system that permits instant information from around the world, the biotech researchers and Big Pharma business executives are poised to do no less than reinvent business, economics, and even life, in the twenty-first century.

From Lab to Life Around the Planet

As described earlier, the advances in the understanding and manipulation of biology and genetics grew slowly over a 7000-year period. Individual researchers, often working alone or in small groups, began to develop important insights into the workings of plants, animals, and people in the 1800s. In the first half of the twentieth century, more organized efforts, usually in large government or university labs, began to sketch the overall picture of biological mysteries. Today, a detailed understanding of at least the human portion of the picture is within sight. The addition of well-funded, private labs with a profit motive spurred biotech research from a dribble to a torrent.

Now an industry of global proportions, biotech, commands the interest of investors, scientists, governments, organized religion, and activist groups around the world who are concerned with its impact and effects on humans and nature. While the rapidly emerging public concerns about biotech will be discussed at some length later in the book, suffice it to say here that the industry is no longer a "best kept secret." By late 1998, it had created a huge debate about human cloning among policy makers around the globe, spawned a trade war between the United States and the European Union, and a major political upheaval for the Tony Blair government in the United Kingdom.

The biotech industry will ultimately impact everyone on earth. It will change global economics, ecology, and life itself. In many ways, biotech, more than any technology before it, will be everybody's business, and not the narrow concern of a few businesses or individuals. In the meantime, though, the businesses themselves have begun to cluster in a number of areas around the United States and selected countries around the world as shown in Chapter 5.

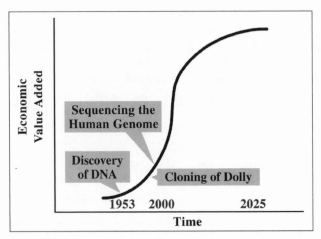

Figure 9-1. Early strategic inflection points of the Bioterials Age.

The Beginning of the Biotech Business . . .

In the growth and development of any industry, there are ups and downs, times when it seems that everything goes right and times when everything seems to go wrong. And there are events and dates that seem to stand out amid the highs and lows. Those dates are the strategic "inflection points" that are seminal in moving an industry ahead with great momentum. (See Figure 9-1.)

Most industries get centuries or multiple decades to weather both the good times and the bad. For the fledgling biotech industry, however, its highs and lows are often measured in months or years. In fact, in the past twenty-five years, the industry has been through several business cycles. These cycles were, at times, invisible to the broader populace as much of the business world focused on the rapidly growing information technology sector. But now the biotech industry is about to emerge on center stage in both the worlds of science and commerce. For biotech, three key years, three "industry inflection points," each almost a decade apart, stand out: 1978, 1988, and 1996.

The "Gene-sis": 1978

In the early 1970s the first stirrings of commercial interest in biotechnologies began around the world, although, at that time, it was largely in the United States. Like so many other technologies and ideas in the last century, many of the early activities that would eventually create the biotech industry started in California, particularly Silicon Valley.

Almost from the beginning, the small innovative companies that considered themselves the pioneers of biotech have had a rather uneasy alliance with the health care giants that are their first and perhaps most important channels to a market eagerly awaiting their discoveries.

In fact, the commercial biotech industry really started in 1978 when a scrappy young company named Genentech signed a deal with pharmaceutical giant Eli Lilly to develop genetically engineered insulin. At the time, financial analysts had trouble even putting a value on the partnership because of the newness of the technology. It became a harbinger of things to come, however, as entrepreneurs and research teams continued to partner with Big Pharma in order to keep their operations afloat and to get their products to market.

Surviving the Crash: 1987

The big players weren't always convinced though. Current biotech powerhouse Amgen had trouble just surviving in the early 1980s. The company arranged a 1984 deal with Japanese brewer Kirin Brewery at a critical stage, allowing it to stay in operation and eventually create a marketable product.

In 1982 Eli Lilly won FDA approval for humulin (human insulin), which was the first gene-spliced product to hit the market. In 1985 Genentech received FDA approval for a human growth hormone. The following year, the genetic research community reached another historic milestone. Research succeeded in tracking down a disease-related gene, despite knowing nothing about the biomedical problems of the disease. This opened the door to faster discovery of disease genes and illustrated the importance of mapping the complete human genome. Partnerships between biotech research labs and big pharmaceutical companies started to become a regular pattern, with 121 strategic alliances set up in 1986 alone.

From 1986 through 1988, the FDA approved only 10 new bioengineered drugs. More important than the number, these new drugs set the pattern for the future. Initial public offerings dropped to zero after the stock market crash of 1987, but the industry otherwise emerged relatively unscathed. Had the industry gone down at this critical point, it might have taken many years to get itself re-established.

Legitimacy, Growth, and Expansion: 1996

Biotech entered the 1990s with over half of the U.S.-based companies setting up global expansion plans, and growing numbers of companies reaching clinical trial stage each month. A pipeline of products was gaining momentum, and those companies with drugs in the market were aggressively seeking ways to expand internationally.

Companies raised a record of nearly $2 billion in the first 6 months of 1991 and had a record year for IPOs.

More importantly, actual sales reached nearly $6 billion. A historic 1993 alliance between SmithKline Beecham and Human Genome Sciences changed the industry's entire outlook, establishing "genes as currency" and recognizing the future impact of genetics on medicine. In this $125 million deal, the principals referred to genes as a "new utility" and established the importance and value of a team's genetic research and information.

The biotech product pipeline soon crossed the psychological double-digit approval number threshold: 16 bioengineered treatments were approved in 1995 and 20 were approved in 1996.

Several IPOs neared the $100 million mark in 1996 and two companies went public simultaneously on two separate international exchanges. It was the point of legitimacy, stability, and growth. The biotech business was real and here to stay. Biotech companies had proven their mettle and the big pharmaceutical companies' alliances with these firms started to bear fruit. No longer were investors putting money into dreams; the investments were translating into marketable treatments for major medical conditions. IPOs increased 537 percent the following year, market capitalization increased 60 percent, and public companies increased their number of employees—mostly scientists—by 22 percent.

In the past 4 years, 76 new genomic drugs and vaccines were approved and over 300 more moved into late-stage trials. Globally, over 1200 antibodies are either on the market or in development for virtually every life-threatening disease or debilitating condition, up from 700 just a year ago. Whereas some medical conditions were previously written off as untreatable by traditional chemical means, genetic solutions are becoming a reality for treating everything from cancer to coronary disease and dwarfism.

Like Fast-Mutating Cells, the Biotechs Explode

Biotech has come a long way since Genentech's pact with Eli Lilly in 1978, to the point where Bayer's deal with Millennium in 1998 was worth $456 million. For a 14 percent stake in Millennium, Bayer acquired the future rights to 256 drug targets—more targets than the entire industry had developed just a decade ago. Close on the heals of that deal, Guilford and Amgen inked another early products arrangement for $466 million.

Market capitalization of the biotechs has increased exponentially. By 1999, Biogen's market cap is over $3.4 billion and Amgen's, led by biotech pioneer Gordon Binder, topped $8 billion. (See "Gordon Binder: Amgen's Leading Man.") Biotech's successful contributions to the big pharmaceutical conglomerates have pushed those companies' worth up as well, with Pfizer's stock price increasing tenfold since 1994.

Gordon Binder:
Amgen's Leading Man

He is chairman and CEO of a company that became the largest independent biotechnology firm in the world before it was 20 years old, and Gordon M. Binder knows that a key to Amgen's astonishing growth was that it literally followed the money.

"Amgen raised $400 million before it sold anything at all," he told an Massachusetts Institute of Technology (MIT) symposium in 1996. "(That) shows why British biotech companies are coming over here (the United States) to raise money. That, combined with the university research base, is why America leads and will continue to lead the world in biotechnology."

Binder's own background might not at first glance seem a natural for someone running a biotech organization. His training, after all, is neither as a scientist nor a biologist. Born in St. Louis in 1935, Binder chose Purdue University, one of the midwest's best-known technical schools, for his undergraduate degree, a B.S. in Electrical Engineering in 1957. From Purdue, Binder did a 3-year hitch the U.S. Navy, and then was off to the Harvard Business School where he was a Baker Scholar (one of the school's most coveted awards).

After stints at Ford and Systems Development Corporation, he joined a new company called Amgen, in 1982. The startup had been founded just 2 years earlier as AMGen (Applied Molecular Genetics) by a small team of scientists and venture capitalists. Their initial investment?: $80,000. Amgen began operations in 1981 with a private equity placement of $18.9 million, which involved venture capital firms and two major corporations. It was an unprecedented amount of financing for a biotechnology firm that did not have a single product on the market.

There were fits and starts in those early days. Amgen at first pursued odd ideas, like generating energy from wood chips. By the mid-1980s, though, the firm had focused its entire energies on human therapeutics.

Binder joined as Amgen's Vice President and Chief Financial Officer in 1982. In his first 5 years, the company, which is traded on the NAS-DAQ under the symbol AMGN, raised money through three public stock offerings, in 1983, 1986, and 1987.

The next year, he was elected CEO, and in 1990, Chairman.

Amgen's first product, the genetically engineered Epogen, finally received FDA approval on June 1, 1989, and was immediately put on the market. The next morning, Binder had red balloons placed all over Amgen's campus and gave everyone the day off. He had reason to feel festive. Epogen was a revolution in the treatment of patients suffering from anemia associated with chronic renal failure. By the end of 1989, $96 million worth of Epogen had already been sold. By 1998, Epogen had become one of the leading pharmaceutical products in the world, with sales that year alone of $1.4 billion.

Neupogen, a recombinant product that counteracted the side effects of chemotherapy and the AIDS drug AZT by boosting the count of white blood cells, got its FDA approval in February of 1991. It, too, soon became an industry standard, generating $1.1 billion in annual sales by 1998. From 1989 to 1997, Epogen and Neupogen were the only products Amgen had on the market. Did this "less is more" approach hurt? Hardly.

Fortune magazine ranked the company *first* among its list of "Shareholder Superstars" for the years 1986 to 1996. In that span, Amgen's average annual return to investors was 67.8 percent, far ahead of second-place Oracle's 53.5 percent. The magazine also ranked Amgen way ahead in revenue growth. Amgen's 108.1 percent easily outdistanced runner-up Sunamerica's 60.9 percent. The *Fortune* analysis of Amgen's strategy was that Binder's company stayed ahead of its biotech competitors by not using the others' approach of waiting for the disease to steer them to the science. Instead, Amgen developed hit drugs by finding promising areas of research that would lead to breakthroughs.

Binder backed this "science first" approach in several ways. First, Amgen invested large sums in research and development, $663 million in 1998 alone. That was a 5.5 percent increase from the previous year. It also had collaborative arrangements with some 200 colleges and universities. That included Amgen's 10-year agreement to pay for up to $30 million of research at MIT, in exchange for patent and technology licensing rights for the products of the research. "We are enthusiastic about this promising collaboration, which could serve as a model for industry-academic partnership," Binder said when the deal was made in 1994.

"This agreement with Amgen represents an essential element in the kind of future I see for MIT: a synergy of basic research efforts at universities and long-term commitments to industry," MIT President Charles M. Vest said. Another major academic partner was Rockefeller University in New York. Rockefeller awarded Amgen a contract for development of its "fat" gene for $20 million and a promise of future payments in 1995.

Amgen also established agreements with corporations, such as Yamanouchi Pharmaceutical Company, Regeneron Pharmaceuticals, Kirin Brewery, Hoffman-LaRoche, and Guilford Pharmaceuticals. The Japanese firm Kirin, for example, formed a joint venture with Amgen for $24 million to develop Epogen way back in 1984. Binder's firm also pays the federal government to do research at labs that once worked with nuclear weapons.

The third Amgen product, Infergen, received FDA marketing clearance in October of 1997. It, too, is a bioengineered drug. Infergen is an interferon used to treat chronic hepatitis C viral (HCV) infection, a liver disease. Just $16 million of the new drug was sold in its first full year on the market (1998). Analysts expect Infergen will always trail far behind blockbuster predecessors Epogen and Neupogen.

The year before Binder joined Amgen, it had exactly seven staff members. By the end of 1998, there were about 5500. Approximately 3500 employees work at the 39-building, 3.8-million-square-foot headquarters campus in Thousand Oaks, located a little north of Los Angeles in Ventura County. Manufacturing operations are based in Colorado. Amgen has a domestic sales force of about 300, and also has facilities in Canada, Europe, Asia, and Australia.

Binder, who turns 65 in 2000, lives in Malibu, a beach town whose residents also include rock stars. He must feel right at home there. He's played a starring role at Amgen since 1982.

Smaller companies have not shared in the run-up though, and have had to look to different sources. Many industry veterans have set up venture capital firms to fill the gaps in funding when companies are at a critical development stage. A typical example is Merlin Ventures in the

United Kingdom, which has just set up a $165 million venture capital fund to finance second- and third-year biotech companies in Europe.

Biotech and the Big Pharma "Marriage of Convenience"

Alliances between biotechs and Big Pharma have become the real backbone of the industry. The number of deals jumped 400 percent during the past decade, reaching several hundred in 1998 alone. This "marriage of convenience" is likely to continue for decades, since the two industries will continue to need each other. Big Pharma needs access to the next blockbuster drugs and small biotech companies need life-sustaining cash and access to markets.

Twenty-one new biotech drugs and vaccines were approved in 1998, up from just three a decade ago. Treatments hit the market for such varied conditions as arthritis, hepatitis, and narcolepsy and four genomic drugs have crossed the $1 billion per year mark in revenues.

The number of companies involved in the industry has expanded both up and out, with the number of players increasing each month and the scope becoming more global. There are now more than 1400 biotech companies and research labs, largely involved in the medical field, with the members of the industry trade group BIO hailing from 26 different nations. Although the United States still leads the pack by a wide margin and Europe and Japan have a large share of the pie, countries such as Canada, Israel, and Korea are developing a stream of commercially viable products. Research labs around the world—from Brazil to Australia—are making new discoveries virtually every day. (See "Canadian Biotech: It's in Their Genes.")

Canadian Biotech: It's in Their Genes

Canada's biotech sector ranks second only to the United States in terms of growth. Although it may lag other industrial nations in capital expenditures, Canada is home to some of the most cost-effective researchers in the world. To back this claim, Canadian analysts point out that Canada ranks third in the world for number of citations in science, engineering, and medicine (nondefense) per dollar invested in R&D. They do so well, despite the size of the market and the lure of better opportunities south of the border, it almost seems that biotech is in their genes! In Canada, government-financed research supports and fosters the BioIndustrial base. A recent study by the U.S. National Science Foundation found that 73 percent of the main science papers cited in Canadian industrial patents during the 1990s were based on research financed by the Canadian government or Canadian nonprofit agencies.

Canadian biotech companies enjoy federal and provincial government tax credits, have access to a strong financial venture capital base, and can generally look to the government for support in developing strategic alliances with other companies, universities, or other nonprofit research groups. This has spurred the industry and, by 1998, it included nearly 300 Canadian companies, investing over $500 million in R&D and generating over $C1 billion annual sales. Employment, which almost reached 10,000 in 1998, is expected to grow at a rate of 10 percent per annum through 2001.

Health care is by far Canada's largest biotechnology sector accounting for 46 percent of the industry compared to 29 percent in agriculture and food. The gap narrows somewhat when sales in the two sectors are compared. Health care accounts for 50 percent of the sales and agriculture 44 percent. Overall in 1998, 100 companies were conducting clinical or field trials of various new products in the pipeline. Following is a summary of Canadian biotech accomplishments and activities in the key sectors:

- *Health care.* New solutions to cancer, AIDS, infections, heart disease, and others are now available in Canada or in the pipeline. Pure insulin developed in Canada has been available since the early 1980s providing diabetic patients with an alternative to bovine insulin. In fact, researchers in Canada uncovered the genetic trait for diabetes. Other examples range from the first drug to treat *E. coli* infection to a tumor-destroying medicine that could revolutionize cancer treatment.

- *Agriculture.* Canadian regulatory agencies have approved genetically engineered crops that require fewer herbicides, such as canola, corn, and soybean; insect-resistant potatoes, corn, and cotton; tomatoes that offer consumers a longer shelf life; and natural microbial fertilizers. The Canadian agrifood product pipeline includes crops to resist drought, fruits and vegetables with enhanced flavor and nutrition, and crops that resist pests and disease.

- *Environment.* Canadian biotech researchers have had numerous successes in improving the environment. They have developed microorganisms for processes such as bioremediation, wastewater treatment, and oil recovery; enzymes for biopulping, biobleaching, and textile processing; and microbial pest control agents for crops and trees. The product pipeline is also full. Researchers are seeking new tools to clean up toxic chemicals and pollutants such as PCBs, new techniques for monitoring and detecting pollution, and advanced methods to convert organic wastes to biofuels.

SOURCE: Canadian Biotechnology '98: Success for Excellence, BIOTECanada, April 1999.

Time and Money: Everyday Challenges

Biotech today faces challenges more daunting than the electronics industry of the transistor age or the early software and computer hardware developers faced just a few decades ago. Most of these challenges deal with time and money.

With information technologies, at least in the early stages, much of the research and product development was handled by "boot strapping" entrepreneurs like Bill Hewlett and Dave Packard. Eventually, when scale was needed, venture capitalists provided seed capital. In fact, the growth of the information industry paralleled the growth of venture capital as an innovation funding source in the United States. And unlike biotech, whose products are often highly specific, information products were often "generic" and immediately applicable to many uses. If one target market wasn't buying, they moved on quickly to another.

Later, IPOs would provide some additional growth capital, but was just as often used by entrepreneurs as well as the venture capitalists as an "exit strategy." The final stage was either the emergence of a "winner take all" (or at least "most") industry leader (such as Microsoft, HP, Dell, Cisco, or Intel) or absorption into a larger entity, often by a cash-laden company outside the industry seeking to reap the rewards of information economics.

Bioterials development, although still featuring innovative and assertive individuals, such as Eric Drexler and Craig Venter, is much different. No garages or untrained entrepreneurs with "insanely great" ideas here. Bioterials demands well-trained scientists doing careful analysis of microscopic cells and subatomic particles in the most advanced labs in the world. The world of bioterials involves expensive equipment in expensive settings used by expensive people.

Senior executives of biotech firms must split their efforts between the science of labs and the huge sums of money required to keep them open. Executives in small and medium-sized enterprises spend much time courting investors to raise enough money to keep afloat. But the "sales pitch" has clearly changed from the early days.

A New Kind of "Cash Cow"

Bruce Henderson, the founder of the Boston Consulting Group, coined the term "cash cow," to describe a company within a larger portfolio of companies that could be "milked" for cash. That is, the corporate entity that owned the portfolio would make very few investments in the future development of the cash cow, but instead would harvest as much cash as it could from the operations. The biotechs, often single entities with no related "cash cows" to draw on, have become reverse cash cows, only this time cash burners! Much of the credit for biotech industry development is owed to executives that have sold a dream to investors.

In the 1970s and 1980s, genetic research firms could get away with selling dreams, but now that the pace of technology has accelerated, investors and partners are not willing to tolerate long periods with no results. The days when investors would accept "paper and promises" are over. Those who have invested money want to see a return through products in the marketplace. When companies go to public markets through IPOs, they're generally not following exit strategies, but "futures strategies," raising money for a big push into a new area of science.

And, virtually every biotech company is in some kind of alignment with Big Pharma, mainly because it's the only way to survive. The average mass-market drug costs $350 to $400 million to develop. Few small and medium-sized companies can then afford to hire an army of salespeople to market their product, especially when there is no other product revenue from past ventures. (Only Amgen has so far been able to simultaneously develop two or more commercially successful products.) Some creative managers have pioneered other financing methods to keep cash flow going, such as buying an unrelated cash-rich company with stock or swapping royalties for enough funds to finance clinical trials.

Many innovative firms get continual funding through venture capitalists and initial and secondary public equity offerings, but investor sentiment and market conditions make this method erratic, at best, for the biotechs. Each time biotech was touted as the next big thing, the money flowed like water, but it dried up just as quickly when investors realized that profits would be a long time coming—a pattern that still continues to this day. For example, in March 1999, the stock price of a small biotech company, Pathogenics, dropped 70 percent in 1 day after they announced slower than expected earnings growth.

At this early stage of industry development, betting on a biotech startup is still rife with casino comparisons, especially when a company is relying on a single discovery to fund the future. This has led to some "banding together" as some of the smaller biotechs form alliances or buy each other for mutual support or increased market presence. Among recent such transactions are the purchase of Cytomed by LeukoSite of Cambridge, Massachusetts, to expand its line of products into treatments for asthma and skin inflammatory diseases, and Organogenesis, Inc. of Canton, Ohio, that formed a research alliance with Novavax.

Big Daddies and Little Orphans

To keep pace and prepare for this increase in therapeutic applications, leading companies, including Merck and Pfizer, have begun shifting their marketing strategies away from the "big daddy," blockbuster drug approach to one of developing more segmented groups of drugs. For example, instead of one class of arthritis drug for everyone, there could be several classes; patients would take a gene test to determine which drug in their class will be most effective. Advances in molecular biology and gene therapy are bringing major changes to the industry. Drug companies will either adapt or fall by the wayside.

Price pressures are a constant worry for the entire drug industry, but the potential of "big daddy" winners, such as a cure for cancer or even the common cold, keep the monies flowing. The smaller companies developing smaller-scale "orphan drugs" (those that treat fewer than 200,000 patients) feel the heat the most. Although HMOs have lately begun to realize that expensive but effective drug treatments can cost less in the end than hospital care, the pricing pressures from managed care and Medicaid keep new wonder drugs from reaching a true market price.

The pharmaceutical industry is unique in that it can routinely take a decade for a drug to go from the laboratory to the pharmacy shelf, with a tremendous number of hurdles along the way. It is estimated that for every drug or treatment that gains FDA approval, 5000 to 10,000 compounds and combinations are tested. Of these, 250 make it to the clinical test stage and only five ever reach the human (phase III) test stage. Only one of these ever crosses the finish line, which is itself no guarantee of commercial success.

During the time that this application testing and approval process is taking place—which costs millions for even the most modest attempt—a company working on its first product is going further into debt every day. Casino analogies abound when many companies are stepping up to the table with only one product—the equivalent of a one-shot single bet on a roulette table. Some industry observers estimate that *only 1 out of every 10* biotech firms succeeds in bringing a product to market.

When a company's carefully nurtured compound beats the odds and finally hits the streets, the patent clock has already started ticking. The 20-year window of exclusivity that patent holders enjoy begins not upon street date, but when the drug is submitted for approval to the FDA. Thus, a vaccine that requires 8 years of trials and reviews may allow its patent holder only 12 years of generics-free marketing time in which to fully collect on it.

Big Bets, Astronomical Payoffs

Despite the long-shot odds, new biotech firms are emerging each week and top universities are being showered with research money. The reason, simply, is that the potential rewards are staggering. A brash young scientist can break out of a university research lab with the next treatment for leukemia and have a multimillion dollar company on its way if he or she can assemble a good team. The president of Bristol-Myers Squibb admitted last year that 60 percent of his company's product targets in testing now came from contracted biotech labs. As the genetic technology improves exponentially, the already nimbler biotech firms are getting faster at discovering promising new treatments and delivering them to the well-oiled marketing machines of the Mercks and Pfizers of the world.

Although biotech needs Big Pharma's money, Big Pharma needs small biotech's speed and intelligence. As industry analyst Richard van den Broek said in 1998, "Any big pharmaceutical company that hasn't made a significant investment in genomics, either internal or external, will be functionally extinct in the next couple of years."

Biotech's weakness in size can also lead to its strengths. Smaller firms can put intense effort into researching one or two treatments and can focus on "orphan drug" cures for diseases that don't affect a large percentage of the population. With a small infrastructure that is focused mainly on research, their operating costs are far lower than Big Pharma's. These firms also tend to take more risks, leading to revolutionary discoveries that the big research labs would never have investigated in the first place. Small firms, moreover, have also accelerated the pace of discovery, cutting down the research time before a drug is ready for clinical trials. They are small and flexible enough to move on to a more refined treatment when the original one runs into obstacles. In some cases, they've found that only the first step of a treatment needs to be researched, with the cells themselves leading the way to the rest of the map.

Although there are now fewer than 15 major players in the pharmaceutical industry, often competing head-to-head on a global basis, there is little direct rivalry in the biotech area. In this early stage of the development cycle, there are plenty of unmet medical needs to focus on and plenty of new processes that a company can focus on without attracting competition. At a later stage, a shakeout and a spate of mergers is likely, but not until the product pipeline gets more competitive and overlap develops.

In terms of pure demographics, few safer long-term growth bets exist than those in the pharmaceutical industry. There are 10,000 more Americans turning 50 every day. The number of people over 100 years old in the United States is expected to exceed some 800,000 by the middle of the next century. The aging population figures in the United States are being mirrored in all developed nations, with the biggest growth after 2005. By 2025, those over 55 years of age are estimated to exceed 30 percent of the total population. Medical and sanitation advances have propelled average life expectancy in the United States from 54 in 1920 to 75 today. As this average moves toward triple digits in the next century, the need for medical treatments will continue to grow. Whoever meets those needs the most effectively will earn a slice of a rapidly expanding market.

Although revenues in the pharmaceutical industry continue to grow at a healthy clip of 6 to 8 percent each year, biotech was up 19 percent in 1997 and 21 percent in 1998. Growth investing is a percentage game, and small companies in new industries are most likely to show the highest percentage growth. Although computer-related stocks are now young adults reaching maturity, biotech companies are still toddlers just taking their first steps, with their rapid-growth phase ahead of them.

Faster and Faster

Industrial companies brought the late-stage mechanical technologies and ideas of the farm, the cotton gin, and the reaper into the factory to spur production and efficiency. The mixture was a potent one, eventually leading to today's technologies and practices such as mass customization and just-in-time logistics. Likewise, the electronics industry grew rapidly by employing these mass assembly techniques of the Industrial Age to rapidly reduce the costs of products. Product features multiplied and production technologies improved at a faster and faster rate every decade.

The bioterials industry will spur its own production technologies further and faster, following Moore's law and by applying the increasing sophistication of electronics in the development, manufacturing, and transportation of products and services.

The Internet has dramatically impacted the information flow of science. When a research lab made a new discovery a decade ago, it would take months for fellow scientists to find out about it. Now that information is available instantly around the globe. This has accelerated the pace of discovery as several teams can jointly push a project forward no matter where those participants are physically located.

Whereas computer hardware and software companies acted independently in developing advances and new processes, the biotech industry is like an organism, growing as rapidly as a living thing through cooperation and shared knowledge. Universities, research labs, and big drug companies can all be working toward a common goal, with each holding a joint proprietary stake.

As described in Chapter 6, a biotech company can now also skip several steps in the discovery process, by accessing genome databases supplied by others. Incyte Pharmaceuticals sells gene databases to subscribers who rely on them to make sense of genetic data. A team of 125 biologists and 175 programmers enable researchers to zero in on specific combinations that will, for example, bust up a harmful virus without affecting human cells. This company, along with other competitors, also sells cloned genes that serve as bacterial guinea pigs. A researcher can purchase from a library of 15,000 different clones, enabling a company in a hurry to skip time-consuming steps and move on to the trial stage within a few months.

Dr. Francis Collins, Director of the National Human Genome Research Institute (NHGRI), points out that the increasingly clearer human gene map has drastically reduced trial-and-error time. "Now, the increasing detail and quality of genome maps have reduced the time it takes to find a disease gene from years, to months, to weeks, to sometimes just days . . ." When the map is completed and databases are better organized, finding genetic disease information could be a process as simple as a web browser search.

Pharmacogenomics

In the near term, a mouthful of a discipline called *pharmacogenomics* is involved in developing specific drugs that treat specific genetic sets of patients. Instead of a shotgun approach where one drug is meant for everyone, precise drugs can be configured for distinctive gene types, leading to custom treatments that are more effective and have fewer side effects. Currently, $8 billion worth of prescribed medicines don't work on patients or must be discontinued because of adverse side effects. Herceptin, a product developed by Genentech, is already on the market, targeted at the 25 to 30 percent of breast cancer patients who have a gene called HER2. In the future, a doctor will meet with a patient, pull up his or her genetic chart, then prescribe or even configure the exact treatment needed for that gene type.

From a business standpoint, pharmacogenomics will be the "niche" phase of medicine, the natural transition to a more customer-centered product. Following in the footsteps of cable TV, special-interest magazines, and all the interactive sites of the World Wide Web, our drugs will cease being blockbuster one-size-fits-all pills, but will be designed specifically for us. The medical industry will then treat the *person,* not the disease.

To keep pace and prepare for this increase in therapeutic applications, leading companies including Merck and Pfizer have begun shifting their marketing strategies away from the "blockbuster" drug approach to one of developing more segmented groups of drugs. For example, instead of one class of arthritis drug for everyone, there could be several classes; patients would take a gene test to determine which drug in their class will be most effective. Advances in molecular biology and gene therapy are bringing about major changes in industry that will require drug companies to either adapt or fall by the wayside.

Everyone Plays in the Biotech "Game"

At least since the Renaissance, academic institutions around the world have played a pivotal role in the development of science, training both the "scientific stars" and the essential journeyman, as well as acting as the center for discussion, debate, and communication of important scientific ideas and insights. Up to now, however, those institutions were seldom "impact players" in the commercial drama. Likewise, large, centralized, national (and often nationalistic) governments have basically played the role of "referee," trying to protect their home turf from any alien commercial invasion, although attempting to maintain control of events within their borders. The other great societal institution, the church, with the exception or the occasional railing against the "evils of modern society" (although making great use of the technology), has also stood aside from the action, leaving secular pursuits to the capitalists.

All that is about to change, however, as the biotech industry counts among its chief players, not just companies, but all-important societal institutions, including universities, governments, and churches around the world. Unlike the past, their role is no longer that of sideline observer, occasionally offering advice, guidance, or creating the rules of the game. They have, or desire to have, important roles in shaping the scope, direction, and role of the industry. And, in the case of both government and universities, they want to directly share in the rewards.

The breadth of knowledge and depth of financial resources required in biotech to transform a vision into a finished product is simply beyond the means of any one individual or firm. Thus, the development of the biotech industry is built on symbiotic relationships such as the mutual interdependence of idea-rich but cash-starved biotech startups and deep-pocketed pharmaceutical firms eager to expand their knowledge horizons. But the university is also a key component of the more basic research discoveries (such as the mapping of the human genome) which underlie even the work of the biotech startups. The academy, in turn, acquires a large proportion of its resources from governments, many of which also directly subsidize private research via preferential tax treatment and targeted subsidies. This web of financial and intellectual interdependence is unprecedented and contrasts sharply with the past.

During the industrial revolution, many of the original insights came from individuals, working alone, usually trying to concoct a new solution to a burdensome commercial problem, such as Whitney's cotton gin or James Watt's steam engine. Some, of course, such as the DuPonts and Henry Ford, also became industrial titans in their own right. These inventors were most often co-opted, though, by great industrialists and financiers of the late 1800s and early 1900s, those that we now call the "Robber Barons," among them Rockefeller, Carnegie, Vanderbilt, and Mellon and their international counterparts such as the Matsushitas, Siemens, and Rothchilds. Despite the negative epithet, they created the industrial revolution, and built the commercial infrastructure of the western democracies. The other great institutions—church, state, and universities—largely played a "supporting" role, although some will argue that the "support" was more often "interference."

Important inventions of the Information Age, starting with Samuel F. B. Morse (the telegraph) and Alexander Graham Bell (the telephone), to the development of seminal products such as the PC (Steve Jobs) and software (Bill Gates), were the result of individuals working alone or in small independent groups with the missionary zeal to create something "insanely great." Of equal importance, of course, were the companies, large and small, such as IBM, AT&T, Siemens, and Northern Telecom and later Intel, Lucent, Compaq, Dell, Microsoft, and Cisco, that also developed or perfected technologies and took the resulting products and services to homes and offices around the world.

Early in the Information Age, governments around the world argued that their role should be largely one of erecting barriers in order to control the direction and flow of the technologies so as to prevent the excesses of the past. Later, of course, recognizing that their actions could do little to stem the tide of innovation and global competition, governments progressively freed the information sector around the world, spurring a huge flow of innovation and new, inexpensive products and services.

Universities

Universities largely played a sideline role in the Information Age, occasionally perfecting an important technology, or acting as an "incubator" for innovations or innovators like Gordon Moore and Marc Andreessen. But the big players, like Jobs and Gates, in the main, avoided the academy, preferring the rough and tumble of the "real world." Information technologies moved too fast for the rather staid world of the academy.

Company successes are truly built on scientific discovery and biotechs are hungry to find the brightest minds wherever they may be. Genentech is a typical example, with partnerships with universities in the United States and three other nations. As company CEO Arthur Levinson said in the company's 1998 annual report, "We have shown that excellent science can indeed serve as a foundation for solid operating results."

Those who manage the budgets at universities with a strong science focus will increasingly find themselves making major forward-looking investment decisions. Today's universities are not just idea incubators, but they are an active part of the medical discovery and development process. Apart from financing issues, the main reason that the United States is a leader in biotech is that technology transfer between universities and industry is easier and faster than in other countries.

The University of California system, a major player in biotech research efforts, earned $63 million in royalties from drugs in 1996 and seven other universities earned over $10 million each. Dozens of others are destined to reach this figure in the next year or two. With higher rewards come higher risks, however, as Boston University found out when it saw the $90 million of endowment money it invested in a drug called Seragen shrivel to a value of only $4 million.

Most universities with strong science school faculties have arrangements with private industry, either for seed money to fund experiments or, more frequently, actual royalty deals whereby the university benefits from any eventual sales of the drug targets discovered. Pfizer, Merck, and Amgen are just a few of the companies that have recently announced plans to set up or expand boutique research and development centers in Boston, primarily to tap into the scientific expertise of the faculty and students there. Some research universities, such as Vanderbilt, have even set up venture funds to stimulate biotech research and commercialize their intellectual property.

Many universities felt they made important contributions to the development of information technologies but were unable to capture the "economic rent" for them. Now, faced with increasing finance constraints, most don't intend, and can't afford, to let that happen again. They are organizing to be key players, part of the scientific action, and reap the rewards of the biotech revolution.

Governments

Governments, too, seek an expanded role as a player in the bioterials industry. Frequently a "funder" of fundamental research, government support of major scientific endeavors was most often undertaken for the "common good." Now, though, governments, such as the U.S. government, want a piece of the action. Vast amounts of U.S. government support for the Human Genome Project and the Advanced Energy Project are coupled with increasing pressure for the government to patent and license their proprietary developments. Increasingly strapped for money, just like the universities, governments around the world are looking to the riches of biotech as an important new source of revenue.

Churches and Activists

The role of the churches, along with both highly organized and loosely coordinated activists groups, also have the biotech industry within their sights. The goals with these groups (and there is a wide spectrum of concerns), however, are not commercial. Some are arguing for a complete halt to all biotechnology research, although others want to stop or redirect selective parts of the effort. Their influence is huge, and is characterized in a later chapter as the "Chinese Wall" of the biotech industry. It to enough to say, at this point, that the biotech industry will get more "guidance," from more quarters, than any other in history.

Activists' concerns will make for significant challenges for this fledgling industry, and there will be no easy "genetic" solution to the issues. For the biotechs, such solutions will be an integral part of the business for many years to come. More immediately, though, the industry faces some significant operating challenges just to keep its momentum.

Biotech is already making its initial impacts on health care, particularly Big Pharma—in the United States a $1 trillion industry with about the same number of dollars being spent in the rest of the world. Almost concurrently, it will revolutionize the agricultural business, transforming plants and animals alike. Bioterials will help "Big Farm" feed some 12 billion people by midcentury. And, at the risk of sounding unsympathetic to health and food-related issues, bioterials will save its biggest, and perhaps most profound, impact for the production and consumption of at least one-third of the world's material goods. It will bring new levels of prosperity to those who chose to embrace it.

In earlier industries, a single individual and a good business model could launch a multibillion-dollar company. The key to success in bioterials, though, is grounded in a talented scientific discovery team, deal makers who can gain continual access to capital, and biotech-savvy partners—companies, governments and universities—who can bring credibility, stability, and vision to the operation. Nowhere is that more starkly obvious than in Big Farm.

10

Betting the Farm

The Bionic Farmer

For all the pests that out of earth arise
The earth itself the antidote supplies.
LITHICA, C. 400 B.C.

On a farm in the south of Wales, a young boy rises at dawn to help harvest fleece from the sheep herd that has been in his family for generations. But the wool he gathers will not be shorn in the traditional way, a 5000-year-old annual ritual. In fact, this herd of sheep has literally shorn itself!

Each sheep in the herd was vaccinated with a genetically engineered protein called "Bioclip" and then fitted with a special "hair net." After one week, the protein caused the fleece to shed as a whole into the net, just as though the sheep stepped out of its coat. There was little or no waste in the process, and each piece of fleece was almost exactly the same length. Only 1 day after shedding, the protein levels in the animals returned to normal and the herd began to grow new wool.

The Life Sciences

What the young boy doesn't know is that he is part of one of the newest, fastest growing, and potentially most important "industries" in the history of the world. Sheep that shear their own wool are just a small, trivial part of the new business of "life sciences." The life sciences business, also referred to by other names such as *agbio,* or *agtech,* includes the genetic modification and use of both plants and animals for improved food, better and cheaper health care, and even industrial and consumer goods.

If the health care biotechs and Big Pharma companies described earlier are in a foot race to develop their respective technologies, the life sciences giants are moving at "Grand Prix" speed to develop theirs. And, unlike the large number of small biotechs working in concert with the large pharmaceuticals companies in the human biotechnology business, the big guys are running this race almost exclusively. While there are a number of small, innovative agbio firms conducting R&D in this field, in the main it is dominated by a few large companies in the United States, Europe, and Mexico. A number of these companies are old-line commodity chemical manufacturers that are rapidly re-inventing themselves as life science and pharmaceutical players.

In the United States, an early leader is Monsanto. The company has largely shed itself of its legacy chemical businesses, and is a "first market mover" in life sciences (even claiming to have coined the term) and biologically based pharmaceuticals. Not far behind Monsanto are former commodity chemical competitors DuPont and Dow—also rapidly moving into the bioterials businesses in agriculture, human health, and industrial materials. From Mexico, ELM (Empresas La Moderna), the world's largest seed and vegetable producer, is moving fast into biologically engineered foods. In Europe, former chemical giants are merging to create formidable life sciences companies, including Novartis (Ciba-Geigy and Sandoz), Aventis (Rhone-Polenc and Hoechst), and AstraZeneca (Astra and Zeneca).

Although the term "life sciences" has been around for less than a decade, its origins are almost as old as life itself. Biotech farming in a primitive form has been around for almost 7000 years. Evidence from the Stone Age has shown that even then farmers found ways to improve their crops through natural selection. At each harvest, they simply chose the largest seeds from the best plants, putting them aside for sowing the following year. As early as 5000 B.C., farmers (mostly women) had learned to cross diverse strains of plants or animals to produce greater varieties. Offspring from these hybrids were selectively bred to produce the greatest number of desirable traits. Maize

(corn), which is one of the first food crops known to have been cultivated by man, was found as early as 5000 B.C. in Mexico. Since no
wild forms of the plant have ever been found, corn is believed to have
been the fortunate result of some ancient agricultural experiment.

In addition to basic agricultural improvements, humans have experimented with biotechnologies to improve food production almost as
long. All producers of wine, bread, beer, cheese, yogurt, and pickling
products are, in effect, biotechnologists who have worked for thousands of years to improve their products. But, just like the young
sheep herder described here, they were probably unaware that they
were the early innovators that helped create one of today's most
important industries.

The Agbio Business

The business of agbio got its formal start with the first systematic
attempt to produce an insect-resistant plant in the eighteenth century, when European grapevine stems were grafted onto resistant
American root stocks to defeat the Phylloxera aphid. A long period
of scientific dormancy followed, as more than 250 years would
elapse before scientists focused seriously on the genetic manipulation of plants. In the case of farm animals and pets, hybridization, or
cross-breeding, has been practiced for over 3000 years, although that
too has only been under serious study by genetic engineers for the
past 50 years.

A breakthrough in the use of selective breeding to increase food
production occurred in the 1960s when Norman Borlaug, an American agriculturist, led a hybridization project that vastly increased
worldwide yields of rice and wheat. In 1970 Borlaug was awarded
the Nobel Peace Prize for his work, which had measurably reduced
hunger throughout the world.

Humans have always been dependent on animals and plants for
sustenance. Animals have depended on plants for food. Plants have
depended on birds, insects, and certain mammals for pollination and
reseeding. But this ancient cycle was greatly modified in the 1970s
with the introduction of hi-tech farming. In less than one generation,
both consumable and decorative plants have become more dependent on humans for cultivation and genetic design to reduce damage
and increase yields.

The modern hi-tech farming era, which began as recently as the 1950s, introduced better methods of soil conservation and irrigation. Improved fertilizers for production of more food per capita, and chemicals to control insects, crop diseases, and weeds, added to the yields. Today, that period is referred to as the "green revolution." *Business Week* magazine, in an April 1999 story, suggested the advent of the agbio industry in the 1990s represented the "second green revolution." But the agbio business is more than just green, as it includes genetically altered animals as well as plants.

The evolving agbio industry reaches into a large number of areas and any categorization of them will invariably be arbitrary. However, in its broadest form, the agbio industry can be thought of as including two major areas: the development of genetically engineered plants, both land- and water-based, and the genetic manipulation of animals, fish, and insects, and other living organisms.

In the case of genetically re-engineered plants (often referred to as transgenic plants), researchers and developers work at three broad but distinct goals: improvement of the inherent genetic quality of the plant itself to improve the growing efficiencies or reduce the negative additives to the soil or air, genetic improvement of the plant so that it is healthier for animal and human consumption or carries new disease fighting substances, and the use of plants for the production of other materials and substances for a wide variety of commercial uses.

As for animals, the same three broad categories apply: improving the inherent genetic characteristics for better, more efficient, animals and animal products; genetic improvement of the animal so that it has enhanced health characteristics; and genetically altering animals and other living creatures (spiders, for example) for the production of new materials for health care and industrial uses.

In addition, some important work is under way on the improvement of food and medicines for pets and the water-based food industries. Purina, among others, is "microdesigning" pet food based on genetic information. It adjusts nutrients in the pet food to interact with genes to improve pet health and minimize disease risks. Other areas of genetic research include "biofilms" to improve the conversion of materials, such as nitrates and ammonia, that are important for aquaculture.

A discussion of the entire field of agbio, such as pet foods and aquaculture, could easily be the subject of an entire book. However, the focus here is on the major lines of scientific inquiry in agbio and their economic implications.

From Information Age Farmer to Bionic Farmer

The transformation of agriculture by information technologies got under way in the 1970s, at the same time that those technologies started to transform industrial firms. By the 1990s, the "Information Age farmer" had helped develop the concept of *precision farming* (also variously known as *prescription farming, site-specific farming,* or *variable rate farming*). These methods utilize global positioning systems (GPS) and geographic information systems (GIS) in a hi-tech approach that collects and transmits data via satellite to create yield maps of fields during harvest. Farmers can use the maps to precisely program their planting and fertilizing so as to maximize production while minimizing the need for fertilizers and fuel. GPS also helps farmers comply with the myriad of government environmental regulations for toxic fertilizers and pesticides.

No sooner had the Information Age farmer become a fixture in agriculture, than a new transformation began, this time to the "bionic farmer." In just 5 years, since the mid-1990s, with the release of the first genetically engineered field crops, the U.S. farm and farmer have been undergoing a dramatic renaissance based on genetically engineered crops. The first new food product to reach the grocery shelf, the genetically enhanced FlavrSavr tomato has been quickly joined by a host of others aimed at the $800-billion-a-year U.S. food industry. Today, estimates are that some 50 percent of all U.S. corn, cotton, and soybeans are genetically enhanced. For a greater understanding of the entire genetic approach to one crop, see "A New Way of Pickin' Cotton."

A New Way of Pickin' Cotton

If there's one crop that affects nearly every man, woman, and child on earth, it's cotton. Diets and staple foods vary worldwide, but nearly everyone has cotton in his or her dresser drawer.

This humble plant is the most important crop in many regions of the world. It is the fifth-largest crop in the United States and number one in many southern states. Through genetic modification, researchers in 42 countries are working on methods to make cotton more resistant to threats and researching ways to make the final product more useful and durable.

Resistance from the Inside

On average, 15 percent of the yearly U.S. cotton harvest is lost to disease and insects. In less developed countries, that number is often double or triple. Insecticides have been useful in the past, but the predators eventually build up resistance and a side effect is that many natural predators are killed as well. Weed killers that fight encroaching vegetation can also harm the plant they're meant to protect. Genetics has become a more targeted, environmentally friendly answer:

- Monsanto's Calgene division launched "Bollgard" in 1996, a genetically altered seed that produces a cotton lethal to bollworms. The bacillus thuringiensis (Bt) bacteria is not effective as a spray because it breaks down in sunlight, can be washed away by rain, and must be eaten by the insects to work. Now that it's part of the cotton itself, however, its effectiveness doesn't fade. If at any time during the growth cycle a bollworm eats the plant, the worm will die.

- Farmers in western Australia are using a similar method to fight two types of caterpillars. After losing the war due to insecticide resistance, Ord Valley farmers are growing cotton on land that has been barren for 25 years. When the caterpillar eats any part of the cotton plant, a protein reacts to the specific pH balance in the worm's stomach, setting off a bacterial attack that kills the insect from the inside.

- Labs in Pakistan and Turkey are developing plants that are harmful to aphids and whiteflies, the biggest crop threat in a dozen Asian and African countries. Whitefly-transmitted geminiviruses have resulted in a decrease in production of 40 percent over 2 years in Pakistan, and the threat can easily spread to other parts of the world through trade shipments.

- Several companies are selling genetically modified (GM) cotton that is resistant to weed killers. The most popular variety is produced by Monsanto to resist Roundup—one of their most profitable products.

- Members of Egypt's Cotton Research Center are working against the clock to develop cotton that will grow in high-saline soil. As environmental degradation has allowed the sea to seep further inland, saltier soil is reducing the amount of land available for cotton cultivation.

- Several researchers are performing trials on faster-maturing plants and drought-resistant plants. The U.S. Department of Agriculture's (USDA's) research arm is developing plants that will have an increased photosynthetic efficiency. If successful, each of these developments will allow cotton harvesting in a wider geographic area than is now possible.

- Several researchers are working on cotton that sheds its seeds more easily, saving labor and fuel by eliminating the need to physically shake the seeds loose from the pod.

The agbios are still at a very early stage in development, however, when it comes to GM cotton. Not all the approaches described here are producing results. Scientists expect to reach a point, though, where cotton fields are free of chemicals and the growth cycle requires less fuel for maintenance.

A Superior Finished Product

The first stage of cotton biotech has focused on making the plant stronger and more resistant, with no real change in appearance or function. The second stage is altering the final product itself to make it more useful or convenient:

- Researchers in Israel, Turkey, and the United States are all developing cotton plants that grow in color. This will make it possible to produce "natural" colored clothing. The payoff will be tremendous in terms of energy savings and a reduction in pollution from the dyeing process.

- Monsanto has developed a cotton fiber that "holds its press" and resists wrinkles, giving it the properties of synthetic permanent press fabrics. The result could give people the best of both worlds and cut down on the production of materials that require more energy and pollutants to produce.

- Scientists at Auburn University, along with others, are introducing protein-based polymers into cotton. The result will increase the fiber strength, thermal characteristics, dye binding, and water absorption.

Whether in the ground or on our backs, the "new" cotton could easily be the "poster product" of the Bioterials Age.

One example is the appearance of new, genetically engineered oil seed crops that grow from canola, an oil seed–producing plant that yields lauric oil, found naturally in coconuts and palm kernels. Canola oil has found wide acceptance among consumers because of its reduced cholesterol content and competitive pricing against cottonseed oil and other generic products. In addition, early bioagricultural achievements have included a new hybrid corn seed that resists the corn borer, as well as improved barley with disease-resistant genes.

Another example of the superiority of genetically modified food compared to a conventionally grown crop is Monsanto's NewLeaf Plus potato. It is more effective against potato leaf roll virus than any insecticide and it also prevents net necrosis, a cause of internal defects. As a result, the potato requires 80 percent less insecticide than conventional potatoes, increasing processor throughput and protecting yields while improving overall quality.

Designer Seeds in the Race for Life

Ever since the first nomadic hunters (Neolithic Man, between 7000 and 8000 B.C.) decided to settle down and grow crops, farmers have battled pests, weeds, and plant diseases. For many thousands of years, the only technical innovation for farmers, developed about 3000 B.C., was the invention of the plough. The invention of the plough created a revolution in farming, and the birth rate of the world's population for the first time exceeded the death rate. The plough set off the agricultural revolution and the population explosion that continues to this day. In the first millennium, by the year 1000 the world had a population of about 300 million. By 1800 it had reached 1 billion people. By 1900, there were some 1.7 billion people in the world, 90 percent of whom still lived and worked on the farm, producing just enough food for themselves and the 10 percent who lived in the cities.

To feed today's hungry world of nearly 6 billion people, farmers plant more than 70 percent of the world's fields with cereal grains (the English word "cereal" comes from the name of the Roman goddess "Ceres"). And, in the last 40 years, spectacular gains have been made, with huge increases in yields per acre, some 80 percent for wheat and corn, and price decreases of nearly 60 percent for these same crops.

Farmers have known for centuries that some plants survive epidemics of disease or insects while others in the same crop succumb. It was not until 1905, however, that Sir Roland Biffen of Cambridge, England, experimented on two varieties of wheat and showed that the ability of a plant to resist a rust fungus was inherited.

Other important events in the development of designer seeds include:

1930s—Plant breeders find that when plants are infected with a mild strain of a virus, they become immune to a more destructive strain.

1938—The first commercial insecticide containing *Bt* is introduced.

1950s—Studies show that proteins produced by *Bt* bacteria kill insects.

1981—A *Bt* toxin gene is cloned at the University of Washington.

1983—Monsanto scientists successfully introduce genes into plants.

1990s—Genetically engineered virus-resistant squash seeds, worm-resistant cotton, and herbicide-resistant strains of soybeans, cotton, canola, and corn reach the market.

Is all of the emphasis on research to improve seeds really necessary?

Yes, in the opinion of agbio researchers, life sciences executives, and population experts who expect food supplies to fall short of demand early in the next century. This forecast has prompted scientists to intensify the search for new ways to use genetic engineering to improve plant and animal agriculture. With world population expected to double to some 12 billion people by 2050, continued advances in agbio are critical. The growth of world agriculture production, however, is expected to exceed that of world population growth only until about 2010.

Today, agbio engineers are producing seeds that can induce plants to resist disease, insects, and herbicides. These new seeds promise to free farmers from their age-old pestilences while eliminating the need for toxic chemicals that degrade the environment. The process of selectively breeding plants to produce more per acre and resist diseases and pests, though, can take more than 15 years to reach the market. This is due to the careful selection and repetitive crossing of progeny that is required. The growth of crop acreage devoted to bioengineered plants will continue to explode as we enter the twenty-first century. Between 1996 and 1997 alone, acreage in bio-engineered crops in industrial countries increased twentyfold.

The race among the major agbio firms described previously is not just a race about pure economics, however. It is a race for life. In North America where modern agriculture is at its height, farmers produce some 17 times more rice, corn, and wheat per acre than sub-Saharan Africa (and almost 3 times that in Europe and Russia and 5 times that in Latin America). In spite of these advancements, farmers worldwide in the 1990s still lost about a quarter of their crops to pests and disease.

Improving rice, for example, is a prime target of biotechnology research. It is estimated that 50 percent of the potential yield of the world's rice crop is lost annually to bacterial and fungus diseases such as leaf blight and blast. Ongoing research at the Ronald Lab at the University of California at Davis has recently discovered a unique interaction between these two diseases. Using genetic and molecular techniques, scientists at the Ronald Lab are attempting to learn how the interaction of proteins in the rice plant can be altered to signal the plant to produce a molecular response that will provide a powerful defense against both leaf blight and blast.

One of the most important areas in the development of transgenic plants is to improve their consumption effectiveness for both animals and humans. Feed crops for animals, for example, are being genetically engineered to improve their health, lower feed costs, and limit ecologically harmful animal waste. In fact, the study of how wild animals use certain plants for their medicinal benefits has even spawned a new science known as *zoo-pharmacognosy,* which is leading to new insights in the benefits of certain herbs and plants for human and animal health.

For human consumption, plants, such as tomatoes, potatoes, soybeans, bananas, and corn, are being enhanced to improve their ability to fight problems such as cancer and heart disease, as well as their ability to produce hemoglobin and improve digestion. Importantly, vegetables, such as potatoes, are being enhanced to produce vaccines that could materially improve the immunization of children in the Third World who are often hard to reach (for both cost and logistics reasons) with classical procedures. To see how some biotech researchers are studying the potato, see "Laura Miller: Vaccine with Her Fries."

Laura Miller:
Vaccine with Her Fries

From her position on the front lines, Laura Miller sees both the joy and frustrations of biotechnology research. Miller is a laboratory manager and a research support specialist in the Plant Pathology Department at Cornell University in Ithaca, New York. Cornell has established strong programs in a variety of disciplines related to biotechnology, with more than 300 faculty members plus 600 graduate students and postdoctoral associates involved in research.

A graduate of Cornell's agricultural economics program, Miller nonetheless was drawn almost immediately to genetic research. Over her 30-year career, she has participated in pioneering research in the field of genetically engineered potatoes. Asked why she finds her work so rewarding, she says, "I like the idea of knowing that, in my lifetime, I'm going to see actual results of some of this work and carry it over into other crops." Miller says. "I like that idea. A lot of other theoretical research may help 20 to 30 years from now, but to see the actual trans-genic changes in a lot of crops is amazing."

Cornell's program has sprung from a belief that a close collaboration between the university's scientific community and the industries that rely on it is critical. Miller says that fast-food giant McDonald's Corporation, which built a great deal of its reputation on french fries, is a major player in the potato business. "McDonald's has been a real shot in the arm for the potato industry," she says. "They are expanding into other parts of the world. McDonald's is very focused on the quality of the product, but the potato they prefer, the Russet Burbank, is very susceptible to virus diseases. So, we are making genetically engineered Russet Burbanks that are very resistant," Miller continued. "We are working on the potatoes to confer, or even piggyback, multiple resistances."

One of the reasons the work of Miller and her colleagues is so vital is that the potato is such a crucial staple all over the world. "It's one of the most important crops worldwide, even in countries that you might not associate with the potato, such as China," she says. "There are areas of China where the potato is very important."

Most of the projects Miller works on are long term. In addition to improving the basic characteristics of the potato, and its resistance to disease and environmental conditions, much work has gone into creating potatoes that produce vaccines against various diseases. Such vaccines would help inoculate people who eat the potato. While not as necessary in western countries, such vaccine delivery mechanisms could be critically important in the Third World.

In such areas as vaccines, it may take years of work before one of the genetically engineered potato progeny that her team has produced and altered can "get out there and do it," she says. The process can often be slowed by what Miller sees as bureaucratic red tape. "We feel that the risk to the public of our own work is minimal," she says. "We understand that for some genetically engineered things the risk may be greater. But we are subject to the same rules and regulations."

How does this affect her research?

"Everything that goes from our greenhouse has to be Autoclaved, a procedure for cleaning that uses superheated steam, before it can be thrown out," Miller says. "The majority of things are not genetically altered, but everything has to be Autoclaved and sterilized before it can be discarded. We understand regulations, but when we want to do field trials it can be frustrating. The fact is that the general public does not understand the very low risks," she says.

Cornell does transgenic work on a small field in Ithaca, and also carries on research at a larger plot in Lake Placid. Lake Placid is a 5-hour drive from the Cornell campus, and it provides some real scientific advantages for the potato project. "It's a very culturally isolated area. Lake Placid's elevation is high, and there's a lot less disease pressure," Miller says. "Not a lot of potatoes grow right there. A lot of diseases can be blown through the air, or carried by insects that are blown through the air. An isolated area is a good idea; it is probably one of the finest areas in the United States to do this," she says.

One of the keys to making a transgenic potato that will be commercially acceptable is keeping the changes to an absolute minimum. "When we alter the potato, we make sure that we really only alter the one thing," Miller says. "We don't want a potato that looks different from the parent or grows differently from the parent."

On the front lines of agbio research, Miller finds great rewards from the work itself. "We're not trying to make money out here," she says. "We're trying to write papers and reveal scientific truth. "We're trying to do things for the greater good."

To ensure an adequate gene bank for breeding and genetic research programs, the USDA has established a germplasm repository at an experiment station in Geneva, New York, under the supervision of Cornell University. The germplasm on deposit there contains important genetic traits that have the potential to boost insect and disease resistance and improve plant quality. This clonal repository, which includes holdings of accessions of apple, grape, buckwheat, celery, vegetable cole crops, onion, petunia, winter squash, and tomato, is one of the world's largest collections of germplasm. The repository is widely considered a biological insurance policy for the future.

Designer Animals

The pressure on field crops, such as wheat, is exacerbated by the trend of the world's population to consume more and more of its average 2740 calories per day in meat rather than grain. It takes about 1 lb of wheat to make 1 lb of bread, but 2 lb of wheat to produce 1 lb of live weight of chicken, 3 lb for a pig, and 8 lb to create 1 lb of live weight of a cow. While animals have always been important to biotechnology R&D for human health, they are now a critical part of the agbio developments. The successful cloning of Dolly portends a day when entire herds could be cloned from cultured cells in the laboratory with precisely engineered traits favorable for food production.

It is estimated that this one genetically engineered market niche could increase gross revenues to the beef and dairy industry by as much as $8 billion. In addition, many scientists believe that these cloning experiments are the first steps toward raising "efficient," disease-resistant herds of many kinds. Lamb, pork, chicken, beef, and dairy producers could eventually guarantee uniform results, thus providing an absolutely consistent product, with, for example, less fat. Because of the significant economic implications, agbio scientists have moved rapidly to understand the genetic composition of a number of important animals.

Like the work on transgenic plants, the genetic re-engineering of animals has a number of objectives. Important among them is the improvement of the inherent characteristics of the breed (bigger, leaner, more production of by-products such as milk), more efficient use of feed, as well as production of materials for health and industrial uses. Closely related are efforts to create optimum balanced animal food to prevent infectious animal diseases such as salmonella in poultry. Other efforts are aimed at lowering animal fat percentage and in similar dietary considerations to enhance human health.

Agbio scientists have also used recombinant DNA techniques to produce "transgenic" (implanting the DNA from one species into the genes of another) animals for other applications. Among them, providing medically useful proteins in animal milk and developing a wide range of vaccines to fight disease. One of the most stunning developments, announced in early 1999, by the magazine *Nature Biotechnology,* was the creation of transgenic goats capable of "manufacturing" a human protein. The protein has the potential for the treatment of heart attacks and for the prevention of blood clots. Other recent developments include:

- Closely following the announcement that Dolly's creators had cloned two more sheep, a Holstein calf was cloned in 1998 in Wisconsin.

- This was quickly followed the same year by the birth in Texas of two cloned calves, named Charlie and George.

- In late 1998 two Japanese scientists announced they had successfully cloned multiple calves from a single adult cow.

The three cloned mice of the late 1980s, followed in the 1990s by Dolly, Charlie and George, transgenic goats, and the other clonings mentioned are important because they were the first mammal clonings, suggesting major commercial potential. Cloning quantities of higher mammals beyond an early embryonic stage, however, presents formidable challenges. Genes in cells at the early stages of life carry the encoded knowledge that enables cells to develop into any part of the body. Skeptics of the process theorize that once cells form into specific body components, they lose the capability to reconstruct the entire organism from the genetic contents of the nucleus. Dolly, in fact, is not a true clone. While she carries most of the genetic characteristics of "sheep A," not all of an animal's genes are found in the cell's nucleus. There are a few dozen genes that reside in the mitochondria, outside the nucleus in the cell's cytoplasm. In Dolly's case, some of these genes were supplied by the donor egg of "sheep B." Nevertheless, the progress in cloning mammals continues.

A primary goal of genetic selection and engineering in animals is to improve the cost effectiveness of production. By inserting growth-hormone genes into embryos, scientists have increased the size of sheep and other animals. Since swine were first domesticated about 8000 years ago, through selective breeding pigs have now become a major source of food for humans. Since the early 1990s, Pfizer has marketed a genetically engineered feed additive, which manipulates the genes to produce growth hormones that help accelerate growth and produce leaner pigs.

Why Waste Waste?

On the BioFarm of the future, incorporating gene technology into new methods for waste management will have a significant economic impact.

For example, the use of genetically altered bacteria can be used to clean up the environment by decomposing many forms of waste and soil pollutants. Bioengineering will find more efficient ways to improve waste recycling to improve the nutrition and health benefits of the crop and to create new biodegradable materials. Research is being conducted by Monsanto aimed at developing gene-spliced bacteria for converting organic waste into sugar, alcohol, and methane.

Another project creates bioterials made from lactic acid produced during the bacterial fermentation of discarded corn stalks. When individual acid molecules are joined chemically, they form a material that has the properties of plastic, but is biodegradable because it is made from organic matter. Widespread production of plastics from this material is expected in the future.

BioFarm or BioGraveyard

Despite all of its positive contributions, agbio is as controversial as biotech activities in health care. No one company, nor one individual, is more at the center of the controversy than Monsanto, and its CEO, Robert Shapiro. It is not an overstatement to suggest that the long-term viability of the agbio industry is at stake, and that Monsanto and Shapiro might single handedly affect the entire industry. (See "Robert Shapiro: A Man for All Growing Seasons.") While relatively minor in the United States and Canada, concerns over genetically engineered foods have reached a fever pitch in Europe, where protesters have dumped genetically engineered soybeans on the door step of Tony Blair, the British Prime Minister, and forced supermarket chains to take certain biotech food products off their shelves.

Robert Shapiro:
A Man for All Growing Seasons

Monsanto CEO Robert B. Shapiro is not exactly trapped by the trappings of power. In fact, he more often resembles the corporate farmers he helps than the traditional corporate power brokers. Employees say they seldom seen him in a suit and that you could walk through the office and have a hard time picking him out as the CEO.

Wearing sweaters and khakis instead of Brooks Brothers suits, Shapiro and most top Monsanto executives work out of cubicles, not executive suites. Shapiro has implemented a "two-in-a-box" form of management in which two co-presidents (typically one from a technical background and one not) run each business unit, instead of the conventional hierarchy with single department heads. Employees say he encourages communication and that his door is always open.

But casual cloths and open doors are not the most sweeping change Shapiro has brought to Monsanto. The big change was Monsanto's corporate mission. Since he took over as CEO in 1995, Shapiro has worked to reinvent Monsanto from a commodity chemicals firm into a life sciences company, with massive investments in biotechnology.

"The most essential task, I believe, that we as a species confront today is the requirement that we reinvent the technologies by which we feed, clothe, and house ourselves and generate such wealth as humanity enjoys," he said in a speech to the State of the World Forum in October of 1998. "The fundamental problem is that the technologies we have today require us to use enormous quantities of stuff in order to create modest economic value."

William C. Miller is a San Francisco-based business author whose 1999 book *Flash of Brilliance* includes a foreword written by Shapiro. "Some of Monsanto's products are controversial," Miller says. "But what you can't argue about Bob Shapiro is that within his belief system, he's absolutely sincere about doing what he thinks is the way to go to address hunger and address nutrition, as the world population explodes from six billion to 10 billion."

Born Robert Bernard Shapiro in New York City in 1938, his career in some ways has followed that of his father, former General Instruments CEO Moses Shapiro (1910–1990). Moses Shapiro, like his son, started out as a lawyer. He became Executive Vice President of Automatic Manufacturing Company in 1953. Two years later, Automatic merged with General Instrument, and Moses was appointed CEO in 1969. He retired in 1977, but stayed on as a director of General Instrument and of other firms, including Toys'R'Us.

Following undergraduate studies at Harvard, Shapiro attended Columbia Law School and graduated in 1962. After brief stints with a law firm and the U.S. government, Shapiro worked as a law professor, first at Northeastern University and then at the University of Wisconsin in Madison. He told David Barboza of *The New York Times* that his teaching helped interest him in ways to create policies that were good for people, a concept he would later take with him to Monsanto.

He returned to New York and joined General Instrument as General Counsel in 1972. Moses Shapiro was CEO by then. Father and son worked together at General until Moses retired in 1977. His Monsanto career actually began indirectly in 1979, when he moved to Chicago to work as General Counsel for a small pharmaceutical concern, G.D. Searle and Company. Monsanto soon bought out Searle. Searle had developed an innovative product called NutraSweet, which Shapiro helped turn into a household name as the Monsanto subsidiary's Chairman, President, and CEO between 1985 and 1995. He took over as Monsanto CEO on April Fool's Day in 1995.

"Bob believes that the right corporate environment comes down to two things: authenticity and caring," says author William Miller. "I've known Bob in other circles as well, and he walks his talk."

It didn't take Shapiro long to unshackle Monsanto from its traditional base, the chemical business. For 96 years, St. Louis–based Monsanto had played in the same league as traditional chemical giants like DuPont and Dow Chemical. It had a range of successful products including acrylic fibers, window guards, and water-treatment solutions.

Enter Shapiro. Exit chemicals. By 1997, Monsanto had spun off its chemical business to its shareholders. The new chemical company was called Solutia, with revenues of $3 billion. Solutia and Monsanto were now totally separate entities.

Monsanto had made the investment in life sciences two decades before, and it was really a natural progression. In the 1980s, the company had started to put together a top-flight team of molecular biologists. These scientists did recombinant DNA research to try to make plants stronger, better tasting, and more resistant to pests and diseases. By the early 1990s, the potential reward of managing the interconnected systems of the pharmaceuticals, food, and agriculture businesses, minus the chemicals, became clear, at least to Shapiro.

To its new list of three global businesses—agricultural seeds and chemicals, pharmaceuticals, and food ingredients—Monsanto added an unusual fourth: sustainable development. "There is a set of leaders emerging who are taking the idea of business driving the change toward sustainability in our business practices," Miller says. "We have a level of cynicism about that, but there are people like Bob who are willing to step out in the midst of that cynicism."

Monsanto also stepped out into the marketplace, and it did not step lightly. Over the last several years, Monsanto spent some $8 billion on R&D and related acquisitions. Soon after Shapiro took charge, the company spent $1.4 billion to buy seed companies like Holder's Foundation Seeds and Corn States Hybrid Services, both in the United States, and Sementes Agroceres in Brazil. There were smaller pharmaceutical purchases in both Argentina and Brazil, and joint ventures with local partners in Argentina and Brazil (for cottonseeds and genetically enhanced cotton, respectively) and in Russia (for pharmaceuticals). To help pay for these acquisitions, it has sold its genetically re-engineered mustard and canola business, which were aimed at producing "naturally" produced and biodegradable plastics.

Fourteen of the 24 genetically engineered seeds that U.S. regulatory agencies approved in Shapiro's first 2 years as CEO were either made by Monsanto or one of Monsanto's partners. Ironically, the product that helped pay for all the experimentation was a 25-year-old herbicide, a farmers' favorite called Roundup. *Fortune* reported in 1997 that Roundup accounted for about 40 percent of Monsanto's operating earnings.

More huge agricultural acquisitions followed. Could the company afford them? Wall Street watched and waited. In 1998, Monsanto paid $2.3 billion in cash to buy the 60 percent of DeKalb Genetics it didn't already own. It invested another $1.9 billion in stock, at Monsanto's then-current share price, to purchase Delta & Pine Land Company.

Forbes was now calling Shapiro "Deal-A-Day Bob." American Home Products even agreed to acquire Monsanto for $34.4 billion in June of 1998. But that deal eventually fell apart, possibly because of the inability of the freethinking Shapiro and AHP's more straight-laced CEO, John R. Stafford, to get along.

Following years of spectacular growth, Monsanto finally slowed down in 1998. The R&D spending, combined with the expensive acquisitions, had driven the company's debt load up dramatically. Earnings dropped. Reorganization charges and employee layoffs were announced.

Monsanto's total agricultural expenditures had climbed over $8 billion by 1999. Spurred on by a need for cash, there were rumors of another merger. This time the reported suitor was one of Monsanto's oldest rivals in the chemical business, DuPont, which had also invested heavily in seed companies in recent years. At the time, Shapiro's hope, sources said, was to find a way to keep Monsanto's innovative business approach intact even after it had been acquired by the more conservative, and much larger, DuPont. That deal as well ended without being consummated.

Meanwhile, Monsanto continued to make headlines. Four of the company's biotechnologists, Robert Fraley, Robert Horsch, Ernest Jaworski, and Stephen Rogers, shared a 1998 National Medal of Technology for their work on transgenic crops.

Others disagreed with Monsanto's direction, sometimes violently. In the process, Shapiro become a focal point for the "anti" biotechnology forces. European environmentalists destroyed crop trials of Monsanto's biotechnological products. In India, there were rumors that the company had put a "terminator" gene (a gene that would not allow reproduction) in its transgenic cotton, but Monsanto said that such a gene was still years away. In academic circles, Monsanto has become somewhat of a dirty word because their patents slow independent researchers.

Concerns about Monsanto, and Shapiro, seem to follow everywhere. For those who know him best, however, Shapiro remains a brilliant and innovative leader.

Shapiro doesn't waste much time worrying about the personal criticism as he steers the company in the direction of his personal vision, using biotechnology and other life sciences to address the food and health care concerns of a rapidly growing world population, while simultaneously helping heal a badly damaged environment.

"The demographics are well-known," Shapiro told the State of the World Forum. "Five point eight billion people in the world today, about one and a half billion of them in abject poverty. About one person in seven, about eight hundred million people in the world, so malnourished that they cannot participate in work or in family life. . . ."

While it might be easy to conclude that the United States and Europe go their separate ways on agbio, several new realities of the global marketplace mitigate against that course. First, the costs of research in this area are so substantial that it is hard to justify them just for the North American market; or conversely, the North American market would probably not "buy" the products from such costly research. Second, public concerns in Europe, if substantial and continuous, are likely to eventually have a profound impact on North American consumers. Finally, agricultural exports to Europe represent a significant market for U.S. farmers. A government or consumer boycott would create severe hardships for U.S. farmers. Clear and distinctive labeling has been suggested as a potential solution to the problem. While "genetic" labeling is, and will continue to be, important, the issues are much more complex and deep to be solved so easily.

European and, to some extent, U.S. consumer concerns center on three broad areas: the qualification, competency, and care and motivations of researchers, companies, and regulators; the impact on the environment, including the potential for "rogue" plants and animals and those that are newly resistant to conventional farming techniques; and economics—the concentration of power in agriculture, potential unequal sharing of rewards, and trade inequities. While not articulated by either side of the controversy, economics has to play a significant role.

Such issues could seriously chill the future of the industry, but more importantly, create significant potential for food shortages as the world's population continues its unprecedented growth. Suffice it to say here that the onus is on the agbio industry to clearly, unemotionally, and scientifically state its case. Far too often, the industry, when pushed, is overly aggressive and defensive in presenting its case. In addition, many in the industry have taken a "wait and see" attitude, allowing one or two companies (often Monsanto) to bear the burden of the debate. Only a united, forthright, and empathetic industry posture will win the day.

As with many such controversies, the activists against agbio progress are unencumbered with having to use real science to validate their claims. Far too often, little of real scientific evidence is presented for debate. Like guerrilla fighters they can attack those with real and substantial interests to protect, and who therefore have to stake out a factual position that must stand the test of time. And the media is all too willing to provide a public platform with little verification of claims. A recent case in point in the chemical materials area involved so-called soft plastics. A recent *Wall Street Journal* editorial pointed out that *Time* magazine, among others, had to apologize for printing the concerns of antiplastics activists, who, it later turned out, had used gross generalizations and no scientific evidence to substantiate its claims.

The stakes are too high, for companies and for feeding the world, to allow the debate to flounder on the rhetorical follies of either side. Unfortunately, much of the value of a substantive debate is lost as innuendo, "demonizing" the opposition, supposition and appeals to fear are used by those who would attack the industry. The very fact that they raise such concerns and resort to such tactics means that the agbio industry has done a very poor job of telling its story. (See "Controversial Issues in Agbio.") A real debate is needed, therefore, because, without sounding melodramatic, feeding the world hangs in the balance. Chapter 12 will attempt to put these issues in context.

Controversial Issues in Agbio

A wide range of issues has been raised about agbio. Among those are

- Fear that pathogenic disease-producing organisms used in some plant-related recombinant DNA experiments might develop into highly infectious forms that could cause worldwide crop epidemics. The NIH has, therefore, set limits on the types of recombinant DNA experiments that can be performed using such pathogens.

- Allergens can be transferred from one food crop to another through genetic engineering. An experiment to increase the nutritional value of the soybean involved taking a Brazil nut gene producing a nutritious protein and transferring it into the soybean plant. However, this caused an allergic reaction in people allergic to Brazil nuts. The project was cancelled.

- Some critics have objected to the idea of companies patenting genetically modified organisms, which could make them the property of a particular company.

- Consumer resistance to bioengineered food is growing. A survey published in *Time* in January 1999 found that 81 percent of those surveyed wanted genetically engineered food labeled as such, and 58 percent of those surveyed said that if it were labeled, they would not purchase it.

- Questions have been raised about grains engineered to resist antibiotics and whether that resistance can be passed on the humans.

- Monsanto's marketing strategy to prohibit replanting of their "Terminator" seed has raised economic opposition in Third World countries where farmers cannot afford to pay for the high-priced seeds. Also, many environmentalists fear the product could spread by wind or pollination and eventually cause worldwide sterilization of crops.

- The Humane Society United States (HSUS) has gone on record in opposition to animal cloning. Organizations such as PETA and Greenpeace are lobbying against commercial biotech products and research.

- In an extension of the Banana War to biotechnology, the United States has threatened sanctions against a long list of European Union products in response to the European Union's refusal to allow the import of American beef that has been treated with growth hormones.

11

Financing the Dream

The BioCapitalists

*People used to think their destiny was
in the stars. Now we know it's in our
genes, our DNA."*
ANN DAY, ARIZONA STATE SENATOR

In every economic era, there are winners and losers. In the Bioterials
Age there will be many more winners and far fewer losers.

Reaping the Rewards: From Few to Many

The big economic winners of the Agrarian Age (the land-owning
elite) were few in number, but were seldom those who actually
invented or developed new technologies. In the Industrial Era, the
inventors of new technologies were more likely to enjoy a financial
payoff from their innovations (DuPont, Ford, Eastman, etc.), but often
the economic "rent" from new ideas went to financial players such as
Rockefeller, Mellon, and Vanderbilt (a.k.a., the "robber barons").

As we approach the end of the Information Age, it is obvious that
the inventors and developers of new technologies and approaches
are participating in the rewards at least as much as the financiers. Bill
Gates, for example has been richly rewarded for his innovations in

PC software. Michael Dell, who pioneered a new method of selling computers, has been rewarded nearly as well as Gates, as was Sam Walton, whose Wal-Mart stores were as much a technology innovation as a retail one. In addition, each new era dispersed the rewards more widely to others, even if they were neither inventors nor financiers.

In the western democracies, in particular, there seem to be many more winners (in terms of investments, lifestyle improvements, etc.) than losers with each successive wave of technological innovation. In fact, each new wave of technology has dispersed greater economic goods to greater numbers of people than the era before it. The financial "fruits" of the Agrarian Age were largely concentrated into a few hands, although, eventually, agricultural technologies led to production beyond subsistence for most parts of the world, and as we have seen, this led to the first real population growth. Industrial Age technologies created many wealthy individuals and a new class of industrial elite. In number, these industrialists far exceeded those who reaped the major benefits in the earlier era. Importantly, though, industrial technologies eventually led to wide dispersion of economic benefits, as the "average" person in countries that embraced industrialization saw his or her income increase steadily.

In the Information Age, certain individuals have benefited enormously from technological innovation, often as the creators or exploiters of standard technologies, but again, there has been a much wider dispersion of economic well-being in the industrialized nations and beyond.

This trend toward broader dispersion of economic "rent" will continue unabated into the Bioterials Age. Craig Venter, CEO of Celera and a major player in the Human Genome research, has pledged, for example, that his company will attempt to patent genes but turn over the results of its genetic research to the public domain. Actions such as this will only accelerate the forces described in the new economic laws of bioterials outlined in earlier chapters. It seems very safe to conclude that more people, in more countries, will experience real growth in incomes than ever before, despite the rapid growth in global population. While some countries and individuals will invariably be slower to realize these gains than others, the Bioterials Age will usher in an era of economic prosperity unparalleled in history.

From Robber Barons to the BioCapitalists

In addition to broadening the numbers of those who reap the rewards of technological innovation, the types and forms of commercialization of biotech and new materials technologies will differ markedly from earlier economic eras. Earlier eras required inventor insights combined with entrepreneurial and managerial sophistication and, most importantly, large doses of financial capital.

In the Industrial Age, this capital was most often from a small group of wealthy financiers. In the United States, this group is often referred to as the "robber barrons." The Information Age, whose technologies often didn't require the same scale of financial capital, saw much of its technology exploitation underwritten initially by venture capitalists (VCs) and then public equities markets. In addition, much of the new technology was invented, developed, and marketed by major corporations. As noted in an earlier chapter, universities and governments played a peripheral role at most.

The evolving economy based on bioterials, though, is predicated on a new level of cooperation between small, innovative biotechs paired with large, established firms, and a new relationship between VCs, business, universities and governments (at the federal, state, and even local levels). This is the result of a convergence of several factors: high costs of technology development, huge rewards financially, and high stakes from a public interest perspective.

Genomic Poker: The BioCapitalists

For almost three decades, VCs have invested heavily in the bioterials revolution. They've brought patient money and a high tolerance for risk. They've needed both. As noted earlier, the biotech business is like a decade-long poker game, with many bets being placed but few big winners. These VCs have to be different because the bets are often long term, complex, and very big. In terms of placing bets on the future, as noted in Chapter 1, old-line industrial firms spend about 5 percent of revenues on R&D, information technology companies, between 5 and 15 percent, while the top 10 largest Big Pharmas spend between 8 and 15 percent. By comparison, the biotechs typically begin their R&D spending at 15 percent. Some, with little or no revenues, spend every dollar on R&D.

Such big, complicated, and long-shot bets make many investors shy away from biotech. In fact, the public equities markets have been nothing if not fickle. The biotechs have gone through periods of being the darlings of Wall Street to being the goats. In the late 1990s, for example, biotechs, with the exception of a few "high flyers" have not been in favor at all. In fairness, however, as a group they were not performing particularly well in this period, and looked much less attractive than many Internet-oriented stocks. Most market capitalizations were very low (some trading near cash values), and a number of IPOs were pulled from the market.

Recent indicators, however, suggest there is a lot of venture capital available and interested in the biotech sector. A number of VC groups have formed with specialized interests in agbio, and the VC market in Europe has blossomed into a major force. And, while the late 1990s public equities markets seem to "belong" to Internet IPOs, there is a strong, consistent investor interest in biotech. What do they expect in return? VCs, of course, expect a superior return on their biotech investments, and, the longer the wait, the higher the expectations. The investing public expects a piece of the new economy, as well as consistent current returns. Although the investing public seemed to be quite taken with Internet stocks in the late 1990s, biotech stocks did very well over the past decade as illustrated in "Investing $10,000 in the Biotech Decade." Whether or not such expectations are met will become the biggest bet in the history of the world!

Investing $10,000 in the Biotech Decade

Figure 11-1 tracks a theoretical investment fund with $10,000 invested in each of four portfolios with a select number of biotech, information, industrial, and pharmaceutical stocks. The investments were tracked over the period January 1988 through January 1999. The share price of each stock within the category as of January 6, 1988 (the first date of the data points) was given equal weighting in terms of initial investment. The investment model assumed an initial investment of $10,000 in each category. Therefore, if there are 10 stocks within one category,

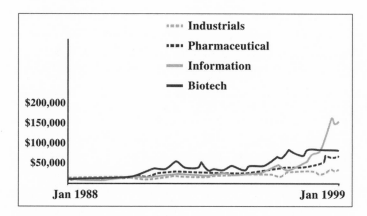

Figure 11-1. Investing $10,000 for 10 years in four public stock portfolios.

each stock is assumed to have a $1000 investment. Or, if there are only eight stocks within the category, each stock received an initial investment of $1250. This provided the portfolio with an initial number of shares per stock.

Monthly tracking data was chosen for simplicity. More specifically, the second Wednesday of every month was chosen to avoid usual holidays (they often create a fluctuation in stock values) and away from Monday and Friday effects (if the second Wednesday happens to fall on a vacation date, the data point for the next Wednesday was then chosen). All selected stocks were reviewed to adjust for stock splits.

The industrials included: Goodyear, Mead, Armco, GM, Boeing, International Paper, Caterpillar, Alcoa, and GE. The information included: Compaq, Intel, AT&T, Texas Instruments, HP, GTE, IBM, and Dell. The pharmaceuticals included: Warner Lambert, Johnson & Johnson, Merck, American Home Products, Glaxo Wellcome, Bristol Meyers Squibb, and Pfizer. The biotechs included: Chiron, Genzeme, Agouron, Genetech, Immunex, Biogen, Amgen, and Monsanto.

The number of shares per stock remained constant throughout the entire 10-year analysis. Portfolio performance was then tracked over the 10-year period according to the performance of its underlying stocks. The performance of all four categories are graphed against each other for comparison.

Although biotech stocks are thought to be quite volatile, and individually they can be, as a group, as a portfolio of stocks, they provided a respectable return to shareholders over the past decade when compared to selected industrials, information, and pharmaceutical stocks.

Those making the bets are a new breed of capitalists this book calls the "BioCapitalists," and relates primarily to those firms innovating in the area of human health biotech, rather than bioterials or agbio. The development of new materials and agbio from a public financing perspective lags that of biotech or is often hidden within the development activities of industrial or life sciences companies.

The Early BioCapitalists: Genetic Pioneers

A new breed of investor, the BioCapitalists, first emerged on the scene with the founding of Genentech in 1976. When the firm went public in 1980 it stock vaulted from $35 per share to a peak of $88 in less than an hour of trading, and the roller coaster ride of biotech investing was launched.

Some of the early BioCapitalists, such as George Rathman, formerly CEO of Amgen, and now the CEO and a major investor in Icos, have become astute financial "riders" on the biotech roller coaster. (See "Icos and the BioCapitalist Roller Coaster.") Others throughout North America are both dedicated and creative scientists and true entrepreneurs who have grown their companies despite formidable odds. If economic conditions and U.S. financial markets have been difficult, those in Canada, particularly in the 1990s, have been nearly impossible. Some like Francesco Bellini have been models of perseverance. (See "Francesco Bellini: The Northern Light.")

Icos and the BioCapitalist Roller Coaster

George Rathman has ridden the biotech financing roller coaster to both the peaks and valleys of the industry. Today, as CEO of the Bothell, Washington-based, Icos, Rathman devotes considerable energy to finding money before he needs it. A developer of biotech solutions for inflammatory diseases, Icos has had to deal with a number of periods of scarce capital.

Rathman, apparently learned that lesson during his tenure as chief executive of Amgen. During one of the industries' periodic financial downturns in the mid-1980s, many of the young biotechs suffered, especially Amgen. During that volatile period, Amgen's share price was literally measured in pennies. According to CEO Rathman, the only thing that kept the struggling biotech firm from merging with a bigger, stable pharmaceutical firm was the fact that Rathman persuaded investors to put up $19 million in capital, nearly four times their initial offer.

Using the same philosophy, in 1990, Icos raised a first-round Regulation D offering of $32 million (Regulation D offerings are limited to a circle of "high net-worth" individuals, one of whom was Bill Gates, who contributed one-tenth of the sum). During a later up trend in biotech issues, Rathman decided to add additional financial stability to the enterprise by making two public offerings for $71 million. When the sector hit a decline that lasted for 3 years, Icos' sizable cash cushion allowed the company to continue to fund research and product development.

During another down period for the sector, in the mid-1990s, Gates and Rathman split the investment in a $23 million rights offering. In May of 1996 the company was able to take advantage of positive market sentiment and completed a $49 million public offering at nearly twice the price per share. The cash enabled Icos scientists to continue their research without compromising quality and the companies to continue producing products without worrying about a diminution of the caliber of their research staff.

In addition, the financial cushion prevented Icos from looking desperate when it came to the inevitable partnering with some of the industries' big players like Glaxo Wellcome. Because of its financial stability, the company was able to preserve important financial rights in these deals.

Francesco Bellini:
The Northern Light

Dr. Francesco Bellini is CEO and co-founder of BioChem Pharma, the most important pharmaceutical company based in Canada and one of the leading biotechnology firms in the world. But trapped in the vise of the Canadian dollar's terrible exchange rate and his country's high taxes, Bellini said in February 1999 that, within a year, BioChem Pharma may have to change strategies.

With likely offers coming from larger American firms, BioChem Pharma as a company would be forced to make the same choice Bellini as an individual made 15 years earlier. "I was, in fact, faced with the prospect in the mid-1980s, when the multinational pharmaceutical firm for whom I worked decided to discontinue its R&D activities in Canada," Bellini recently told the graduating class at the University of New Brunswick. "Although I was one of a few fortunate researchers offered a transfer to the United States, I made two decisions then and there: Number One: I opted to remain in Canada; and Number Two: I vowed to take my future into my own hands, so that never again would some faraway executive of a foreign company decide my fate."

He was born in 1947 in a faraway place, the Italian town of Ascoli Piceno on the Adriatic Sea. Twenty years later, he emmigrated to Canada and has stayed there ever since. Bellini earned a Bachelor of Science from Concordia University in Montreal, then studied at the University of New Brunswick, becoming a pupil of Professor Karel Wiesner. Wiesner and a core group of students, such as Bellini, gave the school an international reputation in the growing field of organic chemistry. Bellini's Ph.D. research focused on a synthetic approach to Delphinine-type alkaloids. On graduation, he then took a job in Montreal with Ayerst Labs, a subsidiary of American Home Products Corporation.

Ayerst left Canada in 1984. Bellini could have taken the safe path and gone with his employer. Instead, Bellini left Ayerst. "No doubt some thought me brash—and perhaps still do!" he says. "But I can honestly say I have never really regretted the path I chose, even on those days when the going seemed particularly tough."

Now on his own, Bellini started small. He became the one-man staff of the Biochemicals Division of the Institut Armand-Frappier (affiliated with the University of Quebec) specializing in the research, manufacturing, and commercialization of fine chemicals. Bellini hoped to develop chemicals that would be used in large research laboratories. Slowly at first, he built a team of researchers producing veterinary products such as embryo transfer kits. The team grew quickly now and they moved on to the problem of treating diseases that affected the human immune system.

Bellini's team became a full-scale commercial venture just 2 years after he left Ayerst. On December 15, 1986, he and four partners launched the initial public offering of IAF BioChem International. Two weeks later, the company (now called BioChem Pharma) had its shares listed on the Montreal Exchange. In 1988, using its expertise in peptide chemistry, BioChem Pharma became the first company in the world to produce an accurate diagnostic kit for the detection of the HIV infection. It was the first do-it-yourself AIDS test kit. Bellini's firm was unable to fully exploit the product in the global market, so it cut a deal with Glaxo in 1990. Glaxo was responsible for the commercialization of 3TC everywhere except in Canada, where both firms would help promote it.

The new product, now commercialized as 3TC or Epivir in over 80 countries quickly gave BioChem Pharma a competitive advantage in the pharmaceuticals industry. In the late 1990s, almost all AIDS drugs were still administered in a cocktail combination that included 3TC. By 1998 sales of 3TC alone reached $808 million, with BioChem Pharma splitting those dollars with partner Glaxo Wellcome.

When Bellini looks back on those early days, he talks about the critical dual role he had to play. It's a balancing act between science and business few have handled so adroitly, though the fiscal challenges now may be Bellini's toughest yet. "I've essentially worn two hats, or more accurately two suits," he says, "the scientist's white lab coat and the traditional jacket and tie of the business executive. In today's intensely competitive business environment, it's often not enough to simply have a great idea. You also have to get your hands on the capital required to develop your product or service to get it to market. So it helps if your inquiring mind is complemented by a little entrepreneurial spirit."

BioChem Pharma's own entrepreneurship spirit has continued throughout its brief history. In 1990, the firm acquired a stake in North American Vaccine, Inc. (NAVA), an American company developing vaccines for the prevention of infectious diseases. In 1991, it purchased 70 percent of two Italian diagnostic companies. A year later, it bought an additional 29 percent of them.

Also in 1992, Glaxo started testing BioChem's next blockbuster drug. This one was called Lamivudine, a once-a-day oral treatment for chronic hepatitis B, the ninth-leading cause of death worldwide. Successful testing of Lamivudine continued for the next 5 years. Glaxo made the first regulatory filings for the drug in 1997. *Fortune* magazine recently speculated that the two-drug success of BioChem might put the Canadian firm in the same favorable position industry leader Amgen had found itself in 7 years earlier, when Amgen's established star Epogen was joined by the new drug Neupogen.

BioChem Pharma explains the complex web of the biotech company and university networking approach this way: "The velocity of science means no one health care company can do it all. So, from the beginning, we have multiplied our internal capabilities through external partnerships. These include synergisitic links with universities, research institutes and smaller companies which focus on basic research, and with the multinationals which are unsurpassed at global-scale clinical development."

It's impossible to say what the future holds for the economic viability of BioChem Pharma, which through almost no fault of its own is in real peril. But it is also impossible not to say that Bellini has battled long odds to help his company, his clients, and his adopted country. He is, by any measure, a Northern Light.

Although VC and public interest in biotech has fluctuated throughout the 1980s, by the 1990s, the major investment firms significantly scaled back their biotechnology investments in favor of Internet-related issues. The rapid run-up in Internet issues caused many broad-based technology VCs, along with many private investors, even those with a strong interest in biotech, to bet their dollars on the "mania" driving Internet valuations. To attract investors back, a number of the biotechs have floated "tracking" stocks designed to separately track the performance of a particular division. Even the bigger players, such as DuPont, were experimenting with such stocks.

Some evidence, though, such as that presented previously here, suggests that investments in public equities in biotech, while volatile over the last two decades, have been a solid investment. The message from the public equities market in the late 1990s seemed to be, "biotech will have to wait." Big Pharma, on the other hand, was willing to step into the void.

The Corporate BioCapitalists: Monetizing Genes

Until very recently, the financial health of the biotechs was largely measured in terms of the interest and funding from VCs and public markets. More recently, however, Big Pharma assets, loans, and even intellectual property in the form of biological compounds have forced a reevaluation of the market value of the biotechs. Most of the deals between the biotechs and Big Pharma have two fundamental principles guiding their execution. The first is a certain degree of flexibility in terms of repayment. This flexibility has produced a wide variety of repayment methods, in some cases even blurring the very definition of repayments. The second, and most common, structure involves options for the pharmaceuticals to provide cash to a biotech partner without negatively impacting the pharmaceutical company's operating results.

If public and VC markets have been unpredictable in recent years, capital from the major pharmaceuticals has readily filled the void. In fact, alliances between small biotech startups and Big Pharma have become the dominant form of industry financing. Industry observers argue that the small biotechs need two such alliances with Big Pharma companies for survival, while each of the Big Pharmas need a dozen different alliances with the biotechs to hedge their bets and ensure a steady flow of innovations. In 1997, the total public capital raised from biotech initial and follow-on offerings was around $2.5 billion. For the same period, however, the total amount contributed to biotech companies by direct investment or alliance was nearly $4.5 billion in the United States alone.

Signals, an Internet magazine, recently argued that 10 big deals over two decades have resulted in the current stable financing model for biotechs (Eli Lilly and Genetech, 1978; Kirin and Amgen, 1984; Glaxo and BioChem Pharma, 1990; Roche and Genentech, 1990; Allergen and Ligand, 1992; Lilly with Centocor's and ReoPro, 1992; SmithKline and Human Genome Sciences, 1993; Ciba-Geigy and Chiron, 1994; Monsanto and Millennium, 1997; and Bayer and Millennium, 1998). In particular, they note that "what was once a Faustian bargain has become the cornerstone of multiple successful biotech business strategies."

The dominant form of participation in small biotechs by Big Pharma has been equities investment. More recently, these alliances have been creating unique funding mechanisms. For example, pharmaceutical companies have provided critical support to their biotech partners by playing the part of bank, guarantor, and fund-raiser.

Many of the most recent alliances have involved loans. After a successful collaboration, in most instances, the loan is repaid using commercial profits from alliance products or the loan is repaid by the biotech's equity, based on market value at the time of repayment. In the case of the Genetech and Scios alliance, for example, Genetech provided a $30 million loan to be used for the late-stage clinical development of Auriculin. Scios has the choice of taking the advance in cash, giving Scios stock at market value, or sharing profits. Other variations on the loan theme are refundable license option payments and royalty participation as a percent of net sales. In addition, several pharmaceutical companies provide loan guarantees to their biotech partners in lieu of actual loans.

In some instances, pharmas have even played the role of fund-raiser for their smaller biotech partners. For example, Allergan not only contributed dollars and development compounds in their alliance with

Ligand's ALRT, but also participated directly in the almost $33 million fund-raising enterprise. According to industry analysts, one of the most unusual examples of "pharma-as-fund-raiser" episodes is Synthelabo's corroboration with Genset. In that deal the pharmaceutical company made an almost $10 million purchase of the biotech's equity, soon after reselling 40 percent of this stake to a private group of investors, essentially acting as Genset's underwriter in a private placement transaction.

In other cases, several major pharmaceutical firms have even provided access to their proprietary compound libraries to their biotech partners, in effect "monetizing" valuable research assets. At the time of one of the original such deals, for example, between SmithKline and Human Genome Sciences, the head of SmithKline's research and development referred to it as "using genes as currency." Craig Venter's Celera Genomics Corporation, a partnership with Perkin-Elmer Corporation, bills itself as an "information company." It intends to put its map of the human genome into public hands, but sell its genetic sequencing information on a subscription (much like Bloomberg or Lexus-Nexis) basis to Big Pharma, the biotechs, academia, physicians, and, eventually, even individuals. In fact, the intersection of biotech and information technology has spawned the latest hot area of biotech investing, bioinformatics.

BioInformatics: Biology Transforms Information

An earlier chapter noted the importance of understanding that the technology of one era is the platform on which new technological eras are built. The technologies of one era become the necessary precondition for the development of the successor technology, often providing core technical ideas and a production base. Information technologies, for example, relied heavily on the chemistry and physics of the Industrial Age. And biology and new materials science, as it turns out, are extremely information-intensive technologies. A particular gene sequence, for example, contains millions of bits of information. No individual scientist or even team of scientists could do the mathematical calculations to sequence a gene (map its structure). Thus, today's rapid progress in bioterials would be unthinkable were it not for computers. Celera Genomics' supercomputer, as an example, is the second largest and most powerful in the world (the other is focused on U.S. national defense).

In turn, however, the new technology transforms the earlier technologies that helped create it. Industrial technologies transformed agriculture, and information technologies are now transforming both industrial technologies (computer-aided design and manufacturing, robotics, etc.) and agriculture. A major contention of this book is that bioterials technology will transform agriculture, industrial production technologies, and even information technologies. Examples of each are found throughout the text, from discussion of agbio to that of the biological computer.

One of the early forms of transformation of information technology is the development of bioinformatics, essentially the development and sale of genetic information. A number of companies, many in Silicon Valley, have pioneered this area. Pharmacopoeia, for example, used combinatorial chemistry to develop some 3.8 million chemical compounds, and offers the information for sale. By comparison, longtime pharmaceutical company, Merck, has developed only 500,000 compounds in its entire existence. Likewise, Incyte Pharmaceuticals and start-up deCode Genetics are using data from the Human Genome Project to compile extensive genetic information databases about many different diseases.

Another group of bioinformatics companies are bringing semiconductor power to bear in the areas of drug discovery and diagnostics. "Gene chip" companies like Affymetrix, Hyseq, and Synteni (acquired by Incyte in 1998) develop semiconductors for analyzing genetic samples. Such companies should radically improve a situation that venture capitalist Bob Nelson of Arch Venture Partners says is immature at best. "PhD's are doing what accountants used to do before spreadsheets," he says, referring to the action of filtering through drug leads without information technologies.

The Cap and Gown VCs: Academic BioCapitalists

The contribution of academic institutions to biotechnology development promises to be far greater than their contributions to either the Industrial Age or Information Age economies. In fact, many industry observers have argued that research universities are a fundamental part of the biotech industry. While alliances with Big Pharma provide critical resources and skills to the biotechs at or near the commercialization stage, the universities play a key role at early stages of discovery. However, from a university perspective, the deals have been far less lucrative than those that Big Pharma has been able to extract form the biotechs. That may be about to change.

Historically, the alliances between universities and biotech companies call for a "one for you, three for me split (25/75) in favor of the biotech companies," in terms of profits or royalties. Often as well, university licenses provide for an alternative royalty mechanism to be used in the event that the technology is subsequently licensed (often to a pharmaceutical firm). Typical arrangements often provide less than 50 percent of the original licensee's financial benefits from the sublicense, including royalties and precommercial payments. For example, the University of California at Los Angeles (UCLA) and Xoma agreed upon a structure whereby Xoma would provide $100,000 in precommercial payments to UCLA plus a 3 percent royalty on net sales. Nine months later, Xoma completed a deal with Pfizer that provided $2 million in up-front payments, the reimbursement of development costs (which were over $28 million over 5 years), and a royalty rate of over 33 percent on net sales. In another case, the State University of New York (SUNY) received a $10,000 up-front fee plus 50 percent of all sublicense royalties from Cortech. Cortech, in turn, licensed its rights to Marion Merrill Dow for around $8 million in equity and milestones, repayment of development costs (over $11 million over 7 years), and 10 percent royalty on net sales.

Thus, while the research universities have historically funded many of the critical early-stage biotech innovations (albeit through grants, gifts, etc., from private and public sources), they have, historically, received a disproportionately small share of the rewards. All that seems about to change. A number of major research universities have set up venture capital funds to invest in the commercialization of their technologies. Although small, they nonetheless are becoming more determined actors in the overall financing of early stage biotech financing. (See "The Cap and Gown VCs.")

The Cap and Gown VCs

As an employee of Vanderbilt University, George "Mick" Stadler almost never wears a cap and gown. He is a true veteran, though, of helping those who often do wear a cap and gown to capitalize on their biotech innovations. Stadler has worked as a foundation manager, a consultant, and now as an "in-house" venture capitalist. Staler has been an important catalyst for the various models universities have developed to reap some of the rewards of their research. It hasn't always been easy, however, even convincing some at the universities that they should. He notes that there's often a tension between academic purity and the move to commercialize innovations.

For most of their history, the academy has been a center of pure science, undertaking research for the sake of research, and freely making the results available in the public domain. There were very few universities that benefitted from basic research done in information technologies, for example, although many of the leading technologists developed their ideas while faculty members. Typically, they would simply leave the university and commercialize their ideas.

For more than two decades, a number of research universities heavily involved in biotech activities have developed various schemes (often related to whether or not they were public or private) to play a more active role. In part, this is a function of the types (from government and private companies, primarily Big Pharma) and amounts (the National Institute for Health gave substantially more than the National Science Foundation) of dollars. It is also driven by the need for both private and public institutions to find new sources of income. Today, virtually all research universities and hospitals and independent foundations and quasi-public institutions doing biotech research have some mechanism for commercialization.

The earliest and still the most common form of university participation in biotech ventures is licensing. Some hold the licenses directly while others, because they are public institutions, such as the University of Washington, have set up a foundation to handle such licenses. Of late, some universities have decided to take equity participation in new ventures started by faculty members, but most have shied away from direct support and involvement in the management of these companies. Basically, those taking equity stakes have acted as brokers, helping make the deal but not directly participating, until now.

Several schools have established venture capital funds either on their own or with partners. Some are funding them entirely with school endowment funds. Typically, a university invests about 5 percent of its endowment into high-risk, high-reward areas such as venture capital. Others, such as the University of Chicago, as a part of Arch Investments (a joint venture with Argonne National Labs), are raising dollars from investors outside the university as well.

One school, Vanderbilt University, has taken the bold step of institutionalizing its venture capital efforts within the school. So they hired veteran Mick Stadler to make it happen.

On the job for just a few months, Stadler already had his first venture organized and operating in early 1999. Former Toshiba executive, Bob Traeger, was coaxed out of retirement to be COO for the new enterprise, named Mxis (*monochromatic x-ray imaging systems*). Capitalized with more than $2 million from the university, the company already has a $2.5 million U.S. Navy contract for its "fourth-generation" light source. Developed at the school's Free Electron Laser Center, this innovative technology is a sophisticated new tool for x-raying, with military, industrial, and health care applications. One of the most promising early applications is for safe, more effective, and more comfortable x-rays for breast exams. It is able to not only detect tumors but also distinguish whether or not they are cancerous or benign and even direct site-specific treatments.

Not resting on his already considerable laurels, Stadler is readying several other "hot" properties, primarily in Vanderbilt's leading bioinformatics research, for the business marketplace.

The BioCapitalist Bureaucrats

In 1997, the North Carolina State General Assembly created the North Carolina Bioscience Investment Fund. It began with a $7.5 million special appropriation to the North Carolina Biotechnology Center, which organized the biotech fund, and selected Eno River Capital (a private investment firm) to manage it. Eno and the Biotechnology Center then raised $8.5 million from NationsBank, Wachovia Bank, and the Burroughs Wellcome Fund in 1999. Rather than an anomaly, the North Carolina fund joins others in states like New Jersey, Massachusetts, Texas, and California that are making critical investments in the economic future of the state by providing seed capital to attract biotech ventures investments.

New Jersey science and technology-related companies, ranging from biotechnology to telecommunications, employed about 168,000 people in 1997 with a payroll of about $9.9 billion. New Jersey produces 43 percent of the pharmaceuticals produced in the United States and has 601 biotech, biomedical, and health care–related firms. Under the state's Economic Development Authority, New Jersey began two financing programs to provide a financial incentive to emerging hi-tech companies. The $100 million Technology Funding Program and the state's Seed Capital Program promote hi-tech expansion and direct assistance in financing. In addition to providing the capital to finance these hi-tech ventures, the state of New Jersey is also providing workspace that will house multiple tenants who receive space for a nominal amount. Local banks provide partial loans at the market rate and the state provides the rest at a below-market fixed rate of 5 to 7 percent. In January 1997, New Jersey Governor Christine Todd Whitman signed a package of bills that created tax credits to help offset the costs of research and development. Under a first of its kind business tax certificate transfer program, companies will be able to sell their unused net operating loss carryover and unused research and development tax credits to other businesses for at least 75 percent of their value. The selling company uses the proceeds of the sale of the tax benefits to help finance their growth in New Jersey while the purchasing company uses the value of the benefits to reduce state taxes.

A number of states are developing programs similar to those of North Carolina and New Jersey. As well, individual cities (with biotech "promotion" programs) from San Diego to Nashville, among others, are attempting to find innovative ways of participating in what National Cancer Institute Director Richard Klausner calls a "golden age of discovery." He could have easily called it "the golden age of financing," as many new groups join the ranks of the BioCapitalists, including federal governments around the world. Foreign government participation will be described later. Meanwhile, the U.S. government's participation in the biotech sector grows more complicated daily.

As noted early in this book, the U.S. government is already a major BioCapitalist with substantial direct investments in bioterials, primarily through health care research funding, its Human Genome project at a cost of $0.5 billion per year, and research into areas such as new energy sources. Indirectly, it participates through funding of various university research projects and, in general, by setting the climate and rules on R&D activities. Government participation in biotech ventures is considerably more complex than for any other BioCapitalist, though, because of the potential divergence of private and public interests. To further its purposes, the industry funds political contributions (some $25 million in 1997) and a major lobbying effort, aimed at raising direct government support in research, paying for education and workforce development programs, and the prevention of inhibiting legislation. Governments, on the other hand, are seeking to balance the interests of the industry and a growing number of vocal activists concerned about biotech research, while simultaneously becoming a major player in the research and seeking new revenue sources from its investments through such activities as patenting its genetic discoveries.

The Global BioCapitalists

Just as the North American BioCapitalists begin to settle in to a period when the major players are known and the core intellectual property (the human genome) is within reach, the global BioCapitalists, particularly those from Europe, are emerging on the scene. An earlier chapter provided a map of biotech activities in Europe and Asia. While significant portions of this activity are supported by governments, particularly outside North America, private capital is increasingly important, especially in Europe. Both private and public, these global BioCapitalists are creating new pools of biotech investment capital for home country consumption as well as the acquisition of U.S. properties. Already a large and growing factor in agbio, through huge global players such as Novartis, Aventis and AstraZeneca, those interested in human genetic research are now increasingly active.

The United Kingdom, a vital force in biological discoveries, leads with over 500 public and private biotech organizations. Others with a sizable per capita biotech industry include Austria, Belgium, Denmark, Finland, France, Germany, Ireland, Italy, The Netherlands, Norway, Poland, Spain, Sweden, and Switzerland. Belgium has some of Europe's most entrepreneurial biotechs, while Denmark has been a leader in developing biotech regulations.

A number of European central and local governments are actively stimulating their biotech industries. Germany, for example, seems to be attempting to "reinvent" itself from an industrial superpower to a spry and entrepreneurial developer of sophisticated hi-tech devices. Biotechnology, and the creation of other hi-tech enterprises in Germany, has flourished as access to venture capital, the availability of government subsidies, and a more entrepreneurial attitude has emerged. This shift in priorities can be seen in the decision made in 1998 by Bavarian state officials to invest as much as DM 2 billion (about $1.1 billion) in numerous technology projects. This mammoth investment was raised by the sale of one of the country's state-owned utilities and was redirected to 50 high-technology enterprises, venture-capital funds, and university research centers.

But deutsche marks seem to be flowing out of Germany as well as within. In 1999 Bayer Corporation, for example, doubled its investment in its operations in Berkeley, California. Since 1992, Bayer's Berkeley division has grown into a biotech company with some $400 million in revenues and over 1200 employees. After sinking $300 million into a new manufacturing facility on its company campus, the company has set a goal of 30 percent annual revenue growth for the next few years.

But it's not just big countries, such as Germany or the United Kingdom, that have embraced biotechnology. Tiny Iceland is at the center of one of the most interesting, potentially important, but clearly most controversial biotech projects in the world. Founded by biotechnologist Kari Stefansson, deCode Genetics is taking on the most complete "bioprospecting" job in the world. Because of Iceland's unique genetic environment (a small and generally "inbred" population), deCode is hoping to map the genetic links to dozens of important diseases and health conditions such as adult onset diabetes and schizophrenia. It raised initial rounds of seed capital from VCs, and in 1998, signed a $200 million deal with Roche pharmaceuticals. Despite its noble intent, and the potential value of its findings, deCode has raised as much controversy over its activities as it has money. In fact, Iceland has become a microcosm not just for genetic research but for controversy as well. In early 1999, the government of Iceland awarded deCode a major contract for its work. At any rate, deCode has brought to the surface many of the public issues (on who "owns" and who "benefits" from genetic research) to be discussed in the next chapter.

Industry observers have noted that, for several years now, the Europeans have been in the United States looking for biotech deals and placing big bets on the U.S. biotech market. The United States is not the only destination, though, for these global BioCapitalists investments. In 1991 the China-EU Biotechnology Centre (CEBC) was created as a communication center servicing the biotech research communities in China and Europe. As the relationship matured, however, the network increasingly began to be used by both European and Chinese biotech-related industries seeking partners, cooperation, or the establishment of joint ventures.

This exposure to European methods and, perhaps more importantly, European capital, was a well-needed push for the struggling Chinese biotechnology sector. Poorly maintained equipment, little, if any, provisions for downstream processing, and a lack of reagents were but a few of the obstacles faced by Chinese biotechnologists. Nevertheless, a BioIndustry Association report suggested that Chinese biotech will be competitive with that of the west in terms of "innovation, quality, and quantity by 2005." Chinese and other Asian governments have often directly invested in technology enterprises, and biotech is no exception. An excellent example is the strategic alliance formed by Dutch companies Skillco and CMO Holland with the Shanghai City Council for the production of tomatoes. Skillco provided the technical expertise in plant breeding while CMO Holland contributed its experience as a manufacturer and supplier of greenhouses.

Genes Don't Need Passports: The Globalization of Biotech

From agriculture to information, each successive technology era has been more global in its development and reach. Bioterials is no exception. The increasing velocity of new discoveries in biotech are matched only by their growing global reach. Biological discoveries, largely North American and European in origin, are now matched daily by those in Asia. While an American company, Amgen, was an early catalyst for the commercialization of biotech, it was a Japanese company, Kirin Breweries, that provided seed capital at a critical juncture. Without it, the field might have taken many more years to develop. Today, while commercial activity is greatest in North America, Europe is closing fast, with Asia not far behind them. For their size, Australia and New Zealand already have large and growing biotech industries. Other parts of the world, such as Latin America and Africa (Israel has over 70 biotech organizations and Argentina and Brazil have budding industries), can be expected to join soon. While trade and then investment were vehicles for economic integration in earlier economies, transnational partnerships among private interests, governments, and universities will be the dominate model for global integration in biotech.

Although precise figures are not available, estimates from various sources indicate that biotech investments into various parts of Asia by the United States, Europe, and Japan (for Japan, into other parts of Asia) increased from about $220 million in 1993 to $570 million in 1997. European investment in Asia is largely centered in Japan, while investment from the United States is more widely dispersed. Within Asia, the mix of government, university, and private—both large and small—mirror the kinds of deals pioneered in the United States. For example, Glaxo has teamed with Singapore National University to screen plants for drugs using microbial technology, while Unilever has established a research center in India to study the potential for enhancing the nutritional value of food.

The manufactured products of industrial technologies traveled the globe in merchant ships and began the integration of the world's economies through the trade in goods. These goods also brought with them a cultural effect, however, that early social observers tagged "cargo cults," as products from other parts of the world began to change local cultures. Today's digital information circles the world instantly as electrons in a network that Marshall McLuhan called a "global electronic nervous system." This global nervous system is at the heart of what has clearly become a global economy. These electrons, like the industrial "cargoes" before them, also carry a cultural "charge." They have created a global consumer culture in which Swiss luxury watches, Japanese electronics, and American computers have eclipsed nationalist urges for domestically produced goods.

Just as the economic and technological eras before it, the Bioterials Age will have immense impact on the global economy and culture. It will, however, complete the job started by the early eras. The genetic code of the biotech era will become like a global chromosomal bond uniting the people of the world. As argued at the beginning of this book, Industrial Age technologies were centralizing technologies, pushing everything up at the center. The technologies of the Information Age, on the other hand, are decentralizing technologies, and pushed everything out to the margins.

The technologies of the Bioterials Age, however, are systemic technologies and will transform everything, including people, from the inside out. Like earlier eras, though, it will not happen quickly, as cultural effects (and their political manifestations) significantly lag technological and economic realities. In fact, at this writing, it seems that we still have a way to go. Craig Venter, in a recent speech, noted the incongruity of the war in the Balkans among people of almost identical genetic makeups. Perhaps, in the not too distant future, the world will recognize that each of us is, in some measure, a BioCapitalist, with genetic as well as economic interdependencies. Such understanding may be obscured though, by the "Chinese Wall," the subject of the next chapter, being built between the biotech industry and the bioactivists.

12

BioEthics

The Chinese Wall

He who fights the future has a
dangerous enemy.

SØREN KIERKEGAARD

The preceding pages have chronicled the unprecedented progress in biotechnology. Throughout the text, reference was made frequently to the ethical issues, referred to here as, "bioethics," which are right now having a dramatic impact on the industry.

Clearly, those involved with cloning and other medical advances are at the center of the action. But no single company is feeling the heat of bioethical concerns more than Monsanto. Now labeled in Europe variously as "Public Enemy Number 1," the "biotech bully boy," and the "Frankenstein food giant," and even (apparently jokingly) by its own employees, "MonSatan." No less than Prince Charles and Paul McCartney, have verbally assaulted the company, while some of the largest food chains in the United Kingdom have sworn off genetically engineered food as a result of the anti-Monsanto backlash in Britain. The hysteria has reached a fever pitch in Europe, threatening not just the company, but the industry and perhaps even a wide-ranging trade war between the United States and the European Union. Much of the concern was generated by a rather un-European public relations campaign undertaken by Monsanto, which came on the heals of the British "mad cow" problem.

Despite little hard evidence to the contrary (the debate is fueled by fear, misunderstandings, and mistrust on both sides, and even, in the case of the activists, hate), concern over biotech foods threatens food and agricultural industries on both sides of the Atlantic. The concern is not limited to the European Union, however, as European concerns are mimicked in many other places around the world.

Researchers and scientists have made unprecedented progress in biotechnology and new materials science in the past several decades. Public concern has yet to focus on new materials, yet that too will come. In the meantime, it is the biological sciences that face intense scrutiny. Indeed, so many advances have emerged, and at such a dizzying pace, that biotech professionals and the public find themselves needing to re-examine some fundamental issues underlying biotechnology. Those issues are the ethics that underscore biotechnology's rapid growth. Those ethical issues, and not the technological and scientific discovery process, also hold the key to determining how quickly the biotechnological revolution will occur.

There are a number of contentious bioethical issues that are well beyond the scope of this book. They include, among others, such concerns as "biohackers," biological warfare, the use of biotech techniques for law enforcement, the legal/political proceedings, thorny medical issues (DNA from OJ and on "stained blue dresses," etc.), and the use of biotechnology for establishing the lineage of historic figures (that is, Thomas Jefferson). Each is important in its own right and deserves careful attention. This book, however, concentrates on those issues that have significant impact, short and long term, on the economy.

As a further disclaimer, this book makes no pretense at trying to resolve those issues, but rather seeks to simply enumerate them and put them into an economic context. Several excellent books have already attempted to outline the complex concerns created by DNA and these tiny living cells. One of the smallest discrete pieces of matter known to humans, the cell and its DNA, is emerging as one of the most complex and intriguing. It is truly amazing that something so small could create a debate so large. No one book, however, could hope to capture and resolve all the emerging issues of the broader subject of the bioterials industry (medical biotech, agbio, new materials, etc.). At best, this chapter outlines the general areas of bioethical concerns and major positions taken by various stakeholders in the debate.

Infinitely Small, Infinitely Large

BioEthics issues have become an inextricable part of the bioterials industry, impacting its scope, direction, and eventual success. Each announcement of the latest scientific breakthrough occasions a debate in many circles around the globe about its efficacy and importance in solving many of life's most intimate secrets. It also raises serious debate about whether or not we really want to know the answers to those secrets.

A huge global public and political debate is fomenting about the uses, and some would say abuses, of biotechnologies. This debate has the potential not just to shape and direct the industry and its technologies, but to even, in the most extreme case, stop it altogether. So critical is the bioethics debate to the future of the industry that it may be the industry's "Chinese Wall."

Some observers, such as Dr. Alicia Loffler at Northwestern University, have argued that, if not properly managed, the bioethical issues will cause the biotech revolution to collapse. Yet other experts would argue that bioethics is more analogous to someone (for example, the public) putting their foot on the brake while someone else (for example, the biotech industry) is accelerating. "The probability of some cataclysmic event occurring that will shut down the process altogether is very low," says Elliott Hillback, Senior Vice President, Corporate Affairs, Genzyme Corporation. The process is not likely to stop, but its pace, scope, and direction are up for grabs. On the other hand, however, biotech is fundamentally different from any previous technological advance. While individual countries could, to some degree, control the flow of goods or information, political power is useless in the face of genetic movements.

No government can stop the free movement of genes.

In practical terms, biotech research that is forbidden or discouraged in one part of the world will simply move to another, more hospitable one. No previous technological innovation—not even information technology—was so highly dependent on intangible intellectual capital. And that intangibility creates great mobility. For one thing, governments will have little effective control over such movements. Perhaps more importantly, however, the potential benefits will be too great for countries to resist. And not just smaller Third World countries: witness the tension in U.S. policy between attacking Chinese human rights abuses and courting its huge commercial market for trade.

The "Chinese Wall," then, serves as an apt metaphor for the role bioethics plays in the development of the industry. The Great Wall of China, the only structure built with human labor visible to the astronauts in space, was built by individual states in the Zhou Dynasty, in the seventh century B.C. Unified by the Qin Shi Huang, individual sections of the wall were joined to create a wall to protect China from the Xiongnu warriors from the north. As a means of preventing entry into the country, its nearly 3000 miles of fortification stands as testament to China's tireless resolve. Ironically, however, even great walls serve only in limited ways as an exclusionary device. The most determined invaders may be slowed down, or rerouted, not stopped. Likewise, issues of ethics will serve as a formidable Great Wall in the dawning biotech revolution.

A Debate as Multifaceted as a Gene

Walls, however, keep things in, as well as out. Unfortunately, the emotional components of bioethics are, in many ways, creating a formidable "Great Wall" in the evolving biotech debate. There is one area, though, where the wall metaphor fails to serve. A wall tends to suggest that there are "two sides" to the bioethics debate. In fact, as it relates to biotech, the old expression, "there's two sides to every story," just isn't true. It seems that there are as many sides to this debate as there are people and organizations debating.

In the end, the Great Wall failed to protect China for all time. In more recent times, China was invaded from the outside many times, and wracked by dissent from within. In the case of biotech, all sides in the debate must ensure that this time the wall will serve its purpose more effectively.

Policy makers must ensure that all sides of the ethics debate get heard. As individual political jurisdictions craft the rules of the biotech industry, they must understand that only a global approach will suffice. Policy makers must ensure that ethics will exclude inappropriate and inhumane manifestations of biotechnology and yet will not restrict the development of viable and productive research.

If the general public is to make an informed decision regarding ethics issues, they need an understanding of the fundamental science. Generally, science education has not kept pace with the rapid changes occurring in all areas of science, but no where is the division more acutely felt than in the biological sciences. Just as computer literacy was crucial to success in the Information Age, bioliteracy will be fundamental to individual, corporate and national success in the twenty-first century.

The biotech industry around the world, while pressing forward with its agenda, must remain open and sensitive to the legitimate concerns of those who suspect and oppose them. All sides must remember, though, that the role of such an ethical debate is to intelligently shape the revolution's future, not to halt its progress.

While some of the bioethical issues appear familiar, with a slightly new guise, others seem unique in their scope and almost unimaginable in their scale. On the other hand, many are at the core of the private-public divide that has been central to all of history. Frankly, at the heart of many of these issues are "property rights," which have dominated the public agenda in one form or another since the Agrarian Age.

From Personal Property Rights to the Property Rights of Our Bodies

The Agricultural Age struggled with the concept of private property, taxation and tithing, the right to fair compensation for labor, and the rights of citizenship. Of all these concerns, the most fundamental of the era was the issue of private property. Ownership of land was almost exclusively held by a wealthy elite or, in some cases, a single ruler. The devolution of property rights, ultimately to individual people, was the basis of the epic political struggles of what is now referred to as the Middle Ages. The ownership of property by the individual was, as well, the spark for the development of the technologies that followed. As owners, people were "invested" in improving their lot, and sought innovative ways to accomplish more.

Although they took new forms, the essential core of these concerns continued into the Industrial Age, particularly the issues associated with property rights: control of capital, management versus labor rights, and the stewardship of ecology. Such issues eventually split the world into many factions along ideological lines and pitted the western capitalist democracies against the so-called workers paradise of communism. Of all the issues that surfaced during the Industrial Age, however, perhaps the most "global" was that of technology's impact on the physical environment. Very much a property rights issue, it focused attention on the ownership rights of the common ecology. As such, it was no longer an issue that could be resolved within national political jurisdictions, and instead became a global concern that required a global response. At last count, several hundred international treaties on environmental issues have been signed by most, if not all, countries.

Near the end of the Information Age, a variety of concerns have arisen such as the growing disparity between the "information haves" and "have-nots" and the nature and protection of intellectual property. However, various concerns related to information and personal privacy are emerging as the dominant issue of these times. Again, this is very much a property issue. While concern about the kind and quantity of information that is available about individuals on the Internet has taken center stage in the debate, the central issue remains: who owns the information about oneself?

The Bioterials Age will likewise have its own set of public concerns. The issues of earlier eras were central to the social, cultural, and economic development of the times. While they each had their own set "logics," they also had emotional components. None of those issues, however, threatened the very existence of the technologies that had created them. The issues associated with bioterials, and biotech in particular, however, will be quite different.

To date, little interest or public concern has been aroused by efforts of physicists and commercial organizations focused on inorganic materials. Most, if not all, have been primarily concerned with the manipulation of organic matter. The resolution (if in fact there can be any resolution) of those ethical issues are at the heart of determining how quickly the biotechnological revolution will unfold or, in fact, if it will even exist. A number of groups and individuals are already questioning the existence of the industry, and some, such as Jeremy Rifkin, have argued for its demise. (See "Jeremy Rifkin: The Unofficial Opposition?")

Jeremy Rifkin:
The Unofficial Opposition?

Like many college students of the 1960s and early 1970s, Jeremy Rifkin marched in the streets to oppose the Vietnam War. Unlike most of his contemporaries, though, his days of political activism were only beginning. Now biotechnology's most vocal critic, Rifkin says he doesn't look back too much on the turbulent days when he worked for Volunteers In Service To America (VISTA) in the Harlem ghetto, organized the 1968 March on the Pentagon, and founded the People's Bicentennial Commission.

Rifkin is the Washington-based author, lecturer, and head of the Foundation On Economic Trends. Many of Rifkin's causes have been based around environmental concerns. He has been president of the Greenhouse Crisis Foundation and head of the Beyond Beef Coalition. Rifkin also worries a great deal about the economy.

"Today smells to me a lot more like 1928 or 1929 than 1969," he says. "In this country, we're living in a bit of a Fantasy Land. We have the highest consumer debt ratio since 1929. We think we're doing well, but millions of people are living on credit cards. There's nothing backing that up. This is an unhealthy economy, mapped with short-term expedients like credit cards. There are a lot of challenges and I'm not despairing, but there are daunting challenges."

The man *Time* magazine called a "self-proclaimed scientific watchdog" was born in Denver in 1945, and is not a scientist himself. Rifkin graduated from the University of Pennsylvania with a B.A. in Economics, and went on to earn his Master's in International Affairs at the Fletcher School of Law and Diplomacy at Boston's Tufts University.

Rifkin's stands usually put him squarely in the line of fire from the business and scientific communities—and, at this time, more than ever. He began to speak out about biotechnology, however, as far back as 1976. One year later, Rifkin and Ted Howard released the book *Who Should Play God? The Artificial Creation of Life and What It Means for the Future of the Human Race*. In 1980 Rifkin and Howard released *Entropy: A New World View* (Viking) and in 1983 Nicanor Perlas and Rifkin teamed up on *Algeny* (Viking), whose title combined the medieval pseudoscience of alchemy with contemporary studies of genetics and biotechnology.

The early 1980s occasionally found Rifkin in court, filing lawsuits against both the University of California at Berkeley and the National Institutes of Health over their research in genetic engineering. Eventually, he enlisted religious leaders, including the well-known fundamentalist Jerry Falwell, to aid his cause. More books followed, such as *Beyond Beef* (Plume) in 1993. The Kirkus review of *Beyond Beef* noted that Rifkin apparently mass-produced environmental rallying cries on a factory assembly line.

His own line is that biotechnology is clearly the wave of the future. That's the subject of his current book, *The Biotech Century—A Second Opinion: The Marriage of the Genetic Sciences and the Technologies Reshaping Our World* (J.P. Tarcher). "There's no doubt we're going into the Age of Biotech," Rifkin says. "I believe we're seeing a major change from the Industrial Age to the Biotech Age. The real issue is, which path will we take? The hard task is the Monsanto agenda," Rifkin says of the St. Louis-based chemical firm which has aggressively invested in biotechnology research. "Monsanto is a tough player. They often skirt the line to the unethical. This 'Terminator Gene' they have is evil."

Rifkin feels he has a better approach to the Age of Biotech. "The soft task is that this can be used in a sophisticated way, preventive agriculture rather than playing God," he says. "The science we're learning about is genes. There's nothing wrong with that. Will we use it to be a second Genesis? The soft path may be preferable." The "second Genesis," as Rifkin sees it, would be a man-made bioindustrial nature designed to remake nature's own schemes of evolution.

This outspoken corporate critic points out that he follows one rule of engagement in rhetoric: He refuses to single out individual executives or scientists within the firms as targets. "I don't ever refer to individuals," Rifkin says. Needless to say, though, he does have an opinion on what he sees as a dangerous initiative that Craig Venter's TIGR is pursuing. "I don't think anybody should be able to patent genes or gene sequences," Rifkin says. "That would be like chemists being able to patent elements when they discovered them." [*Author Note:* Neither TIGR nor Venter's for-profit Celera company plan to patent genes.]

And so the 55-year-old Rifkin marches on into the new millennium, much as he marched on the streets of Washington more than 30 years ago as a student. This man who spends so much time thinking and writing about the future was asked what his own vision of the next century might be.

Is this man who warns of doom and gloom from the advancing technology pessimistic about life after 2000? Or is there still the spark of the 1960s post-Kennedy idealist there, the dreams of the one-time VISTA volunteer for a better tomorrow? "It's funny, I'm getting asked that question a lot lately," Rifkin says. "I never think whether I'm optimistic or pessimistic. A better way to approach the future is, what are the values we believe in? How do we advance the world, in a way that honors the intrinsic value of life?" he continues. "How can we create science and commercial technology that honors intrinsic values, and respect the values of everything on this planet?"

And the bottom line? "I think we should be hopeful," Rifkin says. "I'm always hopeful."

Central to the importance of bioethics in the development of the biotech industry is the evolution of property rights, from land ownership, to concern about the air and water, and finally to the ownership and control of our own bodies. The earliest property rights debates were about the ownership of individual pieces of land. That debate eventually moved on to become focused on the "public" property of the environment and the air and water around us. Most recently, in our largely service-oriented economy, the debate has been directed toward the ownership of information *about us* as individuals. In the biotech era, the debate will focus *on us,* on the very ownership of our bodies, and our genes and cells.

BioLiteracy Replaces Computer Literacy

Just as information technologies, such as the Internet, have had a stimulating effect on the speed of biotech's scientific discoveries and diffusion, these same technologies are speeding up the global dissemination of concerns related to the industry. The global communications infrastructure ensures that every scientific breakthrough and every ethical concern related to it gets instant worldwide exposure. The serious nature of the issue is sometimes lost in the blinding speed of the announcements and the volume at which they assault the public. Toward the end of the Information Age, as computers began to run our lives, there were frequent calls for every person to be computer literate. As the transition to the Bioterials Age begins, the need for bioliteracy replaces that of computer literacy.

The definition of *computer savvy* has changed drastically in the past decade. No longer does one need to know programming language to customize a computer's software or build a web page. Similarly, no longer does one need to be fluent with the family, genus, species, and related classification diagrams that used to define biology. Today's bioliteracy involves acquiring a working knowledge of the basic tenets of molecular biology, the basic building blocks of life. Building a knowledgeable society, one armed with insight into fundamental science, is central to distinguishing real ethical issues from those arising from irrational fears or from a position of ignorance.

Almost all biotechnological activities carry with them either a real or an implied ethical consequence. It is vital, therefore, for the public audiences around the world to face such issues in an informed manner. Society's response to the ethical questions will make or break the development of biotechnology's future. Therefore, it is vital for today's policy makers, industry officials, critics, and the average person to recognize the role they play in determining how biotechnology will be accepted. All people will need to be bioliterate because they will increasingly be called on to make "genetic decisions" about themselves, their family, their community, their country, and their world.

Public Fears...

Most of the ethical issues arise out of fear. Fear primarily because everything we once considered "sci fi" is now a reality. Fear because technologies bring the possibility of drastic changes to life (and society) as we have come to know it. There is also a great fear of a massive biotechnological conspiracy (for example, eugenics) or that all of these technologies might be owned by some ubiquitous power (the *Brave New World* phenomenon) whose primary aim is control through social engineering.

James Watson, the discoverer of the DNA structure, argued in a January 1999 issue of *Time* that "you should never put off doing something useful for fear of evil that may never arrive." And, in reference to the concern that biotech research might create unimaginable new organisms, he argued that "such creations will remain denizens of science fiction, not the real world. . . ." However, without being taught the language of biotech, science will inevitably be misunderstood and subsequently misconstrued by the general public.

If the general public is to make an informed decision regarding ethics issues, they need some fundamental understanding of the science. Generally, science education has not kept pace with the rapid changes occurring in all areas of science, but no where is the division more acutely felt than in the biological sciences.

... and Private Bodies

In addition to being called upon to make informed decisions about the technology and its future, in the near future, every individual will be called upon to make decisions about their own cells, the basic building blocks of life. There will be decisions to be made about our own genes and about how we want them shaped, sculpted, and manipulated. We will have to decide how much information we want to have, or someone else to have, about our genes, or those of people close to us. Whether or not we want our genes to "live" beyond our mortal selves is a question that may confront every person.

Ignoring the Inorganic and Focusing on the Organic

This book makes no claim to identify all the potential issues of the Bioterials Age. It is impossible to enumerate every ethical issue that the bioterial technologies raise. This task is exacerbated by the fact that there are so many issues, but also because many issues haven't even been identified yet. The intensity of debate around bioterials increases dramatically as the science moves from the activities involving inorganic matter to those of organic tissue. In terms of public response, the research of inorganic matter does little more than raise an occasional eyebrow. However, the tenor of public response is raised to exponential heights when it comes to biotechnological discoveries in the way of organic materials. More specifically, it is the genetic and human-related biological developments that are causing ethical controversy.

Within the realm of organic materials, concern likewise increases dramatically as focus shifts from vegetable to animal to human. The issues become more serious, complex, and numerous. Thus, no treatment of bioethics issues can expect to cover exhaustively the range of concerns about biotechnology.

It is important to note that such a division tends to suggest a uniqueness to the issues, when in fact there is none. Some overlap occurs due to the very nature of genetic material. Despite its rich varieties of plants, animals, and humans, nature relies on an amazingly similar set of genes. Therefore, in order to frame the perspective in an artificial, but manageable, whole, five broad areas of concern are considered:

- Genetic manipulation of plants and animals
- Personal health, diagnosis, and treatment
- Reproductive technologies
- Genetic discrimination and issues of privacy
- Cloning

Readers should recognize that these areas are not entirely distinct from one another, nor are they intended to be. Some overlap occurs due to the interrelated nature of current bioscience. The potential ramifications of each area are explained, both positive and negative, along with the highlights of a spectrum of contemporary public opinions.

Readers might also notice that the five areas under examination are presented in an arrangement of least speculative to most speculative. That is, agricultural products are already a reality and are in widespread use. Discoveries centering on health issues occur weekly, and reproductive technologies accelerate with breathtaking speed. Genetic discrimination is happening to a limited extent, and many more cloning advances are to be found in the future than have been presently confirmed.

Genetic Manipulation of Plants and Animals

Human attempts to alter the characteristics of plants and animals to better serve its needs has been going on for more than 7000 years. While most of the effort has been directed to the use of such products for food and clothing, certain efforts have also included less practical pursuits such as the development of ornament plants and the improvements of horse and dog breeds. Nearly every domesticated plant and animal has been the focus of some improvement efforts. An agricultural or food product whose genetic structure has been artificially modified to enhance its value is considered genetically manipulated (GM) or genetically engineered (GE). Once any non-natural gene is spliced into the genetic sequence, the resulting product is considered GM.

Issues concerned with the genetic manipulation of food and agricultural products are most immediate, because a number of genetically altered products are already on the market. The public's response to this fundamental issue will serve as a significant indicator of technological alterations to come.

Interestingly, a sharp dichotomy exists between the North American and European public response to genetically altered food. It seems fair to say that few North Americans seem to know of the existence and especially the widespread availability of genetically manipulated crops. In a similar manner, other biotech critics claim that the large life sciences companies are laying the groundwork so that they may soon be able to dominate the agricultural industry and to ensure that farmers become dependent upon their chemical products.

In Pursuit of Perfect Plants...

The discussion of GM food can be divided into those involving plants and those involving animals. As described in Chapter 10, a wide variety of GM crops are now commonly cultivated in North America, especially corn, tomatoes, and soybeans. Value is added to such GM products in a number of ways, including enhancing their positive attributes or minimizing its negative ones. (See "Accentuating the Positives" and "Adding Value through GE.")

Accentuating the Positive

Genetic engineering may be used to positively alter plants as follows:

- To augment their nutritional value (such as the implanting of genes from pea plants in order to create rice with higher protein value) or to stimulate plants to grow faster, bigger, or sweeter.

- To produce stronger stems, more fruit, or leaves.

- To facilitate breeding (radicchio) or to produce higher yields.

- To slow down the process of decomposition so that fruits and vegetables will last longer or will have greater market attraction. The Flavr-Savr tomato, developed by Monsanto, offers a delayed ripening time so that it might enjoy a longer shelf life on the fresh produce market. Many fruits and vegetables are picked still underripe to allow them to reach the market at peak firmness and freshness. The FlavrSavr manipulation turns off the plant's inherent softening gene; thus, the process of rapid decomposition is delayed. The genetic manipulation that results in delayed ripening is now being extended to apples, peaches, strawberries, bananas, melons, and sweet peppers.

- To reduce the saturated fat content of canola, soybean, corn, sunflower, or other oil crops such as DuPont's high-oleic soybean.

- To encourage higher starch content in wheat or potatoes or higher levels of Vitamin C or E in fruits and vegetables.

- To create cheese appropriate for vegetarian consumption. By genetically manipulating the enzyme rather than relying on the normal (animal protein) method, a true vegetarian cheese may be created.

- To allow tropical fruit, such as guava and papaya, to be grown in a more temperate climate (such research is ongoing at Fort Valley State University, Georgia).

Adding Value through GE

Other ways in which value may be added include suppressing undesirable qualities:

- To decrease food-supply losses due to severe weather conditions such as drought or frost [make plants more resistant to drought or frost or to be able to adapt to a wider range of growing conditions (drier, hotter, colder)].

- To make fruits or vegetables that will be more tolerant to aluminum when canned.

- To create resistance to pests and diseases. For instance, the corn borer insect is responsible for destroying significant quantities of the United States' corn crop. Companies, such as Monsanto, Novartis, and others, have altered corn's genetic structure so that the plant now carries with it a protein designed to resist this insect. Current statistics show that 20 percent of the 1998 U.S. corn harvest carried with it the modification needed to resist this pest. National Corn Genome Initiative (NCGI) is fully supportive of undergoing genetic developments designed to produce stronger and more fruitful corn production. Monsanto has developed a similar alteration to fight the Colorado potato beetle in potato crops.

- To breed resistance to viruses, such as the "cucumber mosaic virus," which affects not only cucumbers but also peppers, lettuce, squash, tomatoes, and other crops. The University of Hawaii, in conjunction with Cornell University, is working on breeding resistance against the papaya ringspot virus into their papaya.

- To build in weed control in canola, corn, cotton, and soybeans.

- To allow farmers to determine whether insecticide or herbicide sprays are necessary by offering them safer and less environmentally dangerous options.

... and Animals ...

A touchier but equally important issue for future generations is the development and refinement of modified animal and fish stocks. In the same way scientists are altering plants, they are also attempting to improve the quality and efficiency of animals. Dozens of researchers are committed to genetically improving a variety of consumer livestock—cattle, pigs, chickens—to induce rapid weight gain and a faster time to market. Other scientists alter livestock genes to make the animal adaptable to a broader range of climatic conditions or to promote disease resistance. Genetically enhanced pigs, sheep, cows, chickens, and other animals and fish are being developed in an effort to reduce costs and pollutants associated with animals bred for food production. As noted earlier in this book, animals have been re-engineered to be "factories" for the production of organs for human transplants, eliminating many of the problems associated with transplanting from other humans.

Salmon has been altered with the addition of an antifreezing gene from cod. This alteration makes the salmon able to live in a colder climate. Moreover, research directed by Dr. Garth Fletcher and Dr. Choy Hew has developed Atlantic salmon with an increased growth rate. These fish, sold under the trade name of "AquAdvantage" salmon, demonstrate growth rates four to six times greater than traditional salmon. In 5 months, the traditional salmon's body weight is approximately 80 gs, but the transgenic salmon's weight exceeds 500 gs. Obviously, the opportunities for aquaculture are enormous, especially at a time when world fishing stocks are being depleted and fishing rights are bringing nations to the brink of war. The "antifreeze" gene has also been adopted by some Finnish aquaculturists. Instead of salmon, researchers at the University of Kuopio are attempting to produce transgenic rainbow trout. A secondary benefit is that they intend to program their transgenic fish to utilize less expensive feed.

... But Will the World Eat It?

The general ethical questions brought up regarding GM agricultural plant products (primarily taste and safety of the food product) are mirrored with the subject of genetically altered livestock. The British beef industry has yet to recover from the "Mad Cow Disease" incidents of a few years ago. This tragic chain of events set off a whole-sale slaughter of thousands of animals. It also created a public relations disaster that illustrates what can happen when the public senses that their food isn't safe. Some consumers fear that researchers don't know all the outcomes of what they're pushing forward, and that the health risks of genetically altered livestock will not become clear until years down the line.

The safety of meat is not the only consideration, as consumers raise additional ethical issues surrounding livestock. The primary concern regards animal welfare and animal rights; consumers want to be convinced that livestock animals do not suffer as a result of genetic engineering. Indeed, presenters at the Transgenic Animals and Food Production Conference, in Stockholm, concluded that buyer objections to genetically altered animals for consumption stands as the major obstacle blocking further development.

In the early 1990s, John Polkinghorne, President of Queen's College, Cambridge, was asked to chair a committee formed with the objective of discovering Britain's response to GM food and agricultural products. The Ethics of Genetic Modification and Food Use Committee—now known as the Polkinghorne Committee—found that public responses correlate strongly to religious preferences. For example, most Christian and Jewish groups find GM food acceptable, but Muslims, Sikhs, and Hindus, due to their particular religious convictions regarding animal consumption, raise ethical objections to consuming food altered with animal genes. They also concluded that because GM food is here to stay, ethics do not require research to stop. Another recommendation was that government and industry should actively seek ways of explaining genetic processes to the public, because most concerns rise from misconceptions about the actual technological developments in use. The Committee asserted that clear labeling of all GM foods will be necessary to allow consumers the ability to make an informed choice.

A GM tomato paste, developed by Zeneca Plant Science and being sold in England with clear labeling, outsells traditional pastes. Apparently, consumers are appeased by its bold labeling as well as its superior taste. Supporting the idea of informed choice, virtually all countries throughout Europe and Asia have instituted clear demands that all GM foods should be properly labeled. A recent European Union survey found that 86 percent of the continent's residents believe such food should be labeled. However, the United States,

Canada, Brazil, New Zealand, and Australia call for very limited labeling requirements. The Australia/New Zealand Food Standards Author-
ity proposed adopting the unrestricted method embraced by the
United States. That position requires that only GM foods substantially
different from their originals require labeling. The differences in labeling requirements have already set off several trade wars between the
United States and Europe, and the situation is sure to get more heated
until some standardization agreement is met.

Europe, and the United Kingdom in particular, is generally more
apprehensive about GM food than is the United States. In fact, Prince
Charles devoted his first online forum, in December 1998, to the
topic of GM food. While the Prince has formerly addressed the issue
in speeches and articles, he asserts here that "We should not be med-
dling with the building blocks of life in this way."

In the United States, the public response to GM food has been
shifting dramatically over the years, primarily from the positive to the
negative. A January 1999 *Time* magazine poll found that 81 percent
of Americans feel GM food should be labeled as such. Interestingly,
however, 58 percent said that they would not buy such food. This
contrasts sharply with earlier polls reported by *Time* that showed far
fewer people aware of or concerned about either the food being
altered or labeled. In the main, concerns about food centers primarily on the questions enumerated in "Issues with Genetically Modified
Foods."

Issues with Genetically Modified Foods

The primary public response to GM food centers on these questions:

- Should GM foods be labeled? A January 1999 *Time* magazine poll
  found that 81 percent of Americans feel GM food should be labeled
  as such. Interestingly, however, 58 percent said that they would not
  buy such food (*www.genetic-id.com*).

- What benefits accrue from manipulating food: will it be less expensive, more nutritious, taste better, or other? Will consumers be able to
  easily see that the benefits outweigh the perceived risks?

- Will consumers be able to taste differences between GM and non-GM
  foods?

- Are GM foods safe to eat? Can they be considered "natural?"

- Could GM crops invade other habitats and threaten native plants?
- Could the genetic manipulation of plants have unforeseen effects on human health?
- Will GM agriculture make the traditional farmer obsolete? Will a greater reliance on GM agriculture make the small farmer dependent upon large biotech and/or pharmaceutical corporations? Will it hasten the disappearance of small farms?
- Will concerned consumers flee to the rapidly growing organic grocery store business to avoid GM foods entirely?

Virtually all public opinion polls conclude that taste and labeling constitute primary concerns regarding GM foods. Some health activists and journalists view the lax labeling regulations in the United States as a result of intense agribusiness lobbying. The FDA asserts, however, that if the end product is "substantially equivalent" to the organic variety, then no labeling is necessary. Public opinion regarding the labeling of GM food is strong enough to initiate litigation. In Canada, the biotech industry has taken a proactive stance in dealing with this issue. (See "Canadian Response to Genetically Modified Food.")

Canadian Response to Genetically Modified Food

Joyce Groote, a geneticist who heads BIOTECanada, a consortium made up of the Canadian biotech community, believes that many Canadian consumers are simply not aware of the benefits of bioengineered products. She believes that once people understand how genetic engineering can create crops that resist pests and grow foods with enhanced nutritional value, they will then be more accepting of the technology. She also believes that they will be more accepting when they realize biotech pharmaceuticals can cure their most feared diseases, or that biotech microbes can reduce pollution. She expresses real concern that pressure from activist groups could cause the government to revoke or modify legislation that has created Canada's current favorable climate for biotechnology.

An indicator of consumer attitude is the March 1999 report of a Canadian Citizens' Conference on Food Biotechnology held at the University of Calgary. The report challenges the biotech industry and underlines widespread consumer concerns about the safety and benefits of genetically engineered foods. The following are some of the key recommendations:

- *Ethics.* A code of ethics reflecting Canadian values must be developed to govern genetic modification of animals used in genetic experiments. Such a code of ethics must also cover gene patenting, culture and dietary restrictions, and the negative perception of corporate funding of public research projects.

- *Legislation.* The conference called for the development of an effective labeling policy for genetically engineered foods, which is not required in the United States.

- *Environment.* Concerned that biotechnology could increase pest and disease resistance, jeopardize biodiversity, and create other environmental risks, the conference called for a multidisciplinary peer-reviewed research program to be incorporated into a formal environmental risk assessment process.

- *Consumer health and safety.* To overcome both consumer apathy and anxiety about bioengineered foods, the conference recommended that a comprehensive public communications plan be developed by industry, producers, and the government.

- *Economic and social impacts.* Canadians worry that Monsanto's "Terminator" technology may increase farmers' dependence on seed companies and force those who choose not to grow genetically modified crops out of the industry. They want the government to monitor and assess the impact of what they see as a trend toward concentration of the food industry in a few hands. They also called for a review of current patent laws and their application to food biotechnology.

In May 1998, a coalition of U.S. scientists, religious leaders, health professionals, consumers, and chefs filed a landmark lawsuit against the FDA to insist on mandatory safety testing and labeling of all GM food. Current FDA policy allows modified food to be marketed without any testing and without special labeling. Protesters assert that such a practice not only violates religious freedom but also the consumer's right to know. The coalition says that millions of consumers unknowingly consume GM food. Andrew Kimbrell, Executive Director of the International Center for Technology Assessment, says that the FDA has placed the interest of biotechnology companies ahead of their responsibility to promote public health; consumers unknowingly have been guinea pigs.

Perfecting Personal Health

The ultimate goal of genetic research is to help people. Almost every disease has a human genetic component. Francis Collins, the Director of the Human Genome Project, says "We are all diseased, just not diagnosed yet." The study of natural genetic variation in humans is the basis for medically important, genetically complex human diseases. In early May 1999, *Science* reported that researchers at the University of California, Santa Barbara, had discovered the "genetic master switch" that controls bacteria infections. Know as DMA, the gene may be the most important weapon in fighting the growing number of antibiotic-resistant infections. Infections claim some 17 million lives annually around the world, three times that of cancer. But gene research extends well beyond infections.

According to the Centers for Disease Control, virtually all human diseases result from the interaction of genetic variation with environmental factors such as behaviors and exposures. Diseases currently thought to be related to genetics include: diabetes, asthma, cancer, Alzheimer's, Parkinson, Huntington, ALS (Lou Gehrig disease), cystic fibrosis, sickle cell, and fragile X syndrome. In addition, aging, obesity/diet, memory, heart disease, breast cancer, spinal cord and brain injuries, and occupational and infectious diseases are thought to be related to genetic variations.

All genetic testing (or any medical procedure) is done only after a person is informed and consents to it. This is known in medical and legal circles as *informed consent*. Diagnosis by genetic testing makes it possible for a person to have special treatments that reduce risk of death. Experts in medical ethics cites three primary concerns: autonomy—the freedom of individuals to express themselves and to make decisions that affect their bodies, justice—recognition that each person is deserving of respect and consideration, and beneficence/nonmalfeasance. Patient autonomy is now considered the most important factor in medical decision making.

The amount of information about genes is almost overwhelming, however. It takes some 70,000 sequences to express a gene structure. And Dr. Randall Scott, President of Incyte Pharmaceuticals, in a recent Ernst & Young industry report on biotech, said that "the entire expressed human genome will be available in a single chip microarray format within 3 years at a cost of around $100." Although many worry about the use of genetic information, the sheer volume suggests that the real problem will be in creating a context in which it makes sense for decision making.

Ethical, legal, and social issues must be addressed in applying genetics to the promotion of health and prevention of disease and disability. These five issues are the most often discussed:

- Informed consent in public health genetic research and programs
- Legal issues in public health programs such as mandatory versus voluntary participation
- Equal access to tests and services for all races and income levels
- Privacy concerns in broad-based genetic studies
- Preventing discrimination based on an individual's genetic codes

Industry Ethical Safeguards

The pharmaceutical/biotech trade organization BIO has even drafted recommendations to lawmakers for addressing genetic ethics issues. Their 14-point "Statement of Principles" addresses ethical issues ranging from patient consent to the confidentiality of genetic information (see the Appendix).

President Clinton set up the National Bioethics Advisory Commission in October of 1995 to address the ethical issues of biotech. Its membership is made up of some of the country's brightest scientists and doctors from universities such as Princeton, Johns Hopkins, and the University of Virginia.

Among the more important ethical questions being raised are the following:

- Are there appropriate ways in which genetic information might be used in employment settings? Might it be ethical to use genetic testing to identify employees who could demonstrate a susceptibility to certain employment conditions? Would objections raised as a result of genetic testing make an individual subject to the provisions of the Americans with Disabilities Act?
- In what manner might genetic information be used in cases involving adoption proceedings and the establishment of child custody and child support?
- How might concepts of race and ethnicity impact on genetic testing? Might certain groups be vulnerable to discrimination based on their genetic information?

The U.S. Human Genome Project recently announced that it had successfully completed all major goals in its 5-year plan covering the years 1993 to 1998. A new plan, for 1998 to 2003, was presented in which human DNA sequencing will be the major emphasis. An ambitious schedule has been set to complete the full sequence by the end of 2003, the 50th anniversary of the discovery of the double-helix structure of DNA by James Watson and Francis Crick. If the 2003 date for completion is achieved, it will come in a full 2 years ahead of previous projections. A working draft should be ready by the end of 2001. More recently, a more ambitious schedule was announced. Craig Venter's Celera has argued that if the two projects would join forces, the schedule could be greatly accelerated. At the time of this writing, the federal program had yet to respond. Of the goals set out for the project, some specifically address their ethical responsibility. The project leaders acknowledge that public privacy, ethical responsibility, and policies to protect genetic rights are inalienably attached to their research efforts.

Gene Testing Goes Mainstream

There are currently well over 50 accredited DNA labs in the United States that do genetic paternity testing, but there are many more that "go about their business without bothering to get accredited." One company, Identigene, offers its service on billboards in 30 cities, offering, for example, to quickly identify fathers. Considering that finding suitable DNA material is much easier than getting a blood sample, it's not hard to imagine someone unknowingly or unwillingly being tested. A discarded fingernail or a hair from a comb is now enough for a lab to investigate.

Stem Cells

While a number of vital public health benefits will likely result from research on stem cells, all developments are contingent upon the public resolving their fundamental objections to the use of fetal or embryonic cells from deceased babies in research. Some of the beneficial developments include a greater understanding of developmental biology and related studies of infertility and birth defects, therapies for organ transplantation (to replace diseased, damaged, depleted, or absent organs), treatments for diseases such as Parkinson's disease in which new cells contribute to better health, and the development of new drugs.

While the resolution of this issue in the United States may take some time, it is clearly on the national bioethics agenda. Eric M. Meslin, Ph.D., Executive Director of the federal government's National Bioethics Advisory Commission, advised President Clinton in November 1998 of the commission's intent, to "undertake a thorough review of the issues associated with . . . human stem cell research, balancing all ethical and medical considerations."

Regulatory Responses

Ethics commissions in several nations, including Australia, the United Kingdom (the Warnock Report), the United States (National Institutes of Health Human Embryo Research Panel), and more recently Denmark, have approved research on human embryos up to 14 days old. At 14 days, a structure called the "primitive streak" appears, which will become the brain and spinal column and which differentiates embryo from placenta.

On January 19, 1999, the Department of Health and Human Services ruled that embryonic stem cells do not fall under the 1995 Congressional ban on embryo research. They continued that federally supported researchers can conduct research on the cells as long as somebody else derived them using private money. That same day, Dr. Harold Varmus, Director of the National Institutes of Health (NIH), announced that the NIH may pursue and fund scientific research using human pluripotent (derived) stem cells. In April 1999, however, Senator Sam Brownback (Republican, Kansas) and eight other senators objected strenuously to allowing research on embryonic stem cells to continue, and they accused Donna E. Shalala, Secretary of Health and Human Services, of sidestepping Congress' mandate.

Designer Babies: Genetic Impacts on Reproductive Technology

With the various options for reproductive technology, one child may have as many as five different "parents"—an ovum donor, a sperm donor, a gestational carrier, and two adoptive (rearing) parents. Sociologist Barbara Katz Rothman of the City University of New York, in her

October 1998 book *Genetic Maps and Human Imaginations,* says that current genetic technology regarding reproduction will dehumanize us. It will make us collections of parts. The "book of life," according to Rothman, "will become a catalog" from which the parents-to-be flip through a list of sperm (or egg) donors and select the traits they desire. "Bearing a child is becoming like ordering a la carte."

Some of the events creating new ethical issues for genetic manipulation of reproduction include:

- Twins born the same day (one white, one black) due to a mistake in the embryo implantation process.

- Baby born from a dead man's sperm (harvested 30 hours after he died).

- Baby born to a mother "from beyond the grave" by a surrogate mother from eggs harvested from deceased mother and fertilized by an anonymous male.

- Baby fathered by two gay males; baby genetically linked to both men.

Since 1990, gene therapy has generally meant slipping a healthy gene into the cells of a diseased patient. Soon, it may mean something much more momentous: altering a fertilized egg so that the baby who develops will carry a gene that scientists, not its parents, bequeathed to him. If an unborn fetus is diagnosed with an inherited disease, it is possible that, through genetic engineering, the growing fetus may be cured before birth. But if the introduced genes slip into the fetus' sperm (or egg) cells, the genetic change would reproduce throughout his/her successive generations.

The possibility leaves many bioethicists nervous. With such a potent tool—the ability to irrevocably shape generations to come— some scientists claim that we may have the ability to control our own evolution. James Watson, says "We might as well do what we finally can to take the threat of Alzheimer's or breast cancer away from a family." And polls show that as many as 20 percent of parents have no problem with the idea of genetically improving their children.

UCLA geneticist John Campbell has argued there is a way to alter a baby's genes and still not violate the fundamental ethic principal of informed consent. Certain genes could be paired with an on-off switch. If it's "on" and the patient desires it to be turned "off," he would take a prescribed drug to turn the switch. Researchers are also trying to introduce genetic self-destruct modes so that the alterations given to one generation would not be passed on to future generations.

International Responses

In general, issues involving human reproduction have not received wide attention, except in the Third World, where couples are using such devices primarily for sex selection. Laws prohibiting using pre-natal diagnosis for sex selection, however, are not working in some countries. In China, the province of Shandong outlawed the use of the ultrasound to identify the sex of a fetus in early 1999. A national Chinese law existed—the Maternal and Infant Health Care Act of 1994—which made use of prenatal diagnosis for sex selection illegal, but apparently the national law was not being enforced, and a stronger law was required.

In India, national law also forbids sex selection, but just as in China, such laws are not working. While prenatal diagnosis is intended to identify fetuses with genetic or chromosomal disorders, most prenatal diagnoses are used to determine the gender of the fetus. If the test results cause the parents to choose an abortion, it is invariably because the fetus was found to be female.

Is Genetic Testing Really Reproduction Eugenics?

Eugenics really carries with it two definitions. The first is to prevent the birth of unhealthy (or "inferior") children (negative eugenics). The second is to produce healthier children, better babies, or posi-tive eugenics. Historically, public concern focused on negative eugenics, but new discoveries in genetics could make positive eugenics a reality for the first time.

Basic prenatal care, maternal and infant nutrition, and immuniza-tions are all part of basic health care and should not be considered an attempt to artificially produce healthier children. There is no coer-cive element present, therefore, they are not "eugenics." The Ameri-can Society of Human Genetics has issued a statement on eugenics, basically condemning all forms of coercion but supporting individual decisions about reproduction. *Euphenics*—coined in 1929 by Russian biologist N. K. Koltsov and meaning improvement of the phenotype (body) not the underlying genotype (gene)—might, therefore, be a better word. This improvement is facilitated through biological, not genetic, means. Consequently, using genetic methods to decrease birth defects or eliminate harmful genetic traits at the start should not be looked upon as an attempt to create perfect children. Rather it is an attempt to eliminate the causes of suffering and anguish.

Genetic Discrimination

Genetic testing has advanced rapidly in the recent past. Not only has the knowledge and application of genetic testing grown exponentially in recent years, but also the information produced by such tests has grown in importance. While valuable for medical treatment, bioactivists are arguing that genetic information is increasingly being used in ways that might be contrary to the interests of the individual. This practice, called *genetic discrimination,* appears most often in either employment issues or with insurance issues.

Some 200 cases of genetic discrimination have been raised over the past few years. Clearly, as the number of genetic tests available increases every year, the number of lawsuits will almost certainly increase. The concern is that employers and insurers might base decisions on genetic tests that may tell only part of the story. The amount of genetic information about one individual is so staggering, however, that biotech scientists, such as Craig Venter, doubt that it can ever be seriously used.

Genetic Discrimination in Insurance?

On the other hand, the American Council of Life Insurance (ACLI) asserts that insurance companies should be allowed to utilize genetic information to assign risk categories to potential subscribers. Furthermore, they want to reserve the right to refuse policies to individuals who carry a high degree of risk. According to 1997 figures, approximately 100 million Americans either lack health insurance entirely or are seriously underinsured. The danger is that more and more consumers will be unable to afford life insurance or disability insurance.

Strong legislative protections will surely be enacted to counter genetic discrimination. Representative Louise Slaughter (D, New York), Senator Pete Domenici (R, New Mexico), Representative Nita Lowey (D, New York), and several other members of Congress are already actively pursuing passage of bills restricting genetic discrimination. At least 60 bills in 18 state legislatures provide protection against genetic discrimination in either insurance or employment arenas. Donna Shalala, Secretary of Health and Human Services, says "We must enact bipartisan legislation to stop genetic discrimination."

Genetic Discrimination in Employment?

In addition to insurance, genetic discrimination might occur if employers decide to hire employees who are least likely to have future health problems and extensive absenteeism. Some employers may avoid hiring people they fear will be "bad risks." The Equal Employment Opportunities Commission issued revised guidelines in 1995 to say that individuals who are currently healthy but who have a genetic predisposition for a disease will be perceived as disabled (and, thus, fall within the scope of the Americans with Disability Act). Some feel that if alcoholism or other forms of addiction or mental illness become included under a label of genetic disease, economic and social resources currently available are likely to disappear or be diverted into finding biomedical "cures."

Genetic discrimination might be interpreted in a slightly different way. With a growing number of biometric identification techniques—including the reading of finger and/or hand geometry, facial scanning and/or iris recognition, handwriting and/or voice recognition, for example—the possibilities increase for individual loss of privacy. The most feared biometric technique is DNA matching. In October 1998, the FBI launched a national DNA database containing 20 percent or so of the 600,000 DNA profiles collected in criminal cases. According to a 1998 issue of *US News and World Report,* New York Mayor Rudolph Guliani believes that genes might be collected from newborns to assist in their recovery, should they become missing children.

The United Nations Educational Scientific and Cultural Organization (UNESCO) has outlined the first international treaty setting out ethical guidelines for genetic research. It argues that such human rights abuses as genetic discrimination should be prevented, and practices that are "contrary to human dignity" should be banned. Scientists are urged only to follow research that offers relief from suffering. Few specific research areas are identified because the treaty "has been designed to establish lasting ethical principles at a universal level," says UNESCO's International Bioethics Committee Chief Noelle Lenoir.

Cloning

Since the "birth" in 1997 of Dolly, the ethical issues surrounding cloning have commanded the world's attention. Virtually no one, except the implausible Richard Seed from Chicago, and scientists from South Korea, claims to have mounted an attempt at human cloning.

Apparently, in December 1998, a team of Korean researchers at Kyunghee University Hospital, led by Professor Lee Bo-yeon, claimed that they had cloned a human embryo. Their method, they said, was to replace the nucleus of a woman's egg cell with the nucleus of a cell from her body, transferring her entire DNA to the egg. They then managed to coax the egg to divide twice, creating an embryo of four cells. Had that embryo continued to develop, it would have been a clone of the woman. According to an Associated Press story dated January 28, 1999, American experts said that, to their knowledge, this was a medical first. But a panel of the Korean Doctors Association concluded, after a 25-day investigation, that Professor Lee's team had kept such sloppy records that their accomplishment could not be verified and the results were in doubt.

The sides are clearly drawn regarding whether human cloning should proceed, and no more central bioethical question is being raised.

A number of prominent and respected individuals stand in favor of the pursuit of human cloning. Among them are Stephen Hawking, who says "The fuss about cloning is rather silly; I can't see any essential distinction between cloning and producing brothers and sisters in the time-honored way."

Senator Thomas Harkin (D, Iowa) has spoken out in support of human cloning. Harkin said that he welcomes human cloning and he called the anticloning fervor "rubbish." Senator Harkin is noted for being a friend of all forms of medical research. He said: "This has enormous potential for good. There should be no limits on human knowledge, none whatever. To those like President Clinton who say we can't play God, I say OK, fine, you can take your side alongside Pope Paul V who in 1616 tried to stop Galileo; they accused Galileo of trying to play God too. . . . I don't think cloning is demeaning to human nature, to attempt to limit human knowledge is demeaning. It's not legitimate to try to stop cloning. What nonsense, what utter, utter nonsense to think we can hold up our hand and just say 'stop.' Cloning will continue, the human mind will continue to inquire into it. Human cloning will take place and it will take place in my life-time, and I don't fear it at all. I want to be on the side of the Galileos and those who say the human mind has no limits, rather than trying to stop something that's going to happen anyway."

Indeed, the venerable *New England Journal of Medicine,* in its March 26, 1998, issue, asked "Should Human Cloning Research Be Off Limits?" They outlined their position as follows:

Cloning captured public attention when Scottish scientists startled the world by announcing the birth of a sheep named Dolly that had been cloned by combining the nucleus of an adult mammary cell and an enucleated sheep egg. Interest intensified when Richard Seed, a physicist with no expertise in cloning, no institutional affiliation, and no funding, announced that he would clone humans for a fee. Fear that human-cloning factories might soon appear before anyone had a chance to digest the implications of this new technology sent Congress into action. Legislation was introduced in both the Senate and House of Representatives that would ban human cloning indefinitely or impose a long moratorium on it. Such a moratorium was more or less uncontroversial, given the preliminary nature of the technology required to clone animals and the unknown risks of cloning humans.

Unfortunately, the impetuously drafted bills in both the Senate (the Bond-Frist bill) and the House (the Ehlers bill) would go far beyond restricting the cloning of humans. These bills would put a stop to all cloning experiments that use human cells, in particular, research into what is known as somatic-cell nuclear-transfer technology. Such bills would create important precedents because Congress has never before passed legislation to halt a single kind of scientific or medical research.

And Lee Silver, a biologist at Princeton and author of *Remaking Eden: Cloning and Beyond in a Brave New World,* believes that just as clinics developed to assist infertile couples conceive children, likewise, he believes cloning will eventually be accepted and "used by a small minority of people in special circumstances." He suggests that enhancement through germ-line gene therapy, along with conscious mating between the "enhanced" could lead to a superior gene pool (the "Gen-Rich"). He says: "The huge gap between the rich and the poor shows itself in what parents can do for their children. I see that continuing and becoming more pronounced in the future, and extending into the genetic realm."

Why, the reader may ask, should the First World be concerned with the affordability of genetic therapies in the Third World? Beyond that of pure humanitarianism, there are important economic and geopolitical reasons as well. The economies of the world, and the world's political stability, are so integrated that peace and prosperity in the First World is now highly reliant on those characteristics in the Second and Third Worlds.

If there is a lighter moment in the cloning debate, perhaps it is to be found with the scientists at Texas A&M University, who are involved in a project to clone a wealthy couple's dog. The project, dubbed the Missyplicity Project (after the dog's name) is being tracked not only by scientists internationally but also by a cadre of devoted cybersurfers. Accompanying the project is a sophisticated website recently featured in *Salon* magazine.

Those taking a firm stand against cloning typically rely on arguments citing religious objections or fears that scientists are not in final control of the technology they are embarking upon.

President Clinton, in a radio address to the nation on January 10, 1998, said "there is virtually unanimous consensus in the scientific and medical communities that attempting to . . . clone a human being is untested and unsafe and morally unacceptable. . . . I call on Congress to act now to make it illegal for anyone to clone a human being."

Whether or not it is outlawed, the fact remains that, technically, life can be created in the lab as well as in the bedroom. Craig Venter is prepared to give it a try. He has asked a leading bioethicist, Dr. Arthur Caplan, at the University of Pennsylvania, to form a "blue ribbon" committee to determine whether or not the experiment should be conducted.

Biotech: A Family *Matter*

Environmental pollution, the major issue of the Industrial Age, arose only near the end of that era. Companies and governments have spent billions of dollars to restore damaged sections of the ecology and billions more to devise many new technologies to prevent any further damage. While this issue served to reshape the practices of governments, industries, and the public, it never threatened the survival of various industrial activities and technologies. Likewise, the growing debate over privacy, the major issue of the Information Age, will likely shape the contours and practices of the various information industries. It will not, however, seriously threaten the survival of the industry or its technologies.

The ethical issues around biotechnology, however, threaten the industries' very survival.

It is clear from the debate that

- The closer agbio gets to impacting the entire food supply, the greater the negative pressure on the industry.

- The first signs of global hunger will create a new set of public activists aimed at unqualified support for the industry.

- The closer the industry gets to eliminating various diseases, such as cancer, HIV, and creating replacement organs, the more positive the industries' support.

- The further along the spectrum from inorganic to organic matter, the greater the public and government concern.

- The further along the organic spectrum, from bacteria to insects, plants, animals, and eventually to humans, the larger and more vocal the antibiotech lobby.

- Public approval, so necessary for the industries' survival and growth, is a harsher and "trickier" approval process than the FDA or its international counterparts.

- The closer some biotechnologists get to human cloning and creating "life in the lab," the greater the negative focus on the entire industry.

It is incumbent on the industry, government, the public, and activists around the world to set aside partisan concerns and work cooperatively to chart a common course for the evolution of biotechnology. None alone can accomplish their goals.

Conquering matter is truly an issue for the "family of man," and the resolution of its many issues will only be resolved in the court of public opinion.

Afterword

2005: The End of the Beginning

BioAstrology?

No one can really know the future. In this book I claim only one possible scenario for an economic and technological future. Many will disagree with my views in both content and enthusiasm, but I make no excuses for either.

Projecting the future of bioterials, a technology so complex and a business so pervasive, is at once both a perilous and exhilarating task. To predict the future runs the risk of being placed in the category of a long line of "professions" that have tried similar tasks: prophets, swamis, tarot card readers, mystics, shamans, and astrologers, to name just a few.

Futurists today have several advantages, should they care to use them, over futurists in the past. Most important, they have the vantage point of history to understand how the earlier soothsayers erred. In writing this book, I have tried to understand the mistakes of prophets past, but to keep myself open to the potential of the future. Even so, to proclaim the end of the Information Age and the beginning of the Bioterials Age makes one pause. Have I gone too far? Have I gone far enough? Might I be consigned to history as the first BioAstrologer?

In the process of writing this book, however, I became increasingly convinced about the enormous potential of bioterials and their imminent arrival as the central driver of the global economy. After the exhaustive study of the industry that formed the basis of this book, I reached the conclusion that the biotech revolution is not coming, it's already here. The technologies are breathtaking, and the business potential almost unfathomable.

Predicting the final shape, direction, and impact of bioterials is akin to attempting, in 1947, to predict the power and influence of the Internet based solely on the discovery of the transistor. However, several dimensions of the bioterials revolution are already quite clear.

Global. In many ways the industrial revolution sparked the first movement to a global economy. But the technologies of industrialization were primarily centralizing technologies that created domestic economic transformation that were replicated independently in different countries. The priority of every new industrial economy, and the nation states they created, was, first and foremost, domestic self-sufficiency. The ideal economy of the Industrial Age, as epitomized by the United States, was a totally self-contained domestic economy. Obviously, as the industrial economy grew, there was some inter-country and interregional trade, but it related primarily to comparative advantage based on domestic raw materials or labor.

On a broader scale, industrial technologies transformed the world from a global agrarian economy and divided it into the three economic divisions we now refer to as the First, Second, and Third Worlds. Information technologies blurred the distinction between the First and Second World. The decentralizing and empowering technologies of the Information Age touched off the retreat from left and right totalitarian political regimes and began a liberalization of markets that will see economic progress in much of the Second World rival that of the First.

Bioterials technologies will create the first truly global economy with the benefits shared by all who participate. Unlike earlier technologies, there will be little opportunity for countries or individuals to "opt out" of the bioterials revolution, because unlike chemistry, biology respects no political barriers. And while information technologies moved more freely throughout the world than industrial technologies, governments found ways to hinder and delay them for many years. There will be little opportunity to do so with biological technologies, which move without the constraints of the political world. Clearly, certain countries will try to legislate against them as the European Union appeared poised to do in the waning hours of the twentieth century. In the end, however, governments will be powerless to stop biotechnologies. The overpowering economic logic of bioterials will force capitulation. If fully embraced, these new technologies will catapult the Third World into parity with the First World.

Instant. The time delay between scientific discovery and commercial exploitation has narrowed dramatically from the Industrial Age to the Information Age. The chemist pursuing pure science in the lab of the 1800s was largely isolated from like scientists around the world, and even further removed for those who could commercially exploit any discoveries. Without a computer, the chemist of that era was hampered by the need to use slow and cumbersome mechanical devices to test theories and track progress. Scientific knowledge was shared slowly, if at all.

Today, however, scientists creating technology breakthroughs have elaborate networks for speedy dissemination of new knowledge. The Internet itself has become an increasingly important source for both creation and exploitation of new science. The Internet is ensuring that what biologists discover today is commercially exploited tomorrow. The interaction between mature, ubiquitous, and comparatively inexpensive information devices is ensuring that the bioterials revolution happens instantly. In fact, it is reducing the lag time between science and commerce to zero. The full realization of the commercial value in industrial technologies took centuries. The exploitation and commercialization of information technologies was measured in years. The commercialization of bioterials technologies will be measured in days and eventually minutes. Bioterials is the first "front-loaded" economic revolution.

Infinite. The physical properties of the core technologies of earlier economic revolutions are finite. Chemistry can create innumerable compounds, but it is limited to the mathematical combinations of the base elements. Information technologies are limited to the laws of physics. Biology, however, is quite different. Cells are in a constant state of regeneration, and DNA constantly re-creates itself in similar and new forms. Chemistry and electronics are limited, but biology fuels itself in a never-ending spiral of new creations. Its potential is vast; its technologies infinite; its economics unlimited. Bioterials will conquer matter, and in so doing, create a world of wonders the like of which we can not imagine.

Tsunami Economics

Full realization of the bioterials potential will not be long in coming. In fact, the central thesis of this book is that bioterials (and, in particular, biological) technologies are well along the introductory phase of their growth curve and about to reach the first "inflection point," the "mapping"—or more technically, "sequencing"—of the human genome. It will occur by 2001 at the latest.

At this early stage, biologists need not unravel all the secrets of biology. Complete knowledge of the human genome, for example, is not necessary to touch off the revolution in biotech medicine. Recall that chemists needed to know only a fraction of the basic components in the periodic table of the elements, to accurately predict the rest. Likewise, biologists will use the critical first pieces of sequencing information to predict the balance of the human genome.

This early-stage information is in fact the inflection point for the Bioterials Age. And it is the inflection point not just for the science but for the economics as well, attracting vast new pools of capital that stimulate the search for new commercial applications. In fact, the economic growth rates predicted in Chapters 3 through 6 could be reached easily by 2005. But even they do not include the dramatically stimulating effect of breakthroughs in the genetic sciences or new discoveries by the subatomic physicists, for example, in understanding such phenomena as antimatter. The achievement of such milestones portend a period of global economic growth and prosperity that will rival all the accumulated growth of history.

Perhaps more important than the economic gains is the potential for the industry to do countless good: to feed an estimated population, early in the next century, of 12 billion people with excellent foods at a reasonable price; to end much of the heart break of genetic disorders that lead to disease and untimely death; to produce a plethora of consumer products, cheaply, efficiently, and with little environmental damage. Who could ask for anything more?

It is already clear, though, these advances will come with a price, in some cases, an unusually high one.

A "Jurassic Park" of Issues

The first hint of the enormous ethical and moral issues that this technology revolution will engender are explored in an earlier chapter. They need not be repeated here. Throughout the book, I have tried to present the facts and concerns of the various players—industry, scientists, and biotech supporters and opponents—fairly and with an even hand. Despite my strong disagreement with some (most notably the anti-biotech lobby led by Jeremy Rifkin), I have saved my own observations for the final few paragraphs.

Genetically Modified (GM) Foods

The age-old question about whether art imitates life, or vice versa, is rendered mute as concerns about cloning and genetically altered foods are attacked with little scientific fact but generous quantities of emotion. Such propaganda plays into the public's uncertainties and creates a climate of fear that inhibits real dialogue about important issues.

More than governments, the global court of public opinion has the power to temporarily derail or significantly slow much of biotech's progress. For more than a century now the public has been increasingly conditioned to think of biotechnology in a negative way. Perhaps the first biotech "villain" to intrude on the public consciousness was the mythical Dr. Frankenstein. But as important as books have been in steering the public agenda and debate on biotech, the really negative impact on the public imagination has come more recently from movies and television.

The first movie depicting cloning was the 1965 B-movie *The Human Duplicators*. Although not widely viewed at the time, it is still available on video. It was followed 12 years later by the popular *The Boys from Brazil*. More recently a rash of new movies have picked up the theme with *Multiplicity* (1996), *Gattaca* (1997), and *The Matrix* (1999). Although only now becoming a subject for TV, a 1993 episode about cloning on the *X-Files,* called "All About Eve," has become a cult favorite. The 1993 thriller *Jurassic Park* is probably the most important and widely viewed film about biotech. Since its release, the portrayal of many aspects of biotech have been increasingly negative and distorted. By 1999, television news was reporting almost nightly on the growing anxiety about genetically modified foods, particularly in the European Union.

Clearly, biotechnology research is less predictable than many earlier types of scientific research simply because less is known about the behavior of cells and the ways in which genetic information controls cell activity. Such lack of understanding should lead for calls for more science, not less. The emotional and irrational out bursts of the anti-biotech lobby is fear-mongering of the worst kind. It clouds and distorts the needed debate, and seriously impedes the scientific discoveries that could be the key to so many of the world's most pressing problems: global hunger, disease, and overpopulation. Even those who focus their anger solely on GM foods, but favor new biotech science for human health, need to understand that much of this science comes as a package: Destroy one avenue of inquiry and you seriously jeopardize the rest.

Equally disturbing as these "BioLuddites," however, are members of the food industry such as the European food chains and producers like Gerber who cave into demands of the few emotional voices. They need to reserve their judgments and restrain their knee-jerk reactions until all the information is in. To jump at the first sign of unsubstantiated concern is to imperil the industry, embolden the opponents, and further unsettle the public.

Also of concern are European governments that are capitalizing on the issue and using it as a chit in an escalating global agricultural trade war. Much of the budget of the European Union government is comprised of transfer payments for agriculture. Farmers in many countries wield unusual and disproportionate political power, but no where more so than in Europe. Agriculture is always a sensitive issue in international trade, and concerns about GM foods have been seized upon by European trade negotiators as the latest pawn in the debate. It would be understandable, and forgivable, if there wasn't so much at stake.

The GM foods issue is *the* ethical barometer for the bioterials revolution. Public concerns notwithstanding, little can ultimately be done to stop the science. What is banned in one country will rapidly move to another. But this is no excuse to let the concerns about GM foods go undebated. What is needed is a dispassionate global dialogue, conditioned by facts not fears. There is too much at stake to do otherwise.

Human Cloning

Just as with GM foods, the public is fed more disinformation than solid science about human cloning. Few among biologists or the commercial biotech industry are actively working on human cloning or think it a high scientific priority. But the science is close and the probability is high that human cloning will be possible in the near future. While scientists await the guidance of bioethicists, a global public debate should be undertaken immediately. The issue is too important to be left to either the scientist or the ethicists. All perspectives must be represented, and emotions set aside in favor of rational contemplation of the technology that could fundamentally alter reproduction, the most basic of human instincts.

Patient Investors and Impatient Governments

Investors must come to understand the long-term potential of bioterials and be willing to invest "patient capital," that is, money that is mindful of the enormous long-term potential of the industry. The complex nature of biotechnology research means that vast resources must be invested simply to develop a promising lead. Because it is so hard to predict what profitable products, if any, will result from a given research agenda, attracting capital to underwrite it is extremely difficult.

Until recently, the stock market has proven to be a valuable resource for raising research capital, thanks in part to a number of high-profile releases of "blockbuster" biotech drugs in the late 1980s which drew investor attention. The peak year for capital raised through public stock offerings was 1991—$3.3 billion. Public equity markets cooled considerably during 1992 and 1993 (at least for biotechnology offerings) but have picked up steam again recently, averaging over $2 billion of biotechnology stock offerings annually. Many industry observers attribute this to the continuing maturity of the industry. As young companies have gained managerial and technical experience, investors seem more confident that the time between the beginning of research and actual product development will shorten.

Governments must also be encouraged to provide faster turnaround time on product approval, particularly in the case of pharmaceutical products. They must become as impatient as the public to reap the rewards of biotech, particularly in agriculture and health. The cooperation between sovereign governments for faster approval of new plant, animal, and human biotech products needs to continue and even increase. Further, governments must be encouraged to understand the long-term value of the entire biotech industry and not to fall prey to a vocal minority that would halt the research on emotional rather than scientific grounds.

Genes as Intellectual Property

Resolution of whether or not genes are intellectual property is of real concern and must be settled soon. Even with the many positive developments in biotech, the challenge of creating a "biological periodic table"—identifying the properties and behavior of a diverse group or organisms—is ·beyond the means of any single company, scientist, or university and will require partnerships across firms and between the private sector and academia. A large part of the biotech research agenda is what economists call "basic" research, in the sense that it consists of public knowledge which is not "owned" or "licensed" by a single company.

Just as the periodic table and the chemical properties of the elements can be freely obtained via academic journals to support proprietary product development, so the basic laws and regularities of biotechnology (the vast majority of which have yet to be identified) will need to be identified in order to facilitate the applied research and product development of companies. This implies the need to develop and maintain open technology transfer channels between universities and the private sector.

These channels may lead to tension, because thorny questions will arise concerning what knowledge is "proprietary" and subject to patent protection and what knowledge is generic and publicly accessible. Should it be possible for a company (or university) to patent knowledge of a basic cellular process? Where the line is drawn between proprietary discoveries and public-domain basic knowledge will determine the speed at which new products are marketed. If it excessively favors proprietary knowledge, multiple applications of a given discovery ("spillovers" in economic jargon) may never be exploited.

At the other extreme, leaving too much knowledge in the public domain weakens the incentive to invest in applied product development, since the developers of the products may not be able to extract enough income to make such ventures profitable. Economists have noted a close (although not always complementary) relationship between the patent system and the diffusion of technology. While patents do protect discoveries and maintain incentives for innovation, they can also interfere with technology transfer by closing avenues of research to other inventors, especially if it involves a basic cellular process.

Workforce Dislocations

The bioterials revolution will create a major dislocation of the workforce. While it has become popular in recent times to suggest the need for lifelong learning, the dimensions of what that means is just now coming into focus. As we discovered at the beginning of the Information Age, it was difficult to turn autoworkers into software programmers. The Bioterials Age will force much of the working population into new jobs that require vastly different skills. How will software programmers adapt to the biotech lab?

Conjugating a New Verb Tense: The Present Particle

As the computer becomes ever more simple, the need to teach computer literacy diminishes by the day. As bioterials replaces information technology as the engine of the economy, everyone in the workforce will need a basic understanding of biology. In the Bioterials Age, every particle in the universe—organic and inorganic—is subject to modification, and we will need a new language to think and talk about the huge changes this new era will bring. All the issues described above will be conditioned by our facility with this new language of biotech. Therefore, we need to begin *now* to make biology and the science of new materials a required part of every high school and college curriculum.

Everyone will make a "genetic decision" in the next 5 years. Virtually everyone in the world will make a decision regarding genetics in the next 5 years. It may be a personal decision about health care treatment or the use of genetic reproductive technology or how much information about you or your children's genetic makeup you feel comfortable giving to a school, employer, or insurance company. A working knowledge about the technology and the issues is a prerequisite for informed decision making.

In addition, as a country and a member of the world community, we will shortly be engaged in a global discussion about the uses and abuses of biotech. A citizenry informed and conversant in the new language of biotech is the single most important condition in achieving the full potential of this technology.

Every organization will be a bioterials organization. Every industry, every business, as well as every other kind of organization— profit or nonprofit, public sector or private—will be touched by this revolution, whether it makes, uses, or, in some other way, relies on bioterials. Even those organizations seemingly remote from this revolution will be confronted with questions such as how and when to use genetic information about employees.

The biotechnology sector is unique among industries today in that it is defined not by its products but by the enabling technologies it creates for the development and manufacture of other products touching almost every facet of the economy. This distinction, far from being a curiosity, captures quite quickly why developments in biotechnology are likely to have a more profound effect on the structure and organization of the economy than the Information Age and the Industrial Age combined.

Appendix
Statement of Principles*

Preamble

The Biotechnology Industry Organization (BIO) represents biotechnology companies, academic institutions, state biotechnology centers, and related organizations throughout the United States and in many other countries. The members of BIO apply biological knowledge and techniques to develop products and services for use in health care, agriculture, environmental remediation, and other fields. The benefits of these products and services include saving lives threatened by disease, protecting the blood supply from some infectious agents, improving the abundance and quality of food, and cleaning up hazardous wastes.

While biotechnology can greatly improve the quality of life, we recognize that this new technology should be approached with an appropriate mixture of enthusiasm, caution, and humility. Biotechnology can provide useful tools for combating disease, hunger and environmental contamination, but it should not be viewed as a panacea or as miraculous. For example, lifesaving medicines may have serious side effects, and, while our expanding knowledge of genetics can help create the next generation of medicines, it can also raise important ethical issues.

With these considerations in mind, we have adopted the following statement of principles. While some of these principles are codified in government statutes and regulations, this statement is intended to provide guidance to our industry that goes beyond legal requirements.

Because biotechnology is changing and growing rapidly, this statement may be expanded from time to time to address new issues that arise.

*SOURCE: BIO, 1625 K Street NW, Suite 1100, Washington, D.C.; www.bio.org. Reprinted with permission.

We respect the power of biotechnology and apply it for the benefit of humankind. We will pursue applications of biotechnology that promise to save lives or improve the quality of life. We will avoid applications of our technology that do not respect human rights or carry risks that outweigh the potential benefits.

We listen carefully to those who are concerned about the implications of biotechnology and respond to their concerns. The resolution of bioethical issues requires broad public discourse. We acknowledge our responsibility to consider the interests and ideas of all segments of society and to be sensitive to cultural and religious differences. We will seek dialogue with patients, ethicists, religious leaders, health care providers, environmentalists, consumers, legislators, and other groups who share an interest in bioethical issues

We help educate the public about biotechnology, its benefits and implications. For informed debate to occur, the public and our elected representatives need greater knowledge and a better understanding about biotechnology and its applications. BIO and its members pledge to advance public awareness and understanding.

We place our highest priority on health, safety, and environmental protection in the use of our products. In the United States, biotech products are extensively regulated by federal agencies such as the Food and Drug Administration, the Environmental Protection Agency, and the Department of Agriculture. Our industry supports science-based regulation by government agencies to safeguard health, ensure safety, and protect the environment.

We support strong protection of the confidentiality of medical information, including genetic information. Individually identifiable medical information must be treated confidentially and safeguarded from misuse. We oppose the use of medical information to promote intolerance, discriminate against, or to stigmatize people.

We respect the animals involved in our research and treat them humanely. Laboratory animals are essential to research on new therapies and cures. We test new treatments on laboratory animals to assess product safety before administering them to humans. We develop "transgenic" animals—those with genes from another species, usually humans—to test treatments for life-threatening diseases. We also develop transgenic sheep, goats, and cattle by inserting a gene that allows them to produce human pharmaceuticals in their milk. We breed animals that may provide tissues and organs for transplantation to humans. We will follow rigorously all government regulations and professional standards in the United States, such as the Animal Welfare Act and the federal guidelines for animal care and use promulgated by the National Institutes of Health.

We are sensitive to and considerate of the ethical and social issues regarding genetic research. We will not, for example, treat genetic disorders by altering the genes of human sperm or eggs until the medical, ethical, and social issues that will arise from this kind of therapy have been more broadly discussed and clarified. Also, we support continuation of the voluntary moratorium on the potential cloning of entire human beings, with the understanding that research should continue on the cloning of genes and cells to benefit humankind.

We adhere to strict informed consent procedures. For clinical research conducted in the United States, the National Institutes of Health and the Food and Drug Administration require informed consent from all participants and approval by a national or local review board. We adhere to these requirements in our medical research, except in situations in which obtaining consent is not necessary (for example, research on anonymous information) or not possible (for example, emergency care of unconscious patients).

We will abide by the ethical standards of the American Medical Association and, where appropriate, other health care professional societies to ensure that our products are appropriately prescribed, dispensed, and used. These ethical standards are designed to ensure that health care professionals do not receive monetary or other compensation that might adversely affect how they care for their patients.

We develop our agricultural products to enhance the world's food supply and to promote sustainable agriculture with attendant environmental benefits. There are significant advantages to increasing the yield of crops. Farmers must produce increasing amounts of food per acre to feed a growing global population. We will strive to make this possible while reducing the amount of external supplements (fertilizers, pesticides, etc.) necessary. We will develop our products with an eye toward good stewardship of our agricultural and environmental resources and the sustainability of such development. With regard to the development of new agriculture crops, we pledge to abide by established standards of environmental safety at home and abroad.

We develop environmental biotechnology to clean up hazardous waste more efficiently with less disruption to the environment and to prevent pollution by treating waste before it is released. Many environmental engineering firms, industry, and governments are using biotechnology to harness the power of naturally occurring organisms to degrade contaminants at hazardous waste sites. We will strive to optimize the cost efficiencies and environmental advantages associated with using biotechnology while protecting human health and the environment. We also will continue to develop and implement more environmentally safe and cost-effective means of treating hazardous waste streams in industrial processes.

We oppose the use of biotechnology to develop weapons. We support the Biological Weapons Convention, a treaty signed by the United States and many other nations banning development and use of biological weapons. We will not undertake any research intended for use in developing, testing, or producing such weapons.

We continue to support the conservation of biological diversity. The genetic variation of animals, plants, and other organisms is a valuable natural resource. The environment is constantly changing, and without an adequate store of genetic diversity, organisms will not be able to adapt. Genetic diversity decreases, however, every time a species, breed or crop variety becomes extinct. Working with governments and other organizations, we will help to catalog and conserve these precious resources.

Index

About the Author

Richard W. Oliver is a professor at the Owen Graduate School of Management at Vanderbilt University in Nashville, Tennessee. He was previously vice president of marketing at Nortel and a marketing executive at DuPont. Dr. Oliver serves on the Boards of Directors of six U.S. companies and consults to organizations around the world. He is the author of *The Shape of Things to Come: 7 Imperatives for Winning in the New World of Business* and coauthor, with William Jenkins, of *The Eagle and the Monk: 7 Principles of Successful Change.*